Translator Self-Training Arabic

Practical Course in Technical Translation

Morry Sofer

Schreiber Publishing
Rockville, Maryland

First Printing

Library of Congress Control Number: 2002105645
ISBN 1-887563-74-1

Printed in the U.S.A. by Schreiber Publishing, PO Box 4193, Rockville, Maryland 20849
www.schreiberpublishing.com

Preface

This practical course is for anyone who would like to pursue technical translation in Arabic and English, in such areas as legal, medical, financial or other kinds of non-literary documents (literary translation is a different discipline from technical).

The course is based on the practical experience of a major translation company which has been translating—routinely and successfully—Arabic-into-English and English-into-Arabic documents in all technical areas for almost twenty years. The assignments in this book are taken from real-life documents which were translated by this company, with names and other information changed in some cases to protect proprietary information.

This book grew out of a correspondence course offered about ten years ago, which became a three-ring binder program for translator's self-training five years ago. During those five years, hundreds of translators have used this program each year, and many have offered unsolicited praise for this program, letting us know that it has improved their translation skills, and in more than a few cases helped the user pass accreditation or certification tests for such organizations as the American Translators Association (ATA).

Nothing sharpens translation skills more than the actual act of translating. But one needs an entry point, either into the technical translation field in general, or into new areas of translation, if one has already been doing one kind of technical translation, such as legal. This course provides the entry point.

We at Schreiber Publishing take a personal interest in translators in all languages and subjects, and are always happy to hear from you.

Enjoy the course!

Morry Sofer

Table of Contents

SECTION 1. GENERAL

INTRODUCTION

Welcome to the **Translator Self-Training / Arabic**. We are very pleased you selected this program, which has been in use since 1990. It has helped aspiring translators around the country get their start in this exciting field, while assisting practicing translators in improving their translation skills. Translation is one of the fastest growing professions in today's world, as different languages and cultures are coming closer together every day. Whether you wish to pursue translation full-time or as a sideline, you will find it to be a highly challenging and quite profitable occupation. The purpose of the following exercises is to help you improve your skills as a translator of Arabic and English.

This program is designed to help you work at your own pace and gain experience through translation practice assignments. These assignments, excerpted from actual translation jobs, were selected to help you determine your own level of comfort and expertise, so that you may go on from there to choose the type of translation work you may like to pursue.

To derive the maximum benefit from these texts, you should carefully read the General Comments, the guidelines, and the specific notes which discuss each assignment. Every comment and every guideline represents years of experience in professional translation work. By carefully following this program, you will be able to achieve *in just a few days* what has taken others years to learn. You will be guided through many of the pitfalls of translation, taught how to avoid them, shown shortcuts in accomplishing a complex piece of translation work, and be given the benefit of comments designed to show you how to produce a translation acceptable to major clients such as government, industry, the legal world, and many more.

Before you read further, we strongly urge you to read Appendix A: Requisites for Professional Translators, and Appendix B: Translation Techniques.

The above-listed Appendices will give you a good overview on how translation work is to be approached and practiced, and how to position yourself in the translation market. Try to keep the contents of these two sections in mind as you translate the following assignments.

You are presented with four different texts, which, for most people, represent an increasing level of difficulty (although if you happen to be a lawyer, for example, it is possible that you will find the second assignment the easiest of the four). They are:

1. **General**
2. **Legal**
3. **Chemical/Medical**
4. **Business/Finance**

At a minimum, you may want to do the first and second assignments. Those two represent a vast body of material which is being translated in the United States on a regular basis, but which does not require a highly specialized vocabulary or technical background. The third assignment requires access to chemical and medical terminology, which can be managed by any intelligent translator. The fourth assignment should be approached with caution. Here one must have an understanding of the world of finance, which not all of us do. For your own self-assessment, you may want to try it (since we provide you with the translation, you can compare the results and see for yourself how you did). But if you find it too difficult, don't be discouraged. It is clearly not for everyone.

We hope you enjoy working with these texts, and we urge you to please be patient with yourself. One does not become an accomplished translator overnight. To learn, one must make mistakes. If your heart is in it, and if you love the challenge of working with two languages you happen to know well, then you are sure to get a great deal out of this program.

A Word about Arabic Translation

Arabic is one of the world's major languages. It is the official language of 18 countries in North Africa and the Middle East. It is the mother tongue of at least 165 million people. It is also the language of the Koran, which makes it the second language for millions of Indians, Iranians, Indonesians and other inhabitants of largely Muslim nations, and the holy tongue of all of the above. Historically, it is one of the major repositories and catalysts of world culture.

The volume of Arabic translation in the English-speaking world is not nearly as large as, say, German or Spanish. Nevertheless, there is always a need for accomplished Arabic translators. Whether or not one should pursue a full-time career as an Arabic translator in the English-speaking world is hard to say. Certainly there is always a need for Arabic freelancers, if only on a part time basis, and there are indeed people who have been successfully pursuing full-time careers as Arabic translators in places like England and the U.S. But clearly their numbers are not legion. As a general rule, if one happens to know Arabic and has a flair for translation, it is certainly worth while to sharpen one's translation skills. If, on the other hand, one chooses to major in Arabic in an American college or university with a view to making Arabic translation a career, one should first examine the range of opportunities.

The conscientious Arabic translator is aware of the generic difficulties in working with two languages such as English and Arabic. First, there are the vast cultural differences between a Western language such as English and a Semitic language like Arabic. One cannot translate these languages mechanically, without paying attention to these cultural differences. In addition, Arabic is in the process of developing technical terminologies for new areas such as computers and telecommunications, and the precise term is not always readily available. Add to this the fact that there are several spoken Arabic dialects which are not always mutually intelligible, such as Syrian and Egyptian, and the fact that even the official written Arabic has different terms and usages in different Arab countries. What all this means is that very often the Arabic translator needs to engage in some additional research to produce a truly accurate translation of Arabic into or from English. When all is said and done, however, meeting the challenge of translating Arabic accurately and elegantly can be a source of great satisfaction.

GENERAL COMMENTS

The following comments are offered with two purposes in mind: the immediate purpose is to help you with the assignments. The long-term purpose is to serve as reference material for actual translation work. Keep them for future use.

A reminder:

The "source language" is the language you translate from.

The "target language" is the language you translate into.

Every language has its own "personality," so to speak. When you translate, pretend you are two different persons - an "Arabic Person" and an "English Person." The Arabic Person reads the original Arabic text, and becomes familiar with it. The Arabic Person then turns to the English Person, and says to him/her, "Okay, now it's your turn to say the same thing your way." Now the English Person takes over, and starts writing the same text in English. You will be constantly switching back and forth between the Arabic Person and the English Person, as the first checks the Arabic word, phrase, sentence structure, and then the second thinks in English and comes up with the right equivalents. Here are some of the main language issues you will have to deal with:

Clarity

We each have our own personal style of expressing ourselves - in any language. Some people make their point clearly and succinctly, while others use more words than necessary, including esoteric words, to make their point. The same holds true in translation. You can translate the phrase, *"Al-ajalat min al-shaitan"* as "Haste makes waste," or you could also translate it correctly as, "Haste is the work of the devil." In the first instance, only three words were used; in the second, seven. Most of the time, the first type of translation is better, because it is simpler and more readily understandable. Make it your point to pursue simplicity whenever possible.

Consistency

Most of the time, if you start out translating the word *"bayt"* as "house," stick to "house," and don't start suddenly shifting to"building," or vice versa. The reader may become confused, wondering why the word suddenly changed. Generally in English, building is bigger than house, and one may wonder whether the dimensions of that particular structure might have changed. If you are familiar with word-processing you know how easy it is to do a "global search and replace" throughout the text, so that if halfway into the document you decide that "building" is better than "house," then go back to the beginning and do a global change, replacing the word "house" with "building."

Sentence Structure

It is difficult, yet very important, to ensure that sentence structure is correct and makes sense, yet still retains the flavor of the original text, particularly if this is written in a flowery, elaborate, or otherwise unique style. This fine line is achieved mainly through practice, but it is definitely helpful to read the original several times before even beginning the translation process in order to gain a good idea of the author's style.

It is not necessary to follow the structure of a sentence literally. A run-on sentence which may make sense in one language may not make sense in the other, and therefore should be divided into two sentences (or more). The converse is also true. You should also avoid being too literal when it comes to word order, or your text will sound stilted, awkward, and artificial. You will need to rely on your own good writing skills in determining the most sensible word order and punctuation so that your translation flows smoothly.

Format

Format should be followed as closely as possible. Ideally, every page of translation should look exactly like the corresponding page of the original, except, of course, for the language. There is a very practical reason for this. It helps the reader, who may or may not know the source language, compare the two texts, make sure all the parts are there, and check a particular word or phrase in the source text. This, however, is not always possible, since a page of translation at times is longer than the same page in the source language. Nevertheless, every effort should be made to keep the format as similar as possible to the original.

Terminology

The use of the right terminology is critical in any translation, especially in any technical subject. Here the right kind of dictionaries and reference literature becomes very critical. Keep in mind, however, that dictionaries, no matter how good, are never complete, and do not provide all the answers. The other source of information is people who work in the field the particular translation covers. Their input is often more valuable than that of the dictionary, since they are the ones who work in the field and represent the potential readers of your translation.

The first thing to keep in mind about terminology - as was discussed before - is consistency. If you translate a word a certain way, do not change in the middle of the text to another synonym of the same word, even though it may be accurate. This will throw the reader off. The second thing is to make sure you are using the right terms, rather than trying to approximate them. Keep a list of those terms to maintain consistency throughout the document, and also for future use. If you continue to translate in the same technical field, these lists will become your most valuable translation tool.

Numbers

The use of commas and periods is reversed in decimals (5,1 in Arabic becomes 5.1 in English). Also, a number within an Arabic text follows the right-to-left direction of the language (2.4 Box In Arabic, which means the second box of Chapter 4, becomes Box 4.2 in English). Not to mention the fact that an Arabic table will run its columns from right to left, and needs to be reversed. These are examples of numbers-related diffrences between the two languages which must be closely observed.

Punctuation

Quotation marks are appropriate in English, but this is not always so in Arabic. Punctuation in general is not always used in the same places. These are just a few examples of how even a highly accurate translation will not always mirror its original text. You will often be called upon to be the judge, which involves a combination of excellent writing skills, knowledge of rules of grammar and punctuation, plus common sense.

Errors in the Source Text

Sometimes you will find that the original has errors, such as a misspelling where it is clear by the context that the author intended to say "*hu*" and not "*hi*," or the sequence in a series of numbered clauses is wrong, or a name that has been in uppercase letters suddenly appears as lowercase, for no apparent reason. You can do a number of things in situations such as these. You can go ahead and make the correction and leave it at that. You can translate the text as is, and use the term [sic] after the error, to alert the reader. Or you can make a translator's note on a separate sheet of paper. Ultimately, the client will have to decide what to do with it.

Untranslatable Words or Terms

You may run into a word, a term or a phrase which cannot be translated, or which should be left in the original language (such as, for instance, "*sheikh*"). If there is a need to explain it, it can be done in a footnote or in parentheses (or brackets, which makes it clearer that the bracketed text is not part of the original) following the word (*Sheikh* [tribal, political or religious leader]). As a general rule, however, it is best not to burden your translation with footnotes or parenthetic or bracketed text.

In Conclusion

The above notes are by no means exhaustive. They do not cover all the issues facing a translator. Language is not mathematics. Keep this in mind, and do the best translation job you possibly can.

GUIDELINES FOR TRANSLATING THE ASSIGNMENTS

1. We are providing you with an Arabic text and an English translation of that same text. Pretend you don't have the English translation. If you read it before you do the assignment, you will not be able to do an honest job, and you will not derive the benefit of learning from your own mistakes.

2. Read the Arabic text once for general comprehension. Underline any difficult words or passages.

3. As you start the translation process by reading the text for the first time (see 2., above), keep track of time, so that when you finish you will know how long it took you to translate the text. This is very critical, because you want to increase your translation speed as you go along. The rule is simple: The more words you translate per hour, the more money you will make. A very low hourly word-count can earn you less than minimum wage, which is not at all desirable. (Note: The hours indicated at the top right hand corner for each assignment include two numbers. The first is for beginners while the second number is for an experienced translator. Therefore, an assignment that would take a beginner 5-7 hours to complete might take an experienced translator 2 hours. The timeframe includes research, draft, and final copy.)

4. Read it again. This time make a list of difficult words, and make any notes regarding things you need to clarify about the text (e.g., look up something in an encyclopedia to better understand some concept or piece of information).

5. Try to determine which dictionaries and reference books you need for this assignment, get hold of them, and keep them nearby.

6. Now you are ready to start translating. Preferably, you will be using a computer. If this is too intimidating, write it out the first time. It will take longer, but you will have more time to think. Remember, your objective is to translate on computer, not in longhand. These days, if you want to earn money translating, you have to submit text on disk. There are hardly any exceptions to this requirement.

7. Do a draft translation. Go over the draft. Do the best you can to make the English sound like good, clear, correct English, which does not sound like Arabic, and does not retain any Arabic forms in either style, format, or any technical points. Be sure you did not omit anything. Ask yourself if you succeeded in conveying the correct sense of every idea and every word in the source text. Be sure you are comfortable with every single word you chose in English, and that you have no doubts or hesitations. If, after all this, you do have some questions, do not worry. No one expects you to do perfect work the first time around. You will do better next time.

8. Now that you have accomplished your translation, figure out the time it took you to reach your final version (including all the previous steps - namely, first reading, research, draft, and final copy).

9. Make a list of the words, passages, and concepts in the text where you encountered difficulty, and keep for future reference. This kind of record keeping will help you improve your performance, and serve as a reminder not to repeat the same mistake twice.

10. Print out your corrected and edited text.

GUIDELINES FOR SELF-EVALUATION

1. Turn to the English translation in Section 3, and compare it to yours. Next read the notes concerning the pitfalls and salient points of this text very carefully, and see how they compare to your own experience with the text. They may not necessarily coincide with everything you experienced personally, but they do provide you with some tips on the do's and don'ts of technical translation.

2. The most important thing for you to keep in mind as you compare your translation to the one in Section 3, is that there is no one absolutely correct way of translating a text. Many words can be translated in more than one way. Many sentences can be structured in more than one way. Many ideas can be conveyed in different words. In fact, your translation may turn out to be just as good, and in some spots even better than the one in the book.

3. Keep track of the shortcomings of your translation. The areas you are interested in are the following:

   Omissions - did you fail to translate any particular word or phrase, or even paragraph?

   Format - does your format follow the original (breaking into paragraphs, for instance)?

   Mistranslations - did you mistranslate any particular word?

   Unknown words - were there any words you were not able to translate?

   Meaning - did you miss the meaning of any particular phrase or sentence?

   Spelling - did you misspell a word?

   Grammar - did you make any grammatical mistakes?

   Punctuation - did you mispunctuate or miss any punctuation marks?

   Clarity - did you fail to clearly convey the meaning of any particular part of the text?

   Consistency - did you call something by one name, and then by another without good reason?

   Style - are you satisfied with the way your translation reflects the style of the original (for example, the original is written in a clear, direct style, while the translation sounds more complex and indirect)?

These are some of the questions you have to ask yourself. As you go on to translate other texts, always keep these questions in mind as you self-assess your translation. By improving your performance in the above areas, you are on your way to becoming an accomplished translator.

Part One

Translation: Arabic into English

SECTION 2. ASSIGNMENTS

6-7/3 hours (*word count*: 840)

ASSIGNMENT 1 - GENERAL

الإطار ٢ ـ ١ : التقدم فى مجال صحة الطفل فى أربعة بلدان

فى الستينات ، كانت فرصة الطفل المولود فى العالم النامى فى البقاء على قيد الحياة خلال السنوات الخمس الأولى من عمره تبلغ ٧٧ فى المائة . وبعد ذلك بما يقرب من ثلاثين عاما تحسنت فرص البقاء فأصبحت ٨٩ فى المائة . فما هو مدى إسهام نمو الدخل والتوسع فى التعليم فى تحقيق هذا التحسن ؟ وما هو دور العوامل الأخرى ، مثل التقدم فى العلوم والطب ؟ يستمد بعض الإجابات على هذه الاسئلة من البيانات المتعلقة بحياة الطفل والمأخوذة من خمسة وسبعين بلدا صناعيا وناميا خلال الفترة بين ١٩٦٠ و١٩٨٧ (انظر ملاحظة جدول التذييل أ ـ ٣) . ويعرض هذا الإطار النتائج بالنسبة لأربعة بلدان تختلف مستويات الدخل فيها وهى ـ كوت ديفوار وكوستاريكا ومصر واليابان (انظر جدول الإطار ٢ ـ ١ وشكل الإطار ٢ ـ ١) .

وكان جزء من التحسن فى صحة الطفل فى البلدان الأربعة جميعها راجعا إلى المستويات الأولية لتعليم السكان فى ١٩٦٠ وإلى مستويات دخل الفرد فى نفس العام . ونظراً لأن التعليم ودخل الفرد يحققان منافع صحية عادة ما تبقى على مر الزمن ، فإن صحة السكان يمكن تحسينها بمجرد الإبقاء على المستويات الأولية للتعليم والدخل . ففى كوستاريكا ، حيث كان دخل الفرد فى ١٩٦٠ عاليا نسبيا ، وكان التعليم منتشرا كانت الظروف الأولية مسؤولة عن ٥٨ فى المائة من التحسن فى صحة الطفل بين ١٩٦٠ و١٩٨٧ . وفى كوت ديفوار ومصر ، حيث كانت مستويات التعليم ودخل الفرد متواضعة فى ١٩٦٠ ، أسهمت الظروف الأولية بنحو ما بين خُمس وربع التحسن فقط . وفى اليابان أيضا ، أسهمت هذه الظروف الأولية بخمس التحسن فى صحة الطفل ، لكن هذا لا يدعو للدهشة فى بلد كانت فيه فرصة الطفل الرضيع فى البقاء طيبة جدا بالفعل فى ١٩٦٠ .

بالطبع إن الدخل والتعليم قد تحسنا فى الواقع فى كل هذه البلدان ، وأسهمت هذه التحسينات فى تحقيق مزيد من التحسين فى بقاء الطفل . ففى كوت ديفوار أسهم تحسين التعليم بالقدر الأكبر فى تدعيم صحة الطفل ، اذ كان مسؤولا عن ٦٦ فى المائة من التحسن بين ١٩٦٠ و ١٩٨٠ . وعلى النقيض من ذلك بالنسبة لمصر لم يتجاوز الرقم ٢١ فى المائة . والمقارنة بين كوت ديفوار ومصر توضح القضية . ففى كلا البلدين ، بدأ احتمال البقاء للسنوات الخمس الأولى من العمر بمستويات متماثلة وتحسن بمعدلات متشابهة . بيد أنه فى كوت ديفوار بدأ تعليم الكبار من مستويات أدنى كثيرا منها فى مصر ، لكنه زاد أسرع منها خمس مرات . وكان دخل الفرد فى كوت ديفوار نحو ضعف دخل الفرد فى مصر فى ١٩٦٠ لكنه نما بعدئذ بسرعة تبلغ ٦٠ فى المائة فقط . وهكذا ، فإن التحسين فى التعليم كان أكثر أهمية فى كوت ديفوار ، فى حين كان نمو دخل الفرد فى مصر مسؤولا بالكامل عن نصف التحسن فى صحة الطفل .

وبدا فى كوستاريكا واليابان نفس النمط الذى بدا فى مصر : فقد أسهم نمو دخل الفرد فى تحسن صحة الطفل بأكثر مما فعل التحسين فى التعليم . بيد أن التقدم التقنى (والذى قُدر على أساس معدله مضروبا فى الفترة الزمنية) ، كان مهما فى اليابان ، فى حين كانت أهميته فى كوستاريكا ومصر أقل من أهمية التحسين فى التعليم . وفيما عدا اليابان ، حيث كان الناس بالفعل متعلمين تعليما جيدا فى ١٩٦٠ ، ربما بخس التحليل قيمة إسهام التعليم ، لأنه تناول تعليم الكبار جميعهم وليس المرأة وحدها . وقد تأثرت صحة الطفل بصفة خاصة بتعليم الأم ، ومن المحتمل أن عدد سنوات الدراسة التى تلقتها النساء الأصغر سنا قد زاد بصورة أسرع كثيرا بين ١٩٦٠ و ١٩٨٧ مما كان عليه الحال بالنسبة للسكان الكبار ككل .

جدول الإطار ٢ ـ ١ صحة الطفل ، دخل الفرد ، وسنوات التعليم فى كوستاريكا وكوت ديفوار ومصر واليابان ، ٦٠ ـ ١٩٨٧

المؤشر	كوستاريكا	كوت ديفوار (أ)	مصر	اليابان
١٩٦٠				
بقاء الطفل على قيد الحياة(ب)	٠,٨٩	٠,٧٢	٠,٧٤	٠,٩٦
دخل الفرد (بدولارات ١٩٨٧ الدولية)(هـ)	٢١٦٠	١٠٢١	٥٥٧	٢٧٠١
متوسط تعليم البالغين (سنوات)	٤,٠	٠,٢	٣,٠	١٠,٧
متوسط النسبة المئوية السنوية للتغير ، ٦٠ ـ ١٩٨٧				
بقاء الطفل على قيد الحياة(ب)	٠,٤	٠,٨	٠,٦	٠,١
دخل الفرد	٢,٣	٣,٢	٥,٢	٥,٣
تعليم البالغين من السكان	٢,٠	١١,٨	٢,٤	٠,٢
مرونة بقاء الطفل على قيد الحياة بالنسبة إلى :				
دخل الفرد(د)	٠,٠٤	٠,٠٦	٠,٠٦	٠,٠٢
تعليم البالغين من السكان(د)	٠,٠٣	٠,٠٤	٠,٠٤	٠,٠٢

(أ) تشير البيانات إلى ٦٠ ـ ١٩٨٠ .

(ب) يشير بقاء الطفل على قيد الحياة إلى احتمال البقاء من المولد حتى سن الخامسة .

(هـ) تم تصحيح الدخل لمراعاة الفروق فى تعادل القوة الشرائية .

(د) تشير المرونة إلى النسبة المئوية للتغير فى احتمال البقاء من المولد حتى سن الخامسة التى تقابل تغيرا فى المتغير المبين بمقدار ١ فى المائة .

المصدر : لاو وآخرون ، ورقة معلومات أساسية .

ASSIGNMENT 2 - LEGAL

اشهاد بطلاق صبير عن يد المأذون

رقم الدفتر ٢٨٦٤٦٢ صفحة رقم ١٤

رقم الاشهاد ٤٤٥ - ٢٢٧

انه في يوم الخميس الثالث من شهر ربيع الأول ١٤١٦ هـ الموافق العاشر من آغسطس ١٩٩٥ بحضوري وغن يدي أنا محمد علي يماني مأذون نظام احالة التابع لمحكمة الديخيلة اسكندرية للأحوال الشخصية فني الساعة ٧ م حضر لدي الرجل المسلم المصري المكلف/السيد علي عامر اسماعيل مساعد رئيس قطاع بشركة الفنادق المصرية - فندق فلسطين مواليد الاسكندرية ١٩٥٠/٢/١٢ المقيم بشارع ٦٠ سيدي بشر بطاقة عائلية ٧٩/١٠/١٢//٥٥٥١٤ المنتزه قيد ٨٥٥ وأسم أمه سيدة فيصل. وحضرت معه زوجته عيشة ثريا جمال رشدي لا تعمل مواليد اسكندرية ومقيمة في ٢٢ شارع مالك بسيدي بشر بطاقة شخصية ٨٩/١١/٢//١٨٢٢٢٨ المنتزه وأسم أمها فاطمة محمد حمادى وثابت زواجها بوثيقة عقد زواج رقم ٩ بتاريخ ٧٤/٧/٢٥ لدي المرحوم مصطفى الصاوي مأذون حتيتي سيدي بشر بمحكمة الرمل سابقا وبعد التحقيق من زواجها شرعاً واعترافها بالدخول والمعاشرة الزوجية بحضور وشهادة المكلفين محمود علي جباري مقاول مواليد اسكندرية ١٩٦١/١/٢١ ومقيم ٢٥ شارع سيدي بشر بحري رقم بطاقة شخصية ٧٧/٢/١٢//٦١٧٨٩ المنتزه والسيد أحمد شيتي سعيد ميكانيكي سيارات مواليد اسكندرية ١٩٥٩/٣/٢١ ومقيم في ٢٧ شارع جهاد بالقرب من المطافئ بطاقة عائلية ١٣/١٢/٢٢//١٠٤١٣٧ المنتزه قالت الزوجة المذكورة لزوجها المذكور أبرأتك يازوجي من مؤخر صداقتي ومن نفقة عدتي حتى تنتهي من ذلك شرعا ومن متعتي ومن جميع حقوقي الزوجية الشرعية طلقني على ذلك الآن فأجابها فورا بقوله لها أنت يازوجتي عيشة ثريا جمال رشدي طالق من الآن على ذلك الابراء وتصادقا أن هذا الطلاق هو أولى الطلقات فبانت منه بذلك بينونة أولى صغرى لا تحل له الا بعقد ومهر جديدين باذنها ورضاها كما عرفناها بذلك وتحرر بذلك أربع صور سلم كل منهما صورة وثالثة سجل والرابعة للمحكمة ورسم قدره ٥٥٠ خلاف من الاشهاد والضرائب بعهدي.

الشهود	المطلقة	المطلق	المأذون
محمود علي جبرى أحمد شيتي سعيد	عيشة ثريا جمال رشيدي	علي عامر اسماعيل	محمد علي يماني

شركة البيان للتجارة

الرقم: ٩٥/١٧
التاريخ ١٩٩٥/١/١٢

السيد محمد احمد خليل
- مدير عام شركة كونتيننتال فودز العربية السعودية -

تحية طيبة - وبعد:

قام أحد الأشخاص بتسجيل علامة تجارية تحت اسم (لطيفة أويل)، وذلك بقصد التشويش واستغلال اسم (لطيف أويل)، وقد يقوم هو وشركاؤه بتعبئة الزيوت الرديئة وبيعها في الاسواق السورية تحت اسم (لطيفة أويل).

والذي فهمناه انه ادعى امام مديرية حماية الملكية التجارية والصناعية في سوريا ان لديه ابنة اسمها (لطيفة)، لذا فهو يرغب اتخاذ اسمها كعلامة تجارية، وعلى هذا الأساس تمت الموافقة بتسجيل هذه العلامة.

ونرسل لكم الوثائق التي تشير الى تسجيل هذه العلامة، والى تسجيل علامة (لطيف أويل) والتي نرى الانتباه الى تجديد تسجيلها قبل انتهاء فترة التسجيل.

كما نرجو إرسال توكيل خاص لي من شركة كونتيننتال فودز صاحبة العلامة التجارية (لطيف أويل) من كاتب العدل السعودي مصدقا من السفارة السورية بمنحي كافة الصلاحيات اللازمة لاقامة الدعاوي الجزائية والمدنية ومراجعة الجهات المختلفة وتمثيلنا امامها وتقديم كافة الطلبات وتوكيل المحامين والمطالبة بالتعويض بخصوص كل ما يمس العلامة التجارية (لطيف أويل) او يلحق بها أي ضرر او استغلالها من قبل الغير وخاصة ضد العلامة التجارية المسجلة باسم (لطيفة أويل) فى مديرية حماية الملكية التجارية والصناعية في سوريا تحت رقم ٥٣٣٢٥ تاريخ ١٩٩٤/٣/١٥ وضد كل من له علاقة بهذه العلامة وغيرها بطريق مباشر او غير مباشر. (واسمي :يوسف أحمد بن ابراهيم).

ارجو الاهتمام بالامر والاسراع في اتخاذ الاجراء المناسب ليكون بالامكان مواجهة الأمر منذ بدايته.

وتفضلوا بقبول فائق التحية والاحترام

يوسف أحمد بن ابراهيم

word count: 702

6-7/3 hours

ASSIGNMENT 3: MEDICAL

الإطار ١ - ١ مكافحة العمى النهرى

إن مرض داء المذنبات الملتحية ، أو المعروف بصورة أشيع بالعمى النهرى ينشأ عن دودة طفيلية تنتج ملايين من اليرقات التى تتحرك داخل الجسم وتسبّب هرشاً حاداً وضعفاً وعمى فى آخر المطاف . وينتشر المرض بوساطة ذبابة سوداء صغيرة شرمة فى لسعتها تنقل اليرقات من المصابين إلى غير المصابين .

والأهداف التى يتوخاها برنامج مكافحة داء المذنبات الملتحية الذى وضع فى عام ١٩٧٤ وشمل أحد عشر بلداً فى السهل الإفريقى هى مكافحة الذبابة السوداء بالقضاء على يرقاتها ، وذلك برش المبيدات الحشرية من الجوّ . أما التأثير البيئى للمبيدات الحشرية فتقوم لجنة أيكولوجية مستقلّة بمتابعته بصورة مستمرة بالتعاون مع الحكومات الوطنيّة . وللجنة سلطة كاملة فى فحص المبيدات الحشرية والموافقة على استخدامها أو رفض ذلك . كما تعاون البرنامج مع صناعة الأدوية لاستحداث عقار ، أيفرمكتين ، للاستعمال البشرى وهو يقضى على اليرقات فى الجسم قضاءًا آمناً فعالاً . إلاّ أن تأثير إيفرمكتين فى الديدان البالغة قليل ولهذا يتعين تعزيزه بمكافحة الناقل بالرش من الجوّ . وقد التزمت الشركة المنتجة لإيفرمكتين ، وهى ميرك وشركاه ، بأن تقدم العقار مجاناً طالما دعت الحاجة إليه لمكافحة العمى النهرى .

ولبرنامج مكافحة داء المذنبات الملتحية أربع وكالات تشرف عليه - (منظمة الأغذية والزراعة ، وبرنامج الأمم المتحدة الإنمائى ، والبنك الدولى ، ومنظمة الصحة العالمية) من خلال لجنة توجيهية يرأسها البنك الدولى تضع القرارات المتعلقة بالسياسة العريضة وتراقب العمليات. ولمنظمة الصحة العالمية مسؤولية تنفيذية من خلال فرقة من علماء الحشرات وعلماء الوبائيات والعاملين الميدانيين والروّاد ، و ٩٧ فى المائة من العاملين هم مواطنون للبلدان المشاركة . ويقوم البنك الدولى بتنظيم التمويل ويديره من خلال صندوق استئمانى . كما يساند التنمية الاجتماعية الاقتصادية فى المناطق التى أصابها المرض .

والمعتقد على نطاق واسع أن البرنامج حقق نجاحاً عظيماً . فهو يقى نحو ٣٠ مليون شخص من العمى النهرى ، منهم أكثر من ٩ ملايين طفل ولدوا منذ ما بدأ برنامج مكافحة داء المذنبات الملتحية بتكلفة سنوية تقل عن دولار واحد للشخص . واستعاد أكثر من ١,٥ مليون شخص صحتهم الكاملة بعدما كانوا ذات يوم مصابين إصابة خطيرة ، ويقدر بأن البرنامج سيمنع ما لا يقل من ٥٠٠٠٠٠ حالة عمى بحلول الوقت الذى ينهى فيه أعماله حوالى نهاية القرن . وهو يقوم فعلاً بتحرير ما يقرب من ٢٥ مليون هكتار من الأراضى التى كانت قبلاً أراضى موبوءة لإعادة الاستيطان فيها وزراعتها والنهوض بالإنتاج الزراعى .

والتكلفة المقدرة لبرنامج مكافحة داء المذنبات الملتحية طوال مدة وجوده من عام ١٩٧٤ إلى عام ٢٠٠٠ هى ٥٧٠ مليون دولار على وجه التقريب . والمقدّر أن معدل عائده الداخلى يتفاوت بين ١٦ فى المائة و ٢٨ فى المائة (حسب الوتيرة التى يتم بها استيطان الأراضى التى توافرت مؤخراً ، وحسب الناتج الزائد الذى أضافته الأراضى الجديدة ، وحسب مستوى الدخل فى منطقة برنامج مكافحة داء المذنبات الملتحية ، وحسب معدل نمو الإنتاجية المقدّر) . وهذه المزايا المقدرة لا تشمل آثار البرنامج المواتية على توزيع الدخل ؛ والمنتفعون الرئيسيون هم المزارعون الذين يقومون بزراعة الكفاف والذين يقل دخلهم بكثير عن المتوسط .

الإطار ٥ - ١ جعل الحمل والولادة مأمونين

فى ظل الظروف المثلى ، تنتهى نحو ٩٩٠ حالة من كل ١٠٠٠ حالة حمل تصل إلى الشهر السابع من الحمل بوليد وأم يتمتعان بصحة جيدة . بيد أن الولادة غير مأمونة بالنسبة لغالبية النساء فى بلدان العالم النامى . إذ تلاقى امرأة من بين ٥٠ سيدة فى البلدان النامية حتفها نتيجة لمضاعفات الحمل والولادة ، وذلك بالمقارنة مع حالة وفاة واحدة لكل ٢٧٠٠ حالة ولادة فى اقتصادات السوق الراسخة . ولمعدل وفيات الأمهات نتائج عميقة فى الأسرة ؛ إذ تزداد فرص الوفاة للأطفال دون من الخامسة بنسبة تصل إلى ٥٠ فى المائة عندما تتوفى الأم .

وفى عام ١٩٨٧ ، بدأ المجتمع الصحى الدولى ، بما فى ذلك البنك الدولى ، ومنظمة الصحة العالمية ، وصندوق الأمم المتحدة للسكان ، ووكالات فى خمسة وأربعين بلداً ، مبادرة الأمومة المأمونة . والهدف الرئيسى لهذه المبادرة هو تخفيض عدد وفيات الأمهات بمقدار النصف بحلول عام ٢٠٠٠ . وتتضمن البرامج الصحية الموصى بها بموجب هذه المبادرة تنظيم الأسرة والرعاية المتصلة بالحمل ، والرعاية أثناء الحمل ، والرعاية عند الولادة . (وقد تم تناول خدمات تنظيم الأسرة والإجهاض بصورة أكثر تفصيلاً فى الفصل الرابع) . وتتفاوت مردودية التكاليف الحدية للرعاية المتصلة بالحمل حسب الظروف ، ولكن البنك الدولى يقدر أن متوسط التكلفة لكل سنة من العمر مصححة بعامل العجز بين ٣٠ دولاراً و ١١٠ دولارات ، وهو ما يعادل مبلغاً يقل عن ٢٠٠٠ دولار لكل حالة وفاة يتم لجتنابها .

ويؤدى مد نطاق الرعاية أثناء الحمل ، وعند الولادة ، وبعد الوضع لكى تشمل ٨٠ بالمائة من سكان العالم إلى تخفيض عبء المرض المرتبط بالولادة غير المأمونة بمقدار ٤٠ فى المائة ، وذلك بتكلفة تتراوح بين ٩٠ دولاراً و ٢٥٥ دولاراً لكل حالة ولادة تخضع للرعاية ، أو من ٤ إلى ٩ دولارات للفرد . ويشتمل برنامج معقول من الرعاية أثناء الحمل على ثلاثة عناصر :

● *الاعلام والتوعية والاتصالات* التى تستهدف خلق طلب على الخدمات الاكلينيكية ، تنبيه النساء وغيرهن إلى علامات الخطر التى قد تحدث أثناء الحمل والولادة ، وتعبئة المجتمعات المحلية من أجل نقل النساء اللائى يتعرضن لمضاعفات إلى مستشفيات المركز .

● *طب التوليد القائم على أساس المجتمع* مع هيئة من الممرضات . القابلات المتدربات من أجل توفير الرعاية أثناء الحمل ، بما فى ذلك التحصين ضد شبه سم التيتانوس ، ومعالجة الزهرى ، وتوفير العناصر المغذية الدقيقة (الحديد ، والفوليت ، واليود) ، واكتشاف مضاعفات الحمل والولادة ؛ والولادة الطبيعية ، بما فى ذلك الاستخدام الوقائى للمضادات الحيوية ضد التهاب الملتحمة السيلانى ، والاسعافات الأولية لطب التوليد ، بما فيها المسكنات ضد تشنج النفاس المبكر (النوبات ذات الصلة بالحمل) ، والإزالة اليدوية للمشيمة والإحالة المبكرة الفعالة للمضاعفات الحادة ، والإجهاض المأمون .

● *مرافق المستشفيات بالمراكز* لتوفير خدمات طب التوليد الأساسية (العملية القيصرية ، والتخدير ، استبدال الدم ، الإجراءات اليدوية ، ومراقبة الولادة) ، وإنعاش المواليد الجدد (سفط الافرازات والتنفس المساعد بالاوكسجين) .

وتتوقف درجة التركيز التى تولى للعناصر المختلفة على الظروف المحلية . ولعل طرفها الأقصى من ناحية يتمثل فى المراكز التى تكون الموارد فيها محدودة والنساء معزولات . وهنا ، تكون الاولوية العليا للرعاية أثناء الحمل التى تستهدف بصفة أساسية تصحيح أوجه التصور فى عناصر التغذية الدقيقة ، والعدوى من قبيل الأمراض التى تنقل عن طريق الاتصال الجنسى والملاريا . أما الطرف الآخر فيتمثل فى المناطق الحضرية والمحيطة بالحضر حيث تطغى على مراكز الإحالة حالات الولادة العادية ، وتكون نوعية الرعاية ، منخفضة عادة ؛ وهنا ، يجب تحسين المراكز الصحية ويجب تحسين نوعية الرعاية بالمستشفى لتوفير علاج أفضل لمضاعفات التوليد .

word count: 1352

ASSIGNMENT 4: ECONOMIC/FINANCIAL

خفض الدعم للمجموعات القادرة : ينبغى أن تخفض الحكومات ، ثم تلغى فى النهاية ، الدعم العام للمجموعات الميسورة الحال نسبياً . ويتسنى تحقيق هذا عن طريق تحصيل رسوم بالتكاليف الكاملة من الأشخاص المؤمن عليهم ، الذين يستخدمون المستشفيات والعيادات الحكومية ، مقابل الخدمات غير المتضمنة فى الحزمة الإكلينيكية الأساسية ، وعن طريق إنقاص الإستقطاعات الضريبية مقابل اشتراكات التأمين . وفى جنوب أفريقيا وزمبابوى ، كان يحصل من الأفراد المؤمن عليهم أقل من التكلفة الكاملة للخدمات التى يتلقونها فى المرافق الصحية الحكومية . وبالإضافة إلى هذا ، سمح لهم بأن يستقطعوا من دخولهم الخاضعة للضرائب جزءا من أو كل مدفوعاتهم من دخلهم الخاص للرعاية الصحية ، وكذا أقساط التأمين الصحى عليهم . وبإمكان الموظفين أيضا أن يستقطعوا اشتراكاتهم التأمينية . وتخفض هذه التدابير المبالغ المتاحة لتمويل الخدمات الأساسية . وقد قدر أن الاستقطاعات الضريبية للأفراد فى جنوب افريقيا تعادل ١٨ فى المائة من إجمالى نفقات قطاع الصحة العام فى عام ١٩٩٠ . وفى محاولة أخيرة لعكس وضع مماثل ، قيدت زمبابوى بشكل حاد الاستقطاعات الضريبية للرعاية الصحية والتأمين الصحى ، ورفعت الرسوم ، وكثفت الجهود لتحصيل الرسوم من المرضى المؤمن عليهم بالقطاع الخاص . وتعلمت المستشفيات الحكومية أن بإمكانها غالبا أن تحدد المرضى المؤمن عليهم عن طريق عرض بعض صور الراحة الإضافية غير الطبية عليهم ، مثل حجرات بالمستشفيات الخاصة ، وبإمكانها أن تجعلهم هدفا لاسترداد التكاليف بشكل متزايد إذا ما قبلوا ذلك .

وفى البلدان التى لا يغطى التأمين الاجتماعى بها سوى جزء من السكان ، يكون بوسع الحكومات زيادة نطاق الخدمات الصحية الممولة ذاتيا عن طريق إلغاء الدعم العام للتأمين الاجتماعى . فهذا الدعم ، الواسع الانتشار فى أمريكا اللاتينية ، يفيد الطبقات الوسطى أساسا ولهذا فهو تنازلى . ويؤدى إلغاء الدعم إلى تحرير الموارد لأجل الخدمات الصحية للفقراء . ويفرض الغاء الدعم أيضا انضباطا ماليا على هيئات التأمين الاجتماعى ، التى غالبا ما يسمح لها

بتحقيق عجز يغطى فيما بعد بالتحويلات من برامج الضمان الاجتماعى الأخرى أو من الموازنة العامة للحكومة . ففى فنزويلا على سبيل المثال ، تدعم الحكومة الاشتراكات فى صندوق المساعدات الطبية داخل هيئة الضمان الاجتماعى شبه الحكومية . وعلى الرغم من هذا الدعم ، ففى عام ١٩٩٠ تكبد الصندوق عجزا يعادل ٣٧ فى المائة من نفقاته على الصحة .

توسيع نطاق التأمين : حينما تكون غالبية القوى العاملة موظفة بالفعل ، فإن السياسات الحكومية التى توسع نطاق تغطية التأمين إلى باقى السكان ـ بما فى ذلك المشتغلين لحساب أنفسهم ، وكبار السن ، والفقراء ـ تلغى عدم العدالة الكامنة فى نظم تمويل الصحة متعددة الطبقات ، وتوسيع محتوى خدمة الرعاية المتاحة بصورة شاملة . وحينما تصبح تغطية التأمين شاملة ، كما فى كوستاريكا ، وكوريا ، ينتهى الدعم عادة باستهداف الفقراء بالفعل ، ومن ثم فهو تصاعدى .

لكن قلة فقط من البلدان متوسطة الدخل التى تتوافر لها الموارد المالية الملائمة ، والإرادة السياسية ، والقدرة الإدارية ، هى التى تستطيع تحقيق مثل هذه التغطية الشاملة للتأمين وتبين مبادرة كوريا الجريئة فى إقامة نظام وطنى للتأمين الصحى من العدم فيما بين ١٩٧٨ و١٩٨٩ ، وجهود كوستاريكا فى الثمانينيات لتحقيق الشمول للنظام الذى كان يغطى فيما سبق قوة العمل الصناعية فقط ، أن هذا هدف صعب وإن كان قابلا للتحقيق . وسيكون بلوغ التغطية الشاملة أكثر جدوى إذا ما قصرت الحكومات الحزمة الأساسية من خدمات التأمين على تلك الخدمات ذات المردودية العالية للتكاليف .

خيارات المستهلك : تؤدى المنافسة بين موردى حزمة من الخدمات الصحية محددة بوضوح ومدفوعة مسبقا إلى تحسين النوعية والتشجيع على الكفاءة . وحتى حينما توجد منافسة مباشرة قليلة ، أو لا توجد منافسة مباشرة أصلا بين صناديق التأمين ، كما فى اليابان وكوريا ، فإن مؤسسات التأمين المتعددة شبه المستقلة قد تظل لها ميزات تفوق ما لوكالة كبيرة وحيدة تابعة للدولة ، وتميل صناديق التأمين المحلية التى تديرها مجالس تتكون من ممثلين للعاملين ، وأصحاب الأعمال والحكومة المحلية ، مثلما هو الحال فى ألمانيا ، إلى أن تكون أكثر خضوعا للمساءلة إزاء أعضائها .

وفى عدد من بلدان أمريكا اللاتينية ، فقدت « معاهد » الضمان الاجتماعى المتماثلة ، مصداقيتها بالفعل بسبب عدم كفاءتها وفسادها الإدارى فى الماضى . وتعد المنافسة والخضوع للمساءلة بدرجة أكبر هدفين أساسيين للمقترحات الحالية لإصلاح التأمين الاجتماعى فى الأرجنتين .

احتواء التكاليف: إن الدفع المشترك من جانب الأفراد المؤمن عليهم لقاء بعض الخدمات يمكن أن يساعد على الحد من استخدامهم للخدمات ، ولكنه من غير المرجح أن يكون أسلوبا قويا جدا لاحتواء التكلفة . فالدفع المشترك فى كوريا ، الذى بلغ فى المتوسط ٤٠ فى المائة من النفقات ، لم يفعل سوى التقليل فى إبطاء معدل الزيادة فى الإنفاق على الصحة ، والذى نما من ٣,٧ إلى ٦,٦ فى المائة من الناتج القومى الإجمالى خلال الثمانينيات . وبالمثل ، يبدو أن الممارسة التى أدخلتها جهات التأمين الخاصة فى الولايات المتحدة ، المتعلقة باستعراض استخدام الرعاية الطبية بأثر رجعى تؤدى إلى وفر متواضع يتم لمرة واحدة فى الانفاق على الصحة ، ولكن ليست لها آثار تظل لفترة طويلة على معدل نمو النفقات .

وعلى النقيض من ذلك ، فإن الدفع المسبق لمقدمى الرعاية الصحية يعد نهجا واعدا لاحتواء نفقات الصحة . وبوسع الحكومات تعزيز مثل تلك المشروعات عن طريق إلغاء الحواجز القانونية التى تمنع - فى كثير من البلدان - المؤسسة ذاتها من أن تقوم بدور المؤمن ومقدم الخدمة معا على حد سواء . وفى جنوب افريقيا ، قررت الحكومة مؤخرا السماح بإقامة منظمات للحفاظ على الصحة ، أساسا كوسيلة لاحتواء تكاليف الصحة . وقد أنشىء أكثر من عشرين من تلك المنظمات فى سنوات قليلة فحسب . وقد طبقت رسوم الرؤوس ورسوما تتقرر على أساس التفاوض ، والتى تحد من التكاليف بصورة أكفأ مما تفعله ترتيبات المدفوعات المفتوحة مقابل الخدمات ، والتى استخدمت تاريخيا فى جنوب افريقيا .

word count: 900

SECTION 3. TRANSLATIONS OF ASSIGNMENTS AND NOTES

ASSIGNMENT 1 - TRANSLATION

Box 2.1 Progress in child health in four countries

In the 1960s a child born in the developing world had a 77 percent chance of surviving the first five years of life. About thirty years later, the chances of survival have improved to 89 percent. How much did income growth and expansion of schooling contribute to this gain? What was the role of other factors, such as progress in science and medicine? Some answers to these questions emerge from data on child survival from seventy-five industrial and developing countries for the period between 1960 and 1987 (see note to Appendix table A.3). This box reviews the results for four countries with different income levels - Côte d'Ivoire, Costa Rica, Egypt, and Japan (see Box table 2.1 and Box figure 2.1).

In all four countries, part of the gain in child health depends on the initial levels in 1960 of schooling in the population and of income per capita. Because schooling and income per capita produce health benefits that often persist through time, health in a population may be improved simply by maintaining initial levels of schooling and income. In Costa Rica, where in 1960 income per capita was relatively high and schooling was already widespread, initial conditions accounted for 58 percent of the gain in child health between 1960 and 1987. In Côte d'Ivoire and Egypt, where the levels of schooling and income per capita were modest in 1960, initial conditions contributed only about one-fifth to one-quarter of the gains. In Japan, too, these initial conditions contributed a fifth of the gains in child health, but this is not surprising in a country where a baby's chance of survival was already very good in 1960.

In reality, of course, income and schooling have improved in all these countries, and these improvements contributed to further gains in child survival. In Côte d'Ivoire educational improvements did the most for child health, accounting for 66 percent of the gains between 1960 and 1980. For Egypt, by contrast, the figure was only 21 percent. A comparison between Côte d'Ivoire and Egypt is illuminating. The probability of surviving the first five years of life started at similar levels in both countries and improved at comparable rates. in both, too, the responsiveness of child survival to income per capita and to the schooling of adults was comparable. In Côte d'Ivoire, however, adult schooling started from much lower levels than in Egypt but increased five times faster. Income per capita in Côte d'Ivoire was nearly twice Egypt's in 1960 but then grew only 60 percent as fast. Thus, improvements in schooling were most significant in Côte d'Ivoire, whereas in Egypt growth in income per capita accounted for fully half of the gain in child health.

Costa Rica and Japan followed the same pattern as Egypt: growth of income per capita contributed substantially more to child health gains than did educational improvements.

Technical progress (estimated using the passage of time as a proxy), however, was important in Japan, whereas in Costa Rica and Egypt it mattered less than improvements in education. Except in Japan, where people were already quite well educated in 1960, the analysis probably underestimated the contribution of schooling because it dealt with the schooling of all adults rather than of women alone. Child health is particularly affected by maternal education, and the number of years of schooling received by younger women is likely to have risen much faster between 1960 and 1987 than was the case for the adult population as a whole.

General Comments:

While this text is not highly technical, the complexities of Arabic-English translation are quite obvious in almost every sentence. Aside from the fact that the basic sentence structure has to be rearranged in most sentences, the other constant difficulty facing the translator is the essential difference between Arabic and English, to wit: English is a highly technical and precise language, using such subject-specific terms as "per capita," while Arabic is much more descriptive and circumspect. In short, there is no such thing as being overcautious when translating Arabic into English.

Box 2.1 (line 1) - In Arabic the numbers appear 1.2. Be sure to reverse the numbers in English. This may seem too obvious, but because of the fact that the two languages run in opposite directions, mistakes of this kind can be made inadvertently.

In the 1960s (line 3) - Sentence structure in Arabic-English translation is very critical. Often an Arabic sentence will start with a verb, while this cannot happen in English. You should always look at the entire Arabic sentence before translating it, and decide on the right word order as well as correct meaning before you start writing your English version.

In the 1960s (line 3) - This can be written in several ways, such as sixties, or 60s, or 1960s. or 1960's, or even 60's. Whichever style you follow, be consistent, and don't switch styles for no reason. (If you translate for the U.S. Government, look up this usage on page 170 of the GPO Style Manual, 1984 edition).

77 percent (line 5) - This can be written as 77%, 77 per cent, or 77 percent. Again, be consistent and keep to the same style.

Côte D'Ivoire, Costa Rica, Egypt, and Japan (line 13) - In Arabic, these words are connected to one another by the word "and," while in English we always use commas in a series of items. Also, using a computer, you should have no problem providing the accent on the "o" in Côte D'Ivoire.

Per capita (line 16) - Here is an example of a technical English term which in Arabic is more descriptive and less precise. Finding the correct English technical terms is one important part of good Arabic-English translation.

Box table 2.1 (line 56) - In technical translation you run into a great many graphic items, such as tables, charts, diagrams, etc. Using word processing, it is relatively easy to create these graphic items, which make your translation look professional and "user friendly."

0.89 (line 61) - For decimals, the comma in Arabic is replaced by a period in English.

Lau (line 77) - Since Arabic is written in an alphabet completely different from English, and since Arabic does not have letters for vowels, only for consonants, when a non-Arabic name such as this appears in a text, it may be extremely difficult to figure out how to spell it in Roman letters. There is no easy solution for this problem. A little research may help you find the right spelling. Otherwise, you should translate the name as best you can and put the word [phonetic] following that word, to indicate that it is not necessarily the correct spelling of the name, but a phonetic rendition.

CERTIFICATE OF DIVORCE ISSUED BY AN AUTHORIZED OFFICIAL

Log Number **286462** Page Number 14

Certificate Number: 445-227

I, Mohammad Ali Yamani, official of the Family Court in Alexandria, authorized to issue divorce certificates, state that on Thursday, the 13th day of the month of Rabia I, in the year 1416 [Hijri], corresponding to August 10, 1995, at 7 o'clock p.m., in my presence and under my authority, there came before me Mr. Ali Amer Ismayil, who had been summoned for this purpose. Mr. Ismayil is an Egyptian Muslim male, section assistant chief at the Palestine Hotel of the Egyptian Hotels Company, born in Alexandria on February 21,1950, and residing at 60 Sidi Beshr St., ID Card No. 4/555//10/12/79 al-Muntazah, registration 855, whose mother's name is Saida Faysal. With him came his wife Aysha Suraya Gamal Rashidi, who is unemployed, was born in Alexandria and resides at 22 Malik St., Sidi Beshr, ID Card No. 182338//11/2/89 al-Muntazah, whose mother's name is Fatima Mohammed Hamadi, and whose marriage is confirmed by Marriage Certificate No. 9 dated 7/25/1974, issued by the late Mustafa A-Sawi, then the Authorized Official of Sidi Beshr at Al-Raml Court. After verifying the legality of her marriage and attesting to her first consummation thereof through sexual contact, and in the presence and testimony of the summoned Mahmud Ali Jabari, a contractor born in Alexandria on January 21, 1961 and residing at 45 Sidi Beshr Bahari St., ID Card No. 61789//2/12/77 al-Muntazah, and Mr. Ahmed Shiti Said, an automobile mechanic born in Alexandria on March 31, 1959 and residing at 37 Jihad St., next to the fire station, ID Card No. 104137//2/22/93 al-Muntazah, the above wife said to her above husband: "I have absolved you, my husband, of the remainder of my dowry, and of my support during the legal waiting period required of me before remarrying, and until it is legally over, and of my pleasure, and of all my legal marital rights; divorce me as such right now." He immediately answered her, saying: "You my wife, Aysha Suraya Gamal Rashidi, are divorced from me right now on such an absolvitor." They agreed that this divorce is the first of the divorces, whereby she is separated from him at the first minor level. However, she shall not be lawful to him except with a new contract and dowry which meets with her consent and satisfaction, as we have advised her.

Four copies were issued. Each received one, the third was for registration and the fourth for the court. A fee in the amount of 550 Egyptian pounds for the certificate and taxes was entrusted to me.

Witnesses:	Divorcee:	Divorcee:	Authorized Official:
Mahmud Ali Jabari Ahmed Shiti Said	Ali Amer Yismayil	Aysha Suraya Gamal Rashidi	Muhammad Ali Yamai

AL-BAYAN COMMERCE

Number: 17/95
Date : 12 January 1995

Mr. Ibrahim G. Ibrahim
General Manager, Continental Foods, Saudi Arabia

Greetings:

A person has registered a trademark under the name Latifa Oil with the aim of creating confusion with, and exploiting the trade name of Latif Oil. This person and his partners might bottle poor quality edible oils and market them in Syria under the trademark Latifa Oil.

It is our understanding that this person had alleged at the Department of Industrial and Commercial Proprietorship Protection in Syria that he had a daughter named Latifa, and so he wanted to use that name as a trademark. His request to register that trade name was thus granted.

We are hereby forwarding the documents pertaining to that trademark, as well as pertaining to the Latif Oil trademark. Please make sure that the latter is re-registered before the expiry date.

We also request that you send us a special authorization from Continental Foods, which owns the trademark of Latif Oil. The authorization should be issued by the Saudi Justice Clerk and endorsed by the Embassy of Syria. This authorization should give me the necessary powers to file criminal and civil suits, represent the company, contact all specialized agencies and departments, submit all the necessary applications and requests, hire attorneys, file claims for compensation for matters affecting the trademark Latif Oil and for damage sustained as a result of the trademark having been exploited by others, especially claims against the trademark Latifa Oil registered with the Department of Commercial and Industrial Proprietorship Protection in Syria under number 53325 and dated 28 July 1994, and against all personnel having anything to do, directly or indirectly, with this trademark or any other matter. (My name is Yusef Ahmed Ben Ibrahim).

Please take this matter seriously and take swift and appropriate action so that we can counter this problem and resolve it at this early stage.

My best regards.

Yusef Ahmed Ben Ibrahim

ASSIGNMENT 2 - NOTES

General Comments

The two samples included under the "legal" section represent a divorce certificate and a business letter related to a registered trademark. The first thing to bear in mind in doing this type of translation, is that each type of legal document has its own specific style and format, which should be followed as closely as possible in the translation. This applies to both the text itself and to the format. To the extent possible, an original page should correspond as closely as possible to the translation page.

Having said this, however, it is clear in the first document, namely, the divorce paper, that the Arabic opening sentence, which is one long run-on sentence, is just too complex and convoluted to make much sense in English. As a result, the text had to be restructured in translation, so as to become more logical and cohesive.

The business letter, on the other hand, is much clearer and better organized, and does not require much change in translation. Notice the greeting in the beginning of the letter, a much different style from English business letters.

I, Mohammad Ali Yamani (line 5) - The Arabic original starts with the date of the divorce ceremony, and works its way to the identity of the divorce official and the rest of the participants. In English, however, this makes it quite difficult to understand the sentence, which is why it had to be rearranged. The important thing to bear in mind when rearranging a complex sentence, is not to alter any of the meaning, and to make sure every single element of the text is accounted for in the translation. A long, run-on sentence can be broken down into shorter sentences, and punctuation such as commas and semi-colons can be used to further elucidate the meaning of each phrase, eliminating ambiguities.

Family court (line 5-6) - Names of courts vary from country to country. Be sure your rendition of courts (Family Court, Court of Appeal, etc.) is accurate.

[Hijri] (line 4) - Sometimes you need to add a word or phrase in brackets, to indicate that it is not necessarily part of the text, but rather a clarification of the original.

Sidi Beshr (line 9) - Lacking vowels, you could also translate this place name as "Saidi Bishir." Here a general acquaintance with the city of Alexandria, Egypt may help, or else a good atlas.

A person has registered (page 2, line 7), *It is our understanding* (line 10), *directly or indirectly* (line 23) - These are examples of formal writing in an Arabic business letter, which should be adhered to. It is extremely important in business letters to follow the established style, since the image and credibility of the communicating parties is at stake, and no one wants to sound incompetent or out of step with established business procedures.

Controlling river blindness

Onchocerciasis, or river blindness as it is more commonly known, is caused by a parasitic worm which produces millions of larvae that move through the body, causing intense itching, debilitation, and eventually blindness. The disease is spread by a small, fiercely biting blackfly that transmits the larvae from infected to uninfected people.

The goals of the Onchocerciasis Control Programme (OCP), set up in 1974 and covering eleven Sahelian countries, are to control the blackfly by destroying its larvae with insecticides sprayed from the air. The environmental impact of the insecticides is continuously monitored by an independent ecological committee, in cooperation with the national governments. The committee has full authority to screen insecticides and to approve or reject their use. The program has also collaborated with the pharmaceutical industry to develop for human us a drug, ivermectin, that safely and effectively kills the larvae in the body. Ivermectin, however has little impact on the adult worm and so must be supplemented with vector control by aerial spraying. The producer of ivermectin, Merck & Co., has committed itself to provide the drug free of charge as long as it is needed to combat river blindness.

The OCP's four sponsoring agencies - the Food and Agriculture Organization, the United Nations Development Programme (UNDP), the World Bank, and WHO - through a steering committee chaired by the World Bank, make broad policy decisions and oversee operations. WHO has executive responsibility through a team of entomologists, epidemiologists, field staff, and pilots; 97 percent of the staff are nationals of the participating countries. The World Bank organizes the finances and manages them through a trust fund. It also supports socioeconomic development in the areas affected by the disease.

The program is widely regarded as a great success. It protects from river blindness about 30 million people, including more than 9 million children born since the OCP began, at an annual cost of less the $1 per person. More than 1.5 million people who were once seriously infected have completely recovered. It is estimated that the program will have prevented at least 500,000 cases of blindness by the time it is wound up around the end of the century. And it is already freeing approximately 25 million hectares of previously blighted land for resettlement and cultivation, boosting agricultural production.

The estimated cost of the OCP during the whole of its existence, from 1974 to 2000, is about $570 million. Its estimated internal rate of return is in the range of 16 to 28 percent (depending on the pace at which the newly available land is settled, the incremental output added by the new land, the income level of the OCP area, and the productivity growth rate that is projected). These estimated benefits do not include the program's favorable effects on income distribution; its main beneficiaries are subsistence farmers whose incomes are well below average.

Box 5.1 Making pregnancy and delivery safe

Under optimal conditions, about 990 of every 1,000 pregnancies that reach the seventh month of gestation conclude with a healthy newborn and a healthy mother. For most women in the developing world, however, childbirth is unsafe. About one in 50 women in developing countries dies as a consequence of complications of pregnancy and childbirth, compared with only one in 2,700 in the established market economies. maternal mortality has profound consequences within the household; the chances of dying for children under 5 increase by up to 50 percent when the mother dies.

In 1987 the international health community, including the World Bank, WHO, the United Nations Population Fund (UNPF), and agencies in forty-five countries, launched the Safe Motherhood Initiative. The prime goal is to reduce by half the number of maternal deaths by 2000. The health programs recommended under the initiative include family planning and pregnancy-related care, prenatal care, and delivery care. (Family planning and abortion services are discussed more fully in Chapter 4.) The marginal cost-effectiveness of pregnancy-related care varies with circumstances, but the World Bank has estimated that the average cost per DALY is between $30 and $110, the equivalent of less than $2,000 per death averted.

The extension of prenatal, delivery, and postpartum care to 80 percent of the world's population would reduce by 40 percent the burden of disease associated with unsafe childbirth, at a cost of between $90 and $255 per birth attended, or $4 to $9 per capita. A reasonable program of pregnancy-related care would include three components:

• *Information, education and communications* designed to create demand for clinical services, alert women and others to danger signs that may occur during pregnancy and childbirth, and mobilize communities for transport of women with complications to district hospitals.

• *Community-based obstetrics* with trained nurse-midwife staff to provide prenatal care, including tetanus toxoid immunization, treatment for syphilis, provision of micronutrients (iron, folate, and iodine), and detection of complications of pregnancy and delivery; normal delivery, including prophylactic application of antibiotics against gonorrheal ophthalmia; obstetric first aid, including sedatives for early eclampsia (pregnancy-related seizures) and manual removal of the placenta; effective early referral of severe complications; and safe abortion.

•*District hospital facilities* to provide essential obstetric services (cesarean section, anesthesia, blood replacement, manual procedures, and monitoring of labor) and neonatal resuscitation (aspiration of secretions and assisted respiration with oxygen).

The emphasis given the different components will depend on local conditions. At one extreme are districts where resources are limited and women are highly isolated. Here, high priorities would be prenatal care aimed mainly at correcting micronutrient deficiencies and infections such as STDs and malaria. At the other extreme are urban and periurban areas where referral centers are overwhelmed with normal deliveries and the quality of care is typically low; here, health centers should be improved so that they can deal with normal births, and the quality of hospital care should be enhanced to provide better treatment of obstetric complications.

General Comments

a. Subject matter

Although these particular texts present many examples of specific terminology, the text themselves are straightforward, and present no real difficulty in terms of sentence structure or language style. Unless one is thoroughly familiar with the medical terminology of the text, it would be best not to start translating right away, but first make a list of all such terms in the text one is not certain of.

b. References

A good Arabic-English medical dictionary should have all or nearly all of the technical terms of these texts. If after a thorough consultation with such a source you still have an unknown term, the next thing to do is call someone with an appropriate professional background.

Onchocerciasis (line 2) - This is an example of medical terminology which, if you are not absolutely sure of the spelling, you should look up in the dictionary to verify. Needless to say, in translating medical documents, a high degree of precision is required, since there have been cases where an innocent little mistake, such as changing a letter in the name of a disease, or putting the period in the wrong place in a number pertaining to a dosage, had dire consequences for the end users of the translation, and for the translator as well.

OCP (line 7) - Acronyms are often used in English technical subjects to save space and make communication easier. Arabic is not as prone to using acronyms as English. Besides, because the respective alphabets are so different, and because Arabic does not use vowel-letters, it is often hard to replicate English acronyms in Arabic, or vice versa.

Food and Agricultural Organization (line 20) - Names of organizations may require looking up reference sources. Otherwise, call your clients and find out from them what the exact name of the particular organization is.

97 percent (line 26) - Be consistent in using either "percent," "per cent," or "%."

Community-based obstetrics (page 2, line 30) - Here again we have a very subject-specific English term, while the Arabic is more descriptive.

-REDUCTION OF SUBSIDIES TO BETTER-OFF GROUPS. Governments should reduce and eventually eliminate public subsidies to relatively affluent groups. This can be done by charging full-cost fees to insured persons who use government hospitals and clinics for services not included in the national essential clinical package and by cutting tax deductions for insurance contributions. In South Africa and Zimbabwe privately insured individuals have been charged less than the full cost of the services they receive in government health facilities. In addition, they have been allowed to deduct from taxable income part or all of their out-of-pocket payments for health care, as well as their health insurance premiums. Employers can also deduct their insurance contributions. These measures reduce the amounts available for financing essential services. In South Africa individual tax deductions were estimated to be equivalent to 18 percent of total public sector health expenditures in 1990. In a recent effort to reverse a similar situation, Zimbabwe has sharply limited tax deductions for health care and insurance, raised fees, and intensified efforts to collect fees from privately insured patients. Government hospitals have learned that they can often identify insured patients by offering them extra nonmedical amenities, such as private hospital rooms, and can then target them for aggressive cost recovery if they accept.

In countries where social insurance covers only a fraction of the population, governments can increase the extent to which health services are self-financing by eliminating public subsidies to social insurance. These subsidies, which are widespread in Latin America, mostly benefit the middle classes and are therefore regressive. Elimination of the subsidies would free resources for health services for the poor. Eliminating subsidies also imposes more financial discipline on the social insurance agencies, which are often allowed to run deficits that are later covered by transfers from other social security programs or from the general government budget. In Venezuela, for example, the government subsidizes contributions to the medical assistance fund within the parastatal social security agency. Despite this subsidy, in 1990 the fund ran a deficit equivalent to 37 percent of its health expenditures.

EXTENSION OF INSURANCE. Where the bulk of the labor force is already employed, government policies that extend insurance coverage to the rest of the population - including the self-employed, the elderly, and the poor - remove the inequities inherent in multitiered systems of health financing and expand the content of the universally available package of care. When insurance coverage becomes universal, as in Costa Rica and Korea, subsidies actually end up targeting the poor and are thus progressive. But only a few middle-income countries that have adequate financial resources, political resolve, and administrative capacity will be able to achieve such universal insurance coverage. Korea's bold initiative to create a national health insurance system from scratch between 1978 and 1989 and Costa Rica's efforts in the 1980s to universalize a system that had previously covered only the industrial labor force show that this is a difficult but achievable goal. Attaining universal coverage would be more feasible if governments limited the essential package of insured services to those with high cost-effectiveness.

CONSUMER CHOICE. Competition among suppliers of a clearly specified prepaid package of health services would improve quality and encourage efficiency. And even where there is little or no direct competition among insurance funds, as in Japan and Korea, multiple semi-independent insurance institutions may still have advantages over a single large parastatal agency. Local insurance funds managed by boards composed of representatives of workers, employers, and local government, as in Germany, tend to be more accountable to their members. In a number of Latin American countries monolithic social security "institutes" are already heavily discredited because of their past inefficiencies and corruption. Greater competition and accountability are two of the main objectives of current proposals for reforming social insurance in Argentina.

COST CONTAINMENT. Copayment by insured individuals for some services can help to restrain their use of the services but is unlikely to be a very powerful cost-containment method. Copayments amounting to an average 40 percent of expenditures in Korea have done little to slow the rate of increase in health spending, which grew from 3.7 to 6.6 percent of GNP during the 1980s. Similarly, the practice, introduced by private U.S. insurers of retrospective reviews of utilization of medical care appears to lead to a modest one-time savings in health spending but does not have long-lasting effects on the rate of growth of expenditures.

By contrast, prepayment of health care providers is a promising approach to containing health expenditures. Governments could help to promote such schemes by removing legal barriers that in many countries prevent the same institution from acting as both insurer and provider. In South Africa the government recently decided to allow the creation of health maintenance organizations (HMOs), mainly as a way of containing health costs. More than twenty such organizations have been established in just a few years. They have introduced capitation and negotiated fees, which limit costs more effectively than did the open-ended fee-for-service payment arrangements historically used in South Africa.

Governments can do much to improve the incentives created by social insurance. Where the insured use private providers, fee-for-service payment schemes need to be replaced with an alternative - capitation or annually negotiated uniform fees for doctors and hospitals (based on diagnostic-related groups of procedures, for example) or preset overall budgets for hospitals. Where social insurance covers services by government hospitals, competition with the private sector can improve performance. Other promising approaches ar to allow government hospitals to compete with one another as semiautonomous enterprises, as in the United Kingdom in recent years, and to give hospital managers financial and career incentives to meet performance targets, as in Chile.

The example of Chile (Box 7.2) illustrates the benefits and perils of health sector reform in a middle-income country. Chile has been able to improve efficiency, quality of care, and consumer choice, but the reforms have also created new problems regarding administration, financing, and equity.

General Comments:

a. Financial Translation

In translation, there is a basic difference between translating financial subjects and any other technical subjects, such as legal or medical. While it is relatively easy to master the methodology of working with most technical vocabularies, even if one does not have the technical or professional background in the particular field in which one translates, in financial subjects it is necessary to have at least a general knowledge of the subject. This may be due to the fact that financial terminology and concepts are not always as readily translatable as other technical subjects. The upshot of all this is that one should not be hasty to accept a financial translation assignment if one does not work in this field on a regular basis.

b. Subject matter

This particular assignment consists of a text derived from a publication of an international financial organization. As with most major organizations and corporations, this organization has its own so-called "corporate style," which affects the way this material is translated. Normally, an organization of this magnitude employs its own translators, or uses outside translators on a regular basis, to acquaint them with its style. If called upon to translate this kind of text, be sure to familiarize yourself with the organization's style.

Public subsidies, full cost fees (lines 2-5) - These are examples of very subject-specific English terms. Once again, the Arabic original is more descriptive and implicit, while the English is highly specific. The Arabic word for "subsidies" is actually "assistance," which is not as precise as "subsidies." Nor is the word "cost" specified. This is a major difficulty in handling financial text in the two languages and trying to achieve a high degree of precision.

Cost containment (page 3, line 6) - Here again is an example of a well-established English financial term, which in Arabic is more descriptive, and can be easily mistranslated. Acquaintance with this kind of terminology in English is essential for the accurate translation of financial subjects.

Copayment (line 6-7) - The Arabic refers to "participating payment," which again can be easily mistranslated. Copayment is a term in finance, insurance, health care and other finance-related fields.

6.6 percent (line 12) - Whenever dealing with numbers in an Arabic-English translation, especially in financial text, double check to make sure periods and commas are not transposed, the direction of the numbers is reversed from right to left if necessary, and any other visual pitfalls, such as the use of a period in Arabic to denote zero, are not overlooked.

creation of health maintenance organizations (HMOs) (lines 25-30) - HMOs are a well-established institution in the American health care field, while the Arabic does not take cognizance of this fact, but rather refers to "establishing enterprises to maintain health." It is clear from the context that this refers to the HMO concept, but can easily be missed if you are not familiar with this type of institution.

Part Two

Translation: English into Arabic

5-6/2.5-3 hours

ASSIGNMENT 1 - GENERAL

Box 7.6 Donor coordination in the health sector in Zimbabwe and Bangladesh

The *Zimbabwe* Second Family Health Project (1992-96) is the culmination of a long period of interaction between the government of Zimbabwe, the World Bank, and other multilateral and bilateral donors. The $120 million project, which supports the government's five-year investment program for population, health, and nutrition, is designed benefit directly low-income households, especially women and children. Zimbabwe has entered a period of economic adjustment that will necessitate spending cuts. The project will help poor and vulnerable households from some adverse effects of adjustment by mobilizing additional resources for human resource development and by improving the equity and efficiency of spending.

Zimbabwean participation was emphasized from the project's beginning. The project preparation committee included representatives from various central government departments, provincial governments, and the Zimbabwe National Family Planning Council. The committee set planning guidelines, including a preliminary outline of project components, costs, and financing. Using these guidelines, proposals were prepared locally and were then reviewed by the committee and by interested donors.

Virtually all the major donors to the health sector in Zimbabwe helped with planning the project by assigning agency officials and technical specialists to the donor team that advised the government on design issues. In the end, the project received financing from Denmark, the European Community, Norway, Sweden, the United Kingdom, and the World Bank. Donors monitor project implementation jointly rather than separately, reducing the time needed for donor review and the administrative burden on the government.

In *Bangladesh* the World Bank and ten bilateral agencies together are contributing $440 million to the Fourth Population and Health Project, and the government is providing $165 million, for a total of $605 million over the five-year project period. The United Nations Population Fund, WHO, and UNICEF are supplying project management, procurement, and technical assistance. All the partners in the project belong to the Bangladesh Population and Health Consortium, which has emerged as an important collective force in the health sector. The Asian Development Bank has joined the consortium with a view to ensuring consistency between the project and its own $60 million investment in population and health in Bangladesh.

During project formulation the government and the donors held several workshops in Dhaka and a special conference in Geneva. These workshops were instrumental in forging a consensus on population and health strategies. The consortium approach enables the government and the donor community to agree on an overall strategy and to work out a consistent financing plan for the sector. The consortium operates on the basis of strict equality of all the partners, independent of the size of their financial contributions.

In addition to strengthening Bangladesh's population program and its delivery system for family planning services, the consortium is attempting to reorient the health care system toward public health, including maternal health. It is also trying to make basic services more easily accessible to the rural and urban poor.

Box 7.4 Health assistance and the effectiveness of aid

Recent evaluations of the effectiveness of aid, including a classic 1986 study commissioned by the world donor community, point toward the same conclusion: most aid has been successful, but a considerable share, perhaps a third or more, has been much less so, and a small percentage has failed completely or has even been harmful. These broad-brush averages hide significant regional differences: in Asia and Latin America performance has been better; in Sub-Saharan Africa it has been worse. Aid has been least effective in the poorest countries, where success is most needed.

The reasons for inferior performance lie with both donors and recipients. Poor countries and those experiencing political conflict and instability constitute a difficult environment for aid, as they have little administrative capacity or infrastructure. But these difficulties have in many cases been compounded by unfortunate policies. Aid projects have been poorly designed, both technically and because of inadequate understanding of the human, social, institutional, and political environment. When it comes to coordination, both sides have been at fault. Donors have pursued their own objectives without attempting to ensure that their aid complements that of others. And all too often, aid recipients have played one donor off against another, while ministers and ministries have focused on their own concerns rather than looking to the national good.

Aid for health has generally had a good technical record. It has fit in well with development priorities, especially in recent years, as the concentration on hospitals and high-technology curative medicine has been replaced by an emphasis on primary and preventive care. There have also been major successes - mainly highly focused initiatives such as the program for the eradication of smallpox, the drive against child mortality, and the effort to control river blindness in Africa. What is still lacking is the ability of the aid system to help set in place and sustain locally appropriate public health programs and essential clinical services.

word count: 822

What Everyone Should Know about Asthma

What is asthma?

It's a lung condition that makes breathing difficult.
Asthma may be mild or severe.
Many people with asthma have only mild symptoms. Others have constant difficulty breathing. In rare cases, an asthma attack can be fatal.
The cause of asthma is not known. However, asthma does tend to run in families. It often appears first during childhood.
Asthma cannot be cured, but it can be controlled.
This booklet is not a substitute for an informed discussion between a patient and a health-care provider of the information, procedures or medications discussed in this booklet.

Why should I learn about asthma?

Here are a few good reasons:
Asthma affects millions of people. It affects males and females equally (though childhood cases more often involve boys). Chances are, you know someone who has asthma.
Many people don't know they have asthma, so it often goes untreated.
Treatment is important. People with asthma can learn to:
- prevent many attacks
- recognize warning signals of a coming attack
- seek treatment early, when it's most effective.

Learn more about asthma.

Take a look at the respiratory system:

Air enters through the nose and/or mouth. It travels through the voice box (larynx) and enters the windpipe (trachea).
The windpipe divides into branches. The branches (bronchial tubes) spread throughout the lungs.
The branches lead to tiny air sacs. The sacs (alveoli) are surrounded by tiny blood vessels. Oxygen and other gases can pass between the alveoli and the blood vessels.
Breathing in brings needed oxygen to the bloodstream.
Breathing out allows the body to get rid of waste gas (carbon dioxide) from the blood.

When asthma strikes

Here's what happens before, during and after an attack.
Something triggers an attack. The trigger causes the respiratory system to react. (See pages 8-9 for a list of common triggers).
Muscle spasms grip the bronchial tubes. Muscles surrounding the tubes squeeze tight.
The tubes become inflamed. Swelling makes air passages even narrower.
Mucus production increases. The sticky liquid further clogs the bronchial tubes.
The bronchial tubes remain inflamed. In turn, this inflammation makes the lungs more sensitive to triggers - and more subject to asthma attacks. A vicious cycle can develop.

Asthma can make breathing difficult

Narrowing of the airways can make it hard to breathe in or out.

Symptoms vary from person to person. An asthma attack can cause a variety of symptoms, including:

- wheezing
- shortness of breath, gasping
- coughing
- pain or tightness in the chest.

Symptoms may appear suddenly.
Spasms in the bronchial tubes may lead to sudden difficulty in breathing. Or, symptoms may occur regularly.

Asthma often strikes at night.
People with asthma may awaken struggling to breathe. They may have a hard time sleeping because of nighttime attacks.

These symptoms can also be signs of other health problems. Anyone experiencing these symptoms should seek medical help.

Some people have warning signs of an attack.
In the hours or days before an attack, they may notice:
- an itchy throat or chin
- coughing or sneezing
- a runny nose
- fatigue
- slight changes in breathing.

Recognizing warning signs is important.

By being aware of these signs, people with asthma can take steps to:
- prevent some attacks
- make other attacks less severe.

About asthma triggers

An asthma attack occurs after exposure to a certain substance or situation. Some common triggers include:
Airborne allergens. Allergens are things that people are allergic to. Common airborne allergens include:
- dust and dust mites (microscopic spiders)
- mold
- pollen
- animal dander (tiny flakes of skin).

Infections of the respiratory system:
These include colds, the flu, sore throats and other common illnesses.

Irritants.
Common ones are tobacco smoke, air pollution and perfumes. Chemical used in some workplaces can also trigger asthma.

Certain types of exercise:
People with asthma can and should exercise - but only under a health-care provider's direction.

Aspirin:
Medications containing aspirin can trigger attacks in some people. Certain other drugs can do the same.

Weather:
Cold weather or other extremes or changes in the weather can set off an asthma attack.

Emotional stress or excitement:
Emotions do not cause asthma. But, the body's response to stress or excitement may trigger an attack.
+
Triggers vary from person to person.

How is asthma diagnosed?

If a person is having asthma symptoms, a health-care provider may order:

A physical exam and medical history.
These provide a picture of the patient's overall health.

Lung function tests.
These show how the lungs are working and how they respond to certain treatments.

A chest X-ray.
An X-ray can reveal other problems that may be causing symptoms.

A health-care provider may also recommend the following:

- blood tests
- sputum tests (a study of liquid coughed up from the lungs)
- allergy tests, to help identify asthma triggers.

Keeping asthma under control

People with asthma need to work closely with their health-care provider to:

Identify and avoid triggers
whenever possible. In some cases, treatment to overcome allergies may help.

Control symptoms
with medication. This includes drugs that are:

- taken regularly, to control lung inflammation and prevent attacks
- used as needed, to open bronchial tubes during an attack.

Asthma medication is often inhaled using an inhaler and spacer device. Inhaling the medication can increase its effectiveness and reduce side effects.

Monitor their condition.
- for example, with a peak flow meter. People with asthma can use this device to see how well their lungs are working. Changes in lung function give an early warning of an asthma attack.

Loved ones and others should also learn about asthma, so they can help during an attack.

Some questions and answers

Is asthma contagious?
No. You cannot get asthma from another person.

Can a person with asthma play sports?
Yes! In fact, exercise can be a big part of an asthma treatment program. People with asthma have competed at the highest levels of organized sports.
People with asthma need to work closely with a health-care provider to plan a safe exercise program.

Don't children usually outgrow asthma?
It is possible for children to outgrow asthma. However, there is no way to be sure this will happen or that the condition won't return. Anyone with asthma symptoms should seek medical help right away. They should not wait for the problem to go away.

Does wheezing always mean asthma?
No. Wheezing can have many causes besides asthma. In addition, many people with asthma never wheeze at all.
If you experience wheezing or any other breathing problem, get help right away.

How does secondhand smoke affect people with asthma?
Smoke of any kind is a common trigger for asthma attacks. People with asthma should stay away from known irritants - including tobacco smoke of all kinds.

What's the long-term outlook for people with asthma?
With proper treatment and monitoring, the outlook is excellent! Most people with asthma can control their symptoms and prevent many attacks. New drugs and treatments have fewer side effects, even when taken over long periods.

word count: 1161

Public and private finance of clinical services

Around the world, clinical services are financed through four main channels. Two - out-of-pocket payments and voluntary insurance - are private. The other two are public: compulsory insurance (sometimes known as social insurance) that is either publicly managed or heavily regulated by governments, and funding from general government revenues.

In the poorest countries total health expenditure may be as low as $2 per person a year, and more than half of this comes from private sources, mainly in the form of out-of-pocket payments. Insurance mechanisms in those countries are weak, and the amount of government revenues devoted to health is low. As incomes increase, so do both the percentage of income spent on health (as shown in the upper panel of Figure 5.1) and the share of health spending that comes from public sources (illustrated in the lower panel). In the formerly socialist economies and the established market economies (excluding the United States) public spending accounts for a full three-quarters of total health expenditure.

In addition to the four sources of health financing, there are three ways of organizing clinical health services: public, private nonprofit, and private for-profit. All national health systems use at least two of the twelve possible combinations of financing method and health service organization, and sometimes the different combinations serve sharply differentiated populations. Even so, it is possible to group countries according to income level and the predominant system of providing health care. A principal distinction is whether insurance pays for much care and, if so, what is the dominant type of insurance (Table 5.2).

In low-income countries private out-of-pocket payments account for more than half of the mere $2 to $40 per person spent each year for health care. Most of this sum goes for doctors' fees, payments to traditional healers, and drugs. NGOs, particularly those related to religious institutions, make important contributions to the provision of health services in many low-income countries. In Tanzania and Haiti NGOs operate nearly half of the hospitals, and in Cameroon and Uganda they manage 40 percent of health facilities. In Ghana and Nigeria about a third of all hospital beds are located in mission hospitals. Government spending from general tax revenues generally amounts to less than half of the 2 to 7 percent of GNP allocated to health services. There is little or no insurance.

Until recently, China was an important exception among low-income countries. There, between 1960 and 1980, state enterprises provided health care directly to their workers or contracted with government hospitals to do so. Rural communes were required to earmark a portion of their financial resources for health services for all their members. By the late 1970s insurance covered virtually all the urban population and 85 percent of the rural populations unique achievement for a low income developing country. Since the elimination of communal agriculture and the liberalization of industry in the early 1980s, however, these forms of health insurance and service delivery have weakened considerably. The rural population increasingly relies on a system of government provided health care financed in part out of general revenues, but with substantial cost recovery through user charges, not unlike systems prevailing in other low-income countries.

In the *middle-income countries* there are two major types of health systems, distinguished by whether the government or the private sector provides health insurance. Health spending, at $20 to $400 per capita, is higher than in low-income countries, and both public and private managerial capacity is stronger. In countries with private insurance, such as South Africa and Zimbabwe, the government uses general revenues to pay for health care for middle- and low-income groups, while upper income households (less than 20 percent of the population) use private insurance to pay for private physicians and hospitals or for private rooms in government hospitals.

In countries with social insurance, mandatory contributions from employees and employers, and sometimes government funds, finance insurance for part of the population, including most middle class workers. Health care for the poor is financed from general revenues. This is the system that prevails in Korea, Turkey, and most of Latin America.

In the *formerly socialist economies* of Eastern Europe and the Soviet Union, general revenue financing with government provision of health services was until recently the only officially recognized form of health care. Public spending on health now accounts for 3 to 6 percent of GNP in these countries, or $30 to $200 per capita. Prior to the period of political and economic liberalization in the late 1980s, private payments were frequently made for "public" health services (for example, gratuities were given physicians in government hospitals), and drugs often leaked from the public sector into private markets. Since the political and economic reforms that swept across these countries in the late 1980s, the health systems there have been in crisis. Dwindling public funding and deteriorating government services have created strong pressures for new forms of public and private insurance.

Table 5.1 Rationales and directions for government action in the finance and delivery of clinical services

Area	Conditions that may call for government action: market failure and poverty	Directions for government action
Essential clinical services	Failure to treat, for example, tuberculosis and STDs creates risks for the general population. Public financing can help offset the additional external costs to society. Poor people have limited ability to save or borrow to meet unexpected and uninsured health expenses. Families, including children, can fall into poverty because of ill health.	*Finance* essential clinical services by reallocating current government spending. In low-income countries this may mean increasing public expenditures for health. *Require* through legislation that social insurance or mandated private insurance cover an essential package. *Encourage* more private and NGO provision of essential services, through appropriate legislation and targeted public subsidies.
Clinical services outside the essential package	In insurance markets selection bias leads to lack of coverage for high-risk groups. "Moral hazard," by insulating patient and provider from the cost implications of their decisions, results in overuse of services. The asymmetry of information between patient and provider can cause suppliers to induce excess demand.	*Reduce or eliminate* subsidization of clinical services outside the essential package. Subsidies for public provision of services at less than cost and tax relief for employer and employee health insurance payments often cover services with low cost-effectiveness and primarily benefit the wealthy. *Legislate* compulsory social insurance or mandated private insurance, or define the national essential package comprehensively. *Limit* government involvement in delivery of nonessential services and encourage competition in service delivery by government, NGOs, and the private sector. *Regulate* private insurance by, for example, requiring community risk-rating and forbidding the rejection of high-risk consumers. *Define* the exact content of prepaid packages of care to serve as the products bought and sold in the insurance market. *Encourage* the use of prepayment or salary-based approaches to provider compensation. *Foster* improvements in the quality of private provision by encouraging self-regulation of hospitals, medical schools, and physicians and by disseminating performance indicators.

word count: 837

BOX 6

ELEMENTS OF INSTITUTIONAL COMPETENCE IN MICROENTERPRISE FINANCE ORGANIZATIONS

I. Scale

- The leading microenterprise finance institutions have achieved active portfolios from several million dollars to hundreds of millions, and serve more than 10,000 clients (up to one million); such levels of outreach constitute a potential vision for other aspiring organizations.

- Delinquency is held well below 8 percent and long-run loss ratios are less than 4 percent, often far less.

II. Financial Structure and Institutional Type

- Microenterprise finance institutions can have many different origins and institutional types, underpinning surprisingly similar operations.

- Mature organizations gain access to funding from the local financial system and from their own clients. They must develop strong financial management in order to achieve such access.

- The development of formal financial institutions is emerging as a trend, and it is often necessary to move from depending on international donors to depending on the local financial system.

III. Operational Structure and Productivity

- ***Retail units*** are designed to fit closely with methodology and usually comprise standardized staff functions and routines.

- The ***superstructure*** functions both as a service provider and a control mechanism, and achieves a careful balance between each.

- Retail units must focus on achieving high ***productivity***. Because salaries are such a high percentage of total costs, profitability depends more on high staff productivity than on cost controls. Currently, unit staffs can handle between 11 5 to 280 credit clients per unit staff, and many more savings clients if voluntary savings are offered.

Costs as a percentage of average portfolio range from 12 to 25 percent, with the higher percentages occurring in organizations facing high salary structures. Organizations face pressure to increase loan sizes in order to lower that figure, but must consider whether such a change fits the organization's mission.

IV. Managing Information

- Successful institutions are driven to focus at all levels on a few key indicators of performance. For some, especially growing NGOs, these key indicators are numbers of loans or portfolio quality.

Evolution to a focus on profits internalizes concern with cost control and provides incentives for high productivity directly within retail units. The profit center focus is supplemented by monitoring of portfolio quality and loan size.

- High quality information systems are timely, relevant, and accurate, and serve all levels of an institution, including clients, field workers, supervisors, and policy makers. Information systems must guard against overwhelming users with too much data.

- Computers are not synonymous with information systems. Good information systems are possible without computers at the retail level. Computers should be viewed only as a productivity enhancing tool.

V. Human Resources

- Successful organizations recruit young people with little prior job experience, who demonstrate the ability to work in the informal sector and to absorb the corporate culture.

- In-house training is a process of passing highly job-specific information from existing staff to new recruits. It relies on oral tradition and learning-by-doing, supplemented by classroom reinforcement that emphasizes corporate culture.

- Successful organizations employ a wide range of staff motivators, including commitment to organizational mission, good prospects for career advancement, organization of units as teams, attractive salaries and benefits, and specific incentive programs.

VI. The Living Organization

- Strong leadership is not a matter of "charisma," but does require extended commitment to provide continuity to the institution, as well as a combination of talents such as operational knowledge, external relations, and the ability to motivate people.

- Active boards of directors and competent senior staff are essential, particularly as the role of the executive evolves, and leadership succession is faced.

- Organizations have achieved high growth based on "horizontal" expansion into new geographic areas, often consistently above 20 percent. "Vertical" growth within existing areas is more difficult as it challenges their successful retail unit formula.

- Innovation requires systematic attention to three stages: product and market identification; delivery system design, and organization-wide implementation. In considering new services, the limits in capacity of existing retail units must be respected.

- Leading organizations have shown resilience in coping with inevitable crises that any microenterprise finance organizations may one day face. Swift and sure policy-level action is crucial in helping organizations adjust to major shocks.

APPENDIX

THE RETAIL UNITS OF MAJOR MICROENTERPRISE FINANCE INSTITUTIONS

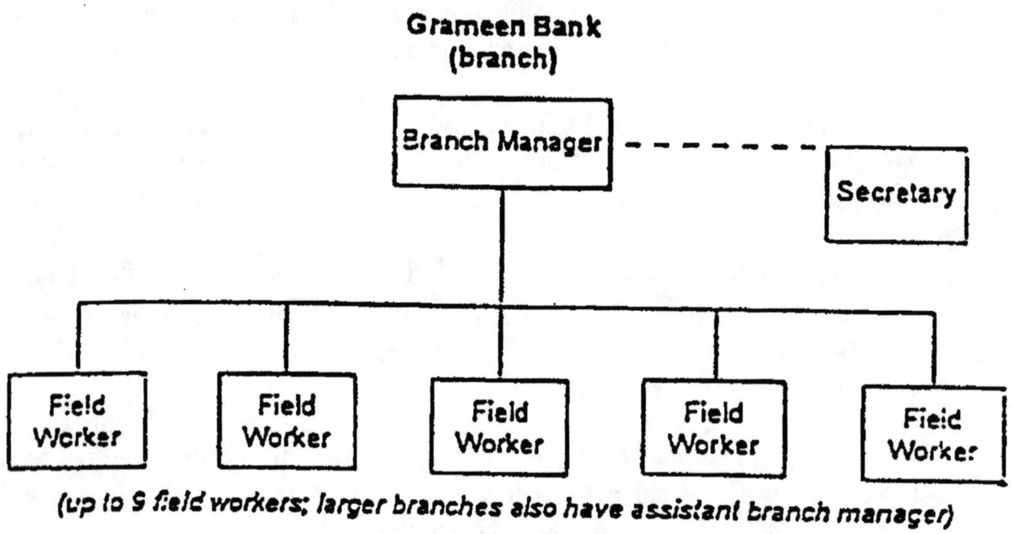

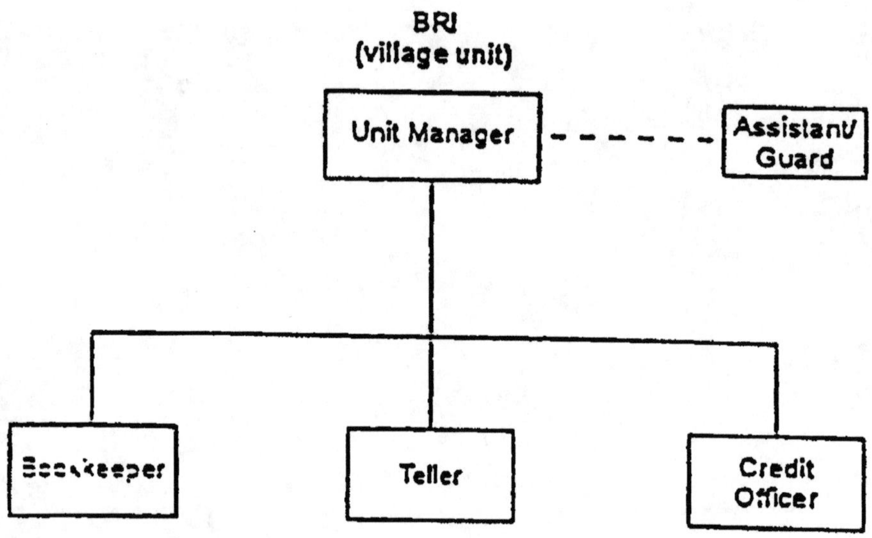

APPENDIX

THE RETAIL UNITS OF MAJOR MICROENTERPRISE FINANCE INSTITUTIONS (cont'd)

BancoSol (branch)

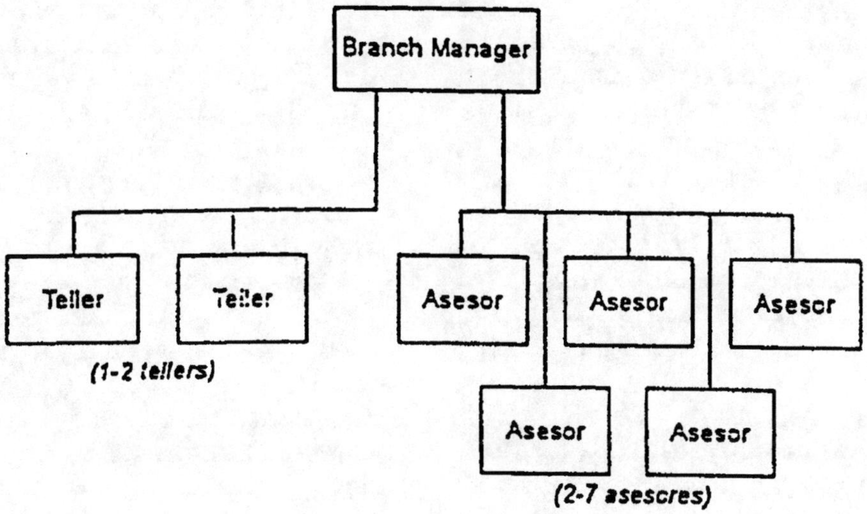

Actuar Bogota (branch)

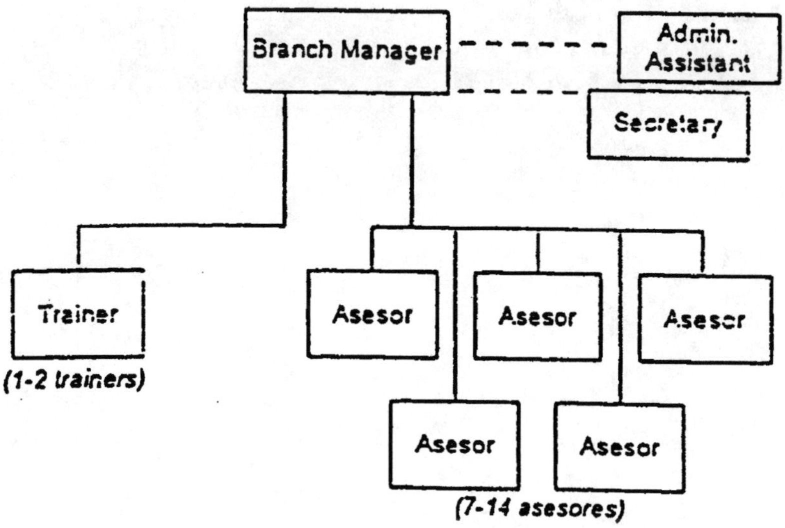

word count: 687

SECTION 3. TRANSLATIONS OF ASSIGNMENTS AND NOTES

ASSIGNMENT 1 - TRANSLATION

الإطار ٧ ـ ٦ : التنسيق بين الجهات المانحة لقطاع الصحة فى زمبابوى وبنغلاديش

يمثل المشروع الثانى لصحة الأسرة فى زمبابوى (١٩٩٢ ـ ١٩٩٦) تتويجا لفترة طويلة من التفاعل بين حكومة زمبابوى ، والبنك الدولى ، وجهات مانحة أخرى متعددة الأطراف وثنائية . وهذا المشروع الذى يتكلف ١٢٠ مليون دولار ، والذى يدعم برنامج استثمارات الحكومة للسنوات الخمس من أجل السكان ، والصحة ، والتغذية مصمم لكى يفيد مباشرة الأسر منخفضة الدخل ، وبصفة خاصة النساء والأطفال ، وقد دخلت زمبابوى مرحلة من التصحيح الاقتصادى تقتضى خفض الإنفاق . وسيساعد المشروع على حماية الأسر الفقيرة والمعرضة للمخاطر من بعض الآثار المعاكسة للتصحيح عن طريق تعبئة موارد اضافية لتنمية الموارد البشرية وتحسين عدالة وكفاءة الإنفاق .

وتم التأكيد على مشاركة أهل زمبابوى منذ بداية المشروع . وضمت اللجنة التحضيرية للمشروع ممثلين من الإدارات المختلفة بالحكومة المركزية ، والحكومات المحلية ، والمجلس الوطنى لتنظيم الأسرة فى زمبابوى . ووضعت اللجنة الخطوط الارشادية للتخطيط ، بما فى ذلك إطار مبدئى لمكونات المشروع وتكاليفه وتمويله . وباستخدام هذه الخطوط الارشادية ، أعدت المقترحات محليا وروجعت بعد ذلك بواسطة اللجنة والجهات المانحة المعنية .

وساعدت جميع الجهات المانحة الرئيسية لقطاع الصحة فى زمبابوى عمليا فى تخطيط المشروع بتحديد المسؤولين بالهيئات والمتخصصين الفنيين فى فريق الجهة المانحة الذى قدم النصح للحكومة بشأن مسائل التصميم . وفى النهاية ، تلقى المشروع تمويلا من الدانمرك ، والجماعة الأوروبية ، والنرويج ، والسويد ، والمملكة المتحدة ، والبنك الدولى . وتتابع الجهات المانحة تنفيذ المشروع بصورة مشتركة وليس منفردة ، وهو ما يقلل الوقت المطلوب للمراجعة بواسطة هذه الجهات ، والعبء الإدارى على الحكومة .

وفى بنغلاديش يسهم البنك الدولى وعشر وكالات ثنائية بـ ٤٤٠ مليون دولار فى المشروع الرابع للسكان والصحة . وتقدم الحكومة ١٦٥ مليون دولار ، بمبلغ إجمالى قدره ٦٠٥ مليون دولار على مدى فترة المشروع ذى السنوات الخمس . ويقدم صندوق الأمم المتحدة للسكان ، ومنظمة الصحة العالمية ، واليونيسيف إدارة المشروع ، وعمليات الشراء ، والمساعدة التقنية . وينتمى جميع الشركاء فى المشروع إلى اتحاد السكان والصحة فى بنغلاديش ، الذى نشأ بوصفه قوة جماعية هامة فى قطاع الصحة . وقد انضم بنك التنمية الآسيوى إلى الاتحاد بهدف ضمان الاتساق بين المشروع وبين استثمارات البنك البالغة ٦٠ مليون دولار فى مجال السكان والصحة فى بنغلاديش .

وخلال صياغة المشروع ، عقدت الحكومة والجهات المانحة حلقات دراسية عديدة فى دكا ، ومؤتمرا خاصا فى جنيف . وكان لهذه الحلقات الدراسية دور كبير فى تشكيل توافق فى الرأى حول استراتيجيات السكان والصحة . ويمكن نهج الاتحاد ، الحكومة ومجتمع المانحين من الاتفاق بشأن استراتيجية عامة ، ومن وضع خطة تمويل متسقة للقطاع . ويعمل الاتحاد على أساس المساواة التامة بين جميع الشركاء بغض النظر عن حجم اسهاماتهم المالية .

وبالإضافة إلى تقوية برنامج السكان فى بنغلاديش ونظامه لتقديم خدمات تنظيم الأسرة ، يحاول الاتحاد إعادة توجيه نظام الرعاية الصحية نحو الصحة العامة ، بما فى ذلك صحة الأمومة . وهو يحاول أيضا جعل الخدمات الأساسية أكثر سهولة من حيث الوصول من جانب الفقراء بالريف والحضر .

الإطار ٧ ـ ٤ : المساعدات الصحية ومردودية المعونة

تشير التقييمات الأخيرة لمردودية المعونة ، بما في ذلك دراسة كلاسيكية في عام ١٩٨٦ كلف بها مجتمع الجهات المانحة بالعالم ، إلى النتيجة ذاتها : أن معظم المعونة كان ناجحا ، ولكن حصة هامة ، ربما الثلث أو أكثر ، كانت أقل نجاحا بكثير ، وفشلت نسبة مئوية صغيرة بالكامل ، أو حتى كانت ضارة . ولكن هذه المتوسطات المعممة تخفى اختلافات اقليمية كبيرة : ففى أسيا وأمريكا اللاتينية كان الأداء أفضل ، بينما كان أسوأ فى أفريقيا جنوب الصحراء . واتسمت المعونة بأدنى فعالية فى أكثر البلدان فقرا ، حيث الحاجة ماسة إلى النجاح .

وتكمن أسباب الأداء المتدنى لدى كل من مانحى المعونة والمتلقين لها . فالبلدان الفقيرة وتلك التى تمر بصراعات سياسية وعدم استقرار سياسى تشكل بيئة صعبة للمعونة ، حيث لديها القليل من القدرة الإدارية أو البنية الأساسية . ولكن هذه الصعوبات تفاقمت فى كثير من الحالات بسبب السياسات غير الموفقة . فقد كانت مشروعات المعونة مصممة بشكل سيىء ، سواء من الناحية الفنية ، أو بسبب الفهم غير الملائم للبيئة البشرية ، والاجتماعية ، والمؤسسية والسياسية . وعندما يأتى الأمر للتنسيق ، فإن كلا الجانبين كان مخطئا . فقد سعت الجهات المانحة لتحقيق أهدافها الذاتية دون حتى محاولة ضمان أن معونتها تكمل تلك المقدمة من الآخرين . وفى الأغلب الأعم ، كان المتلقون للمعونة يثيرون الجهات المانحة ضد بعضها البعض ، فى حين ركز الوزراء والوزارات على اهتماماتهم الذاتية ، لا على النظر إلى الصالح الوطنى .

وكان للمعونة المقدمة من أجل الصحة سجل فنى جيد بشكل عام . فقد تلاءمت مع الأولويات الانمائية ، وبصفة خاصة فى السنوات الأخيرة ، حيث حل محل التركيز على المستشفيات والطب العلاجى ذى التكنولوجيا المرتفعة ، التركيز على الرعاية الأولية والوقائية وتحققت أيضا نجاحات كبيرة ـ تمثلت أساسا فى مبادرات بالغة التركيز مثل برامج القضاء على الجديرى والحملة لمكافحة وفيات الأطفال ، وجهود مكافحة العمى النهرى فى افريقيا . ولا تزال مفتقدة قدرة نظام المعونة على المساعدة فى إرساء برامج للصحة العامة والخدمات الاكلينيكية الأساسية ملائمة ومستدامة محليا .

ASSIGNMENT 1: NOTES

General Comments:
While this is a general, non-specialized text, it is written in a formal style reflecting organizational or corporate language, which should also be reflected in the Arabic version. While Arabic is not nearly as formal as English, it is important to have the translation preserve the style of the English text.

There is no one correct way of translating any text, but it is important in any kind of a technical or semi-technical text to pay close attention to any technical terms, and to preserve the overall style of the original.

Box 7.6 (line 4) - In general, pay close attention to the transposition of numbers in Arabic, as in this case, where the numbers are reversed. This is often a source of mistakes in English-Arabic translation.

World Bank (line 7) - The formal name of an international organization; you want to be sure you know how to render it correctly in Arabic.

$120 million (line 8) - In Arabic the word "dollar" is spelled out rather than rendered by the dollar sign.

Zimbabwe National Family Planning Council (line 18) - As in the case of the name "World Bank," this too is a formal body, which may be rendered in a specific way in Arabic. It may not be as easy to find out how to say it correctly in Arabic as it is to find out the correct rendition of "World Bank," so do the best you can.

WHO, UNICEF (page 33) - The expansions of these two acronyms, namely, The "World Health Organization" and the "United Nations International Children's Emergency Fund," can be found in most good dictionaries. This is not always the case with less well-known organizations, where one may have to leave the acronym untranslated or add a translator's note.

Consortium (line 35) - This is a term which is often mistranslated in Arabic, and requires special attention.

workshops (line 39) - The same is true of this term, because of its variety of meanings.

broad-brush averages (page 2, line 15) - Here is an example an imprecise, rather graphic term used in a formal, technical text, hence hard to translate. There are several ways of rendering this in Arabic. Your task is to pick one that clearly conveys the idea of "rough averages."

ماذا يجب أن تعرف عن مرض الربو

ما هو الربو ؟

هو حالة مرضية تُسبب صعوبة التنفس

الربو قد ياتى بصورة خفيفة أو بصورة حادة.
هناك الكثير من الناس يعانون من أعراض خفيفة للربو. والبعض الآخر يعانى بصفة متواصلة من صعوبة التنفس بسبب الربو. وفى بعض الحالات النادرة، فإن داء الربو قد يصل إلى مرحلة قاتلة قد تسبب الوفاة.

سبب مرض-الربو غير معروف. ولكن من المعتاد أن يتكرر حدوث المرض في العائلة نفسها. وفى الغالب ما تظهر أعراض المرض فى مرحلة الطفولة المبكرة

من المعروف فى الأواسط الطبية أنة ليس بالإمكان علاج مرض الربو ولكن يمكن السيطرة علية.

هذا الكتيب لا يغنى عن المناقشة المفيدة بين المريض والطبيب بخصوص المعلومات والوسائل والأدوية المذكورة فى هذا الكتيب.

لماذا يجب على أن أتعلم عن مرض الربو ؟

اليك بعض الأسباب الجيدة

مرض الربو يصيب الملايين من البشر . وهو يصيب الذكور والإناث بنفس المعدل (علي الرغم من أنها تصيب الأطفال الذكور أكثر من الإناث). من المتوقع أنك تعرف أحد الأفراد الذين يعانون من هذا المرض.

الكثير من الناس لا يدرون أنهم مصابون بمرض الربو، ولهذا لايتلقون أى علاج لهذا المرض.

العلاج مهم. يمكن للمصابين بمرض الربو أن يتعلموا كيف :
- يمنعوا العديد من الأزمات الربوية قبل حدوثها
- يتعرفوا على الأعراض المبكرة وعلامات التحذير قبل حدوث الأزمة

الربويه
. يحصلوا على العلاج المبكر
تعلم أكثر عن مرض الربو . . .

أنظر وتعلم تكوين النظام التنفسى

يدخل الهواء عن طريق الفم والأنف ويمر من خلال صندوق الصوت (العنجرة) إلى أنبوب الهواء (القصبة الهوائية).
الحنجرة Larynx
القصبة الهوائية Trachea

تنقسم القصبة الهوائية لعدة أفرع (شعيبات هوائية) والتى تنتشر فى الرئة.
الشعيبات الهوائية Bronchial tubes

وتؤدى هذة الشعيبات بدورها إلى جيوب هوائية صغيرة تعرف (بالحويصلات - الهوائية)، وتحاط هذة الحويصلات الهوائية من كل جانب بالأوعية الدموية الدقيقة، ويقوم الأكسوچين و الغازات الأخرى بالمرور بين الحويصلات الهوائية و الأوعية الدموية.

الحويصلات الهوائية Aveoli

الشهيق: يوصل الأكسوچين من الهواء الجوى إلى مجرى الدم

الزفير: يسمح للجنسم من أن يتخلص من الغازات الضارة من الدم (مثل غاز ثانى أوكسيد الكربون).

فى حالة الأزمة الربوية هذا مايحدث قبل وخلال وبعد الأزمة:

شيئ ما (غير معروف) يسبب الأزمة مما يسبب رد فعل النظام التنفسى. (أنظر صفحة ٨ و٩ لقراءة قائمة بالعوامل المسببة المعروفة.)

بعدها تحدث تقلصات عضلية تؤدى إلى إعتصار الشعيبات الهوائية أى أن العضلات المحيطة بالشعيبات الهوائية تقوم بإعتصارها بشدة.

لهذا السبب تلتهب الشعيبات مما يؤدى إلى تورمها وبالتالى ضيق الممرات الهوائية.

- يزداد إفراز المخاط. يقوم السائل المخاطى اللزج بسد الشعيبات الهوائية.

تبقي الشعيبات الهوائية على حالة الإلتهاب وبالتالى تكون أكثرتعرضا للمسببات والأزمات الربوية مما يؤدى فى النهاية إلى تكرار حدوث الأزمات بصورة دائمة.

تتسبب الأزمات الربوية فى صعوبة التنفس. ضيق

الشعيبات الهوائية يؤدى إلى صعوبة عملية الشهيق والزفير.

تختلف الأعراض من شخص إلى أخر

قد تسبب الأزمة الربوية عدة أعراض، مثل

- صفير أثناء التنفس
- ضيق التنفس و الإختناق
- السعال
- ألم وضيق فى منطقة الصدر

قد تظهر هذة الأعراض بصورة مفاجئة

تتسبب التقلصات العضلية للشعيبات الهوائية فى حدوث ضيق فى التنفس بصورة مفاجئة، أو قد تظهر الأعراض بصورة تدريجية.

علاة ماتحدث الأزمات الربوية فى فترة المساء

يستيقظ المصابون بداء الربو أثناء الليل وهم يصارعون للحصول على الهواء. وقد يصعب عليهم النوم بالمرة بسبب هذة الأزمات.

هذة الأعراض قد تشير الى مشاكل صحية من نوع أخر، وعلى أى شخص يعانى من هذة الأعراض أن يستشير طبيبا على وجة السرعة.

قد يشعر بعض الأفراد بعلامات للإنذار قبل الأزمة

فى الساعات أو الأيام السابقة للأزمة ، قد يشعر المريض بالآتى:

- حكة بالحلق و البلعوم
- السعال و العطس
- الزكام
- الإرهاق
- تغير طفيف فى التنفس

الوعى بهذة العلامات المبكرة هو فى غاية الأهمية

الوعى بهذة العلامات، يمكن للمريض بالربو أن يتخذ الإحتياطات اللازمة لكى:

- يمنع وقوع بعض الأزمات الربوية
- يقلل من حدة الأزمات الأخرى.

عن مسببات الربو

تحدث حالات الربو عادة كنتيجة للتعرض لمادة أو حالة معينة. بعض العوامل المسببة

المعروفة هى:

العوامل الهوائية المسببة للحساسية

مسببات الحساسية التى تثير الربو هى مواد دقيقة للغاية فى الهواء و من أكثرها شيوعا:

- الغبار و عثة الغبار (وهى عبارة عن عناكب ميكروسكوبية)
- العفن
- غبار الطلع (بويضات تلقيح النبات)
- قشور جلد أو شعر بعض الحيوانات

الأمراض المعدية للجهاز التنفسى

وتشمل نوبات البرد (الانفلونزا)، الزكام، إلتهاب الحلق و أمراض أخرى.

العوامل المسببة (المثيرات)

وأكثرها شيوعا دخان السجاير و تلوث الجو والعطور والكيماويات المنتشرة فى أماكن العمل، كل هذة المثيرات يمكن أن تسبب أزمات الربو.

أنواع معينة من التمارين الرياضية

المصابين بالربو يمكنهم بل يجب عليهم أن يمارسوا التمارين الرياضية شريطة أن تكون تحت إشراف وتوجية الطبيب.

الاسبرين

اية أدوية تحتوى على الاسبرين أو مشتقاتة يمكن أن تثير الازمات الربوية عند البعض. بعض الادوية الاخري لها نفس التاثير.

الطقس

الطقس البارد أو أى تغيير حاد فى الطقس قد يتسبب فى إثارة الازمات الربوية

الإكتئاب أو الإنفعالات العاطفية

التغيرات العاطفية لاتسبب الازمات الربوية، ولكن رد فعل الجسم لهذة التغيرات هو الذى قد يتسبب فى إثارة الربو.

العوامل المسببة تختلف من شخص إلى آخر.

كيف يمكن تشخيص مرض الربو

إذا شعر أحد الاشخاص باعراض الربو فان الطبيب يمكنة أن يطلب:

إختبار طبى شامل و تاريخ طبى كامل للمريض

وهذا بدورة يعطى الطبيب فكرة شاملة عن الحالة الصحية العامة للمريض.

إختبار كفائة الرئة

وهذا الإختبار يتيح للطبيب أن يعرف مدى صحة الرئتين و مدى إستجابتهما لأنواع العلاج المختلفة.

الكشف عن الصدر بالأشعة السينية

الكشف بالأشعة قد يؤدى إلى إكتشاف مشاكل صحية أخرى تسبب هذة الأعراض.

يمكن للطبيب المسئول أن يطلب التحاليل الآتية :

- تحليل دم
- تحليل السائل المخاطى (دراسة السائل المطرود من الرئة أثناء السعال)
- إختبارات الحساسية، وتساعد فى التعرف عل العوامل المسببة أو المثيرات.

السيطرة على مرض الربو

يحتاج مريض الربو إلى الإستشارة المستمرة مع الطبيب المعالج من أجل:

التعرف على العوامل المسببة ومحاولة تلافيها.

فى بعض الحالات فإن علاج الحساسية قد يؤدى تحسن حالة مريض الربو.

السيطرة على الأعراض

عن طريق تناول الأدوية بإنتظام وهى:

- أدوية تؤخذ بإنتظام، للتحكم فى الإلتهاب و منع الأزمات الربوية.
- أدوية تؤخذ عند اللزوم، وتقوم بفتح الشعيبات الهوائية أثناء أزمة الربو.

أدوية الربو تتناول عن طريق الإستنشاق بإستخدام (بخاخات). ميزة الإستنشاق أنة يزيد من تأثير الدواء ويقلل من الأعرض الجانبية.

متابعة حالة المريض

... على سبيل المثال، بإستخدام جهاز قياس التنفس ، يمكن للطبيب معرفة مدى صحة الرئتين ومقدرتهما على أداء العمل. التغيرات المفاجئة فى قرائة هذا الجهاز قد تكون بمثابة إنذار مبكر ضد أزمات الربو.

يجب على الأقارب وأفراد أسرة المريض أن يكونوا على قدر من الوعى بهذا المرض حتى يمكنهم المساعدة أثناء حدوث الأزمة .

بعض الأسئلة والأجوبة

هل الربو مرض معدى؟

لا، لايمكن أن تنتقل العدوى من شخص إلى آخر.

هل يمكن لشخص مصاب بالربو أن يمارس الرياضة ؟

نعم، وفى الواقع فانة من المحبذ أن يمارس الشخص المصاب بالربو بعض الأنشطة الرياضية، وتعتبر هذة التمارين بمثابة جزء هام من النظام العلاجى للربو. وقد إنتظم الكثير من مرضى الربو فى أعلى مستويات المنافسة الرياضية .
ويجب على مريض الربو أن يستشير الطبيب فى أختيار النشاط الرياضى الملائم لحالتة الصحية.

هل يختفى الربو مع نمو الطفل ؟

من الممكن أن يختفى مرض الربو بنمو الطفل، ولكن ليس من المؤكد إختفاء المرض نهائياً، حتى إذا إختفى المرض فإنة ليس هناك ما يضمن عدم رجوعة مرة أخرى . يجب على المريض بالربو أن يسعى للحصول على المساعدة الطبية فوراً والا ينتظر أن يختفى المرض من ذاتة.

هل يعنى حكة الصدر بالضرورة أن هناك إصابة بالربو؟

كلا، هناك أسباب متعددة لحكة الصدر غير مرض الربو، بالإضافة الى ذلك فإن هناك بعض مرضى الربو الذين لا يعانون على الإطلاق من حكة الصدر.
عند شعورك باية حكة فى الجهاز التنفسى، إستشر طبيباً على الفور.

ما هو تاثير الدخان فى الجو المحيط (تدخين السجائر بواسطة أخرين) على مريض الربو ؟

الدخان بجميع أنواعة هو إحد العوامل المسببة للأزمة الربوية. يجب على مرضى الربو أن يبتعدوا عن الدخان و التدخين بكافة أنواعة.

ماهو مصير مرضى الربو على المدى البعيد ؟

بالمواضبة على العلاج الملائم والمتابعة الطبية المستمرة ، فإن مصير مريض الربو هو مصير ممتازا أغلب المرضى بالربو يمكنهم السيطرة على أعراض المرض ومنع الأزمات الربوية فى المستقبل. بالإضافة فإن الأدوية والعلاجات الحديثة لديها آثار جانبية أقل و فاعلية أكبر ضد مرض الربو، حتى إذا استعملوا لفترة طويلة من الزمن.

General Comments

a. Subject matter

Although this particular text presents many examples of subject-specific terminology, the text itself is straightforward, and presents no real difficulty in terms of sentence structure or language style. Unless one is thoroughly familiar with the medical terminology of the text, it would be best not to start translating right away, but first to make a list of all such terms in the text one is not certain of.

However, this particular text is not a professional medical text, but rather a brochure written for the general public to explain a wide-spread health problem. As such, it does not require a medical background, but rather a general understanding of anatomy and medical terms.

b. References

A good Arabic-English medical dictionary should have all or nearly all of the technical terms of these texts. If, after a thorough consultation with such a source, you still have an unknown term, the next thing to do is call someone with an appropriate professional background.

What Everyone Should Know about Asthma (line 3) - This heading is in bold letters. Since bolding does not stand out as clearly in the Arabic printing, it was made somewhat larger than the following text, to make it stand out.

lung condition (line 5) - This is the first of many medically-related terms which should be translated carefully into medically-acceptable Arabic terms.

(trachea), (bronchial tubes), (alveoli) (lines 26-29) - Here the translator kept the English words on the special instructions of the end-user of the translation. Otherwise, the terms need to be translated.

triggers (page 2, line 30) - This is an example of a descriptive American word which can be translated in several ways. Choose a way that makes sense in the context of an Arabic medical text.

التمويل العام والخاص للخدمات الاكلينيكية

يجرى تمويل الخدمات الاكلينيكية ، فى مختلف أرجاء العالم ، عن طريق أربع قنوات رئيسية ، اثنتان خاصتان ، وهما التسديدات المدفوعة من الدخل الخاص ، والتأمين الطوعى . أما القناتان الأخريان فهما عامتان : التأمين الاجبارى (ويعرف فى بعض الأحيان بأنه « التأمين الاجتماعى ») ، وهو إما أن يدار إدارة عامة ، أو أن يخضع للتنظيم الكامل من قبل الحكومات ؛ والتمويل من الإيرادات الحكومية العامة .

وفى أشد البلدان فقراً ، قد تنخفض النفقات الإجمالية على الصحة إلى دولارين للفرد كل عام ، ويأتى أكثر من نصف هذا المبلغ من المصادر الخاصة ، وبصفة أساسية فى شكل التسديدات المدفوعة من الدخل الخاص . وآليات التأمين فى تلك البلدان ضعيفة ، والإيرادات الحكومية المخصصة للصحة منخفضة . وكلما تزايدت الدخول ، تتزايد النسبة المئوية للدخل المنفق على الصحة (كما هو مبين فى الجزء العلوى من الشكل ٥ ـ ١) وحصة الانفاق على الصحة التى تتأتى من المصادر العامة (المبينة فى الجزء السفلى) . وفى الاقتصادات الاشتراكية السابقة واقتصادات السوق المستقرة (باستثناء الولايات المتحدة الأمريكية) ، يمثل الأنفاق العام ثلاثة أرباع الانفاق الإجمالى على الصحة .

وهناك ، بالإضافة إلى المصادر الأربعة للتمويل الصحى ، ثلاث طرق لتنظيم الخدمات الصحية الاكلينيكية : عامة ، وخاصة لا تسعى وراء الربح ، وخاصة تعمل من أجل الربح . وتستخدم جميع النظم الصحية الوطنية اثنتين على الأقل من التوليفات المحتملة الاثنتى عشرة لطريقة التمويل وتنظيم الخدمة الصحية ؛ وفى بعض الأحيان ، تخدم التوليفات المختلفة قطاعات سكانية متباينة بشكل حاد . ومع ذلك ، من الممكن تصنيف البلدان فى مجموعات حسب مستوى الدخل والنظام السائد لتوفير الرعاية الصحية . والفرق الرئيسى هو ما إذا كان التأمين يدفع مقابل قدر أكبر من الرعاية أم لا ،وإذا كان الحال كذلك ، ما هو النوع السائد من التأمين (الجدول ٥ ـ ٢) .

الحكومى من إيرادات الضريبة العامة بوجه عام أقل من نصف النسبة من الناتج القومى الإجمالى المخصصة للخدمات الصحية والتى تتراوح بين ٢ و ٧ فى المائة منه . وهناك تأمين ضئيل ، أو لا يوجد تأمين على الإطلاق .

وإلى عهد قريب ، كانت الصين تمثل استثناء مهما بين البلدان منخفضة الدخل . ففى الفترة بين عامى ١٩٦٠ و ١٩٨٠ ، كانت المشاريع الحكومية هناك توفر الرعاية الصحية بصورة مباشرة لعمالها ، أو تتعاقد مع المستشفيات الحكومية للقيام بذلك . وكان يُطلب من الكوميونات الريفية أن تخصص جزءاً من مواردها المالية للخدمات الصحية المتعلقة بجميع أعضائها . وبحلول أواخر السبعينات ، أصبح التأمين يغطى فعلاً جميع سكان الحضر و ٨٥ بالمائة من سكان الريف . وهو إنجاز فريد بالنسبة لبلد نام ذى دخل منخفض . بيد أنه منذ إلغاء زراعة الكوميونات وتحرير الصناعة فى السنوات الأولى من الثمانينات ، ضعفت هذه الأشكال من التأمين الصحى وتأدية الخدمة الصحية بدرجة كبيرة . ويعتمد السكان فى الريف بشكل متزايد على نظام للرعاية الصحية توفره الحكومة ، ويمول فى جانب منه من الإيرادات العامة ، ولكن مع استرداد التكلفة بدرجة كبيرة عن طريق تحصيل رسوم من المستفيدين ، وهو ما لا يختلف عن النظم السائدة فى البلدان الأخرى منخفضة الدخل .

وفى *البلدان متوسطة الدخل* هناك نوعان رئيسيان من النظم الصحية ، يتميزان بما إذا كان التأمين الصحى توفره الحكومة أو القطاع الخاص . ويعتبر الإنفاق الصحى ، الذى يتراوح بين ٢٠ دولاراً و ٤٠٠ دولار ، أكثر ارتفاعاً مما هو عليه الحال فى البلدان منخفضة الدخل ، كما أن القدرة الإدارية للقطاعين العام والخاص على حد سواء أشد قوة . وفى بلدان التأمين الخاص ، من قبيل جنوب افريقيا وزمبابوى ، تستخدم الحكومة الإيرادات العامة لدفع مقابل الرعاية الصحية للمجموعات ذات الدخل المتوسط والمنخفض ، فى حين تستخدم الأسر ذات الدخل الأعلى (وهى تقل عن ٢٠ بالمائة من السكان) التأمين الخاص من أجل دفع أجور الأطباء والمستشفيات من القطاع الخاص ، أو تسديد رسوم الغرف الخاصة فى المستشفيات الحكومية .

وفى بلدان التأمين الاجتماعى ، تموّل الاشتراكات المالية الالزامية من الموظفين وأصحاب الأعمال ، وفى بعض الأحيان الصناديق الحكومية ، التأمين المتعلق بجزء من السكان ، بما فى ذلك غالبية العمال من الطبقة المتوسطة .

أما الرعاية الصحية للفقراء فيتم تمويلها من الإيرادات العامة . وهذا هو النظام السائد فى كوريا ، وتركيا ، ومعظم بلدان أمريكا اللاتينية .

وفى *الاقتصادات الاشتراكية السابقة* فى أوروبا الشرقية والاتحاد السوفياتى ، كان التمويل من الإيرادات العامة مع توفير الحكومة للخدمات الصحية هو الشكل الوحيد للرعاية الصحية المعترف به رسمياً إلى عهد قريب . ويمثل الانفاق العام على الصحة حاليا ما بين ٣ و ٦ بالمائة من الناتج القومى الاجمالى فى هذه البلدان أو ٣٠ دولاراً إلى ٢٠٠ دولار للفرد . وقبل مرحلة الليبرالية السياسية والاقتصادية فى السنوات الأخيرة من الثمانينات ، كانت المدفوعات الخاصة كثيرا ما تقدم من أجل الحصول على الخدمات الصحية ، العامة ، (وعلى سبيل المثال ، اعطاء بقشيش للاطباء فى المستشفيات الحكومية) ، وكانت العقاقير تتسرب فى أحيان كثيرة من القطاع العام إلى الأسواق الخاصة . ومنذ الاصلاحات السياسية والاقتصادية التى أكتسحت هذه البلدان فى السنوات الأخيرة من الثمانينات ، وقعت النظم الصحية هناك فى أزمة . وقد خلق التمويل العام المتناقص والخدمات الحكومية المتدهورة ضغوطاً قوية من أجل إيجاد أشكال جديدة من التأمين العام والخاص..

الجدول ٥ ـ ٢ النظم الصحية الاكلينيكية حسب مجموعات الدخل

المجموعة القطرية ودخل الفرد فى ١٩٩٠ (بالدولارات)	نفقات الصحة ، ١٩٩٠: كحصة من الناتج القومى الاجمالى (نسبة مئوية)	نفقات الصحة ، ١٩٩٠: بالدولارات للفرد	الخصائص الرئيسية	أمثله
منخفضة الدخل (١٠٠ ـ ٦٠٠)(أ)	٢ ـ ٧	٢ ـ ٤٠	إنفاق خاص مرتفع على الطب التقليدى والعقاقير . الخدمات العامة الممولة من الايرادات العامة . قليل من التأمين	بنغلاديش ، الهند ، باكستان ، غالبية البلدان الأفريقية جنوب الصحراء .
متوسطة الدخل (٦٠٠ ـ ٧٩٠٠) التأمين الخاص	٢ ـ ٧	٢٠ ـ ٣٥٠	الخدمات الحكومية المقدمة للمجموعات المنخفضة والمتوسطة الدخل والممولة من الإيرادات العامة . تأمين خاص وتوفير خاص للرعاية لميسورى الحال (أقل من ١٠ فى المائة من السكان)	جنوب أفريقيا وزمبابوى
التأمين الاجتماعى	٣ ـ ٧	٢٠ ـ ٤٠٠	الخدمة الصحية والرعاية الاكلينيكية للمجموعات منخفضة الدخل والممولة من الإيرادات العامة . التأمين الاجتماعى للقوة العاملة ذات الأجر مع توفير مختلط للدعاية .	كوستاريكا ، جمهورية كوريا ، تركيا
الاقتصادات الاشتراكية السابقة فى أوروبا (٦٥٠ ـ ٦٠٠٠)	٣ ـ ٦	٣٠ ـ ٢٠٠	الخدمات العامة (التى تعتبر منخفضة فى نوعيتها أو آخذة فى الانهيار) والممولة من الايرادات العامة سوق سرية كبيرة للخدمات المقدمة بشكل خاص .	الجمهورية التشيكية ، بولندا الجمهورية السلوفاكية ، جمهوريات الاتحاد السوفياتى سابقا
اقتصادات السوق المستقرة مع استبعاد الولايات المتحدة (٥٠٠٠ ـ ٣٤٠٠٠)	٦ ـ ١٠	٤٠٠ ـ ٢٥٠٠	تغطية شبه شاملة عن طريق الإيراد العام والتأمين الاجتماعى الإجبارى . استخدام مدفوعات الطرف الثالث ذات الحد الأقصى ، والميزانيات الشاملة .	كندا ، فرنسا ، المانيا ، واليابان (تأمين اجتماعى) ؛ النرويج ، السويد ، المملكة المتحدة (إيرادات الضريبة العامة)
الولايات المتحدة (٢٢٠٠٠)	١٢	٢٨٠٠	خليط من التأمين الاختيارى الخاص واستخدام الإيراد العام من الضرائب . تعويض غير منظم ومفتوح للاتعاب مقابل الخدمة . تكاليف إدارية مرتفعة مرتبطة بمقدمى الرعاية الصحية والتأمين	الولايات المتحدة الأمريكية

(أ) مع أن الصين تعتبر بلداً ذا دخل منخفض ، إلا أن نظامها الصحى يقترب من نظام بلد متوسط الدخل لديه تأمين إجتماعى .

المصدر : للاتفاق ، جدول التذييل أ ـ ٩

General Comments:

a. Financial Translation

In translation, there is a basic difference between translating financial subjects and any other technical subjects, such as legal or medical. While it is relatively easy to master the methodology of working with most technical vocabularies, even if one does not have the technical or professional background in the particular field in which one translates, in financial subjects it is necessary to have at least a general knowledge of the subject. This may be due to the fact that financial terminology and concepts are not always readily translatable as other technical subjects. The upshot of all this is that one should not be hasty to accept a financial translation assignment if one does not work in this field on a regular basis.

b. Subject matter

This particular assignment consists of a text derived from a publication of an international financial organization. As with most major organizations and corporations, this organization has its own so-called "corporate style," which affects the way this material is translated. Normally, an organization of this magnitude employs its own translators, or uses outside translators on a regular basis, to acquaint them with its style. If called upon to translate this kind of text, be sure to familiarize yourself with the organization's style.

out-of-pocket (lines 3-4) - This is the first of several subject-specific terms, which should be translated properly into Arabic equivalents. In Arabic, "out-of-pocket" can be translated in several different ways, and hopefully yours is one of the correct ways.

private nonprofit, and private for profit (line 18) - This is another example of economic terms, which should have formal equivalents in Arabic.

NGO (line 27) - Nonprofit NonGovernmental Organizations. Acronyms are one of the problems of technical translation. Especially in going from English into a non-Roman alphabet language such as Arabic, they can be a thorny problem. Make every effort to find out what an acronym stands for. If no answer is available, you may need to put the words [expansion unknown] following the acronym.

GNP (line 32) - anyone familiar with economic or financial texts knows this acronym. If you don't, you may not be ready to translate texts of this kind.

Table 5.1 (page 3) - Make every effort to present the Arabic table (reversed, of course) in a format as similar to the English original as possible.

صندوق رقم٦

عناصر الكفائة التنظيمية لمؤسسات الموارد المالية الخاصة بالمشروعات الصغرى

١- المقياس:

- إن مؤسسات الموارد المالية الرائدة و الخاصة بالمشاريع الصغرى، قد توصلت اليوم أن تتعامل من عدة ملايين إلى مئات الملايين من الدولارات، و هذة المؤسسات قد تخدم من ١٠٠٠٠ عميل إلى
١٠٠٠ ٠٠٠ عميل فى بعض الأحيان، هذا المستوى من الإنتشار يمثل قدوة للمؤسسات الاخرى الطموحة.

- مستوى التاخر فى التسديد أقل من ٨٪ و معدلات الخسارة أقل بكثير من ٤٪ .

٢- نوع البنية المالية و التنظيمية:

- إن مؤسسات الموارد المالية تختلف من حيث الشكل التنظيمى و الأصل، و بالرغم من هذا فإنها تتشابة إلى حد بعيد فى نوع الخدمات التى تعرضها.

- إن طبيعة هذة المؤسسات تمكنها من إستغلال الموارد المالية المتاحة من المؤسسات المحلية و من العملاء على حد السواء. و للوصول لهذة المرحلة الناجحة فإن المؤسسة يجب أن تتميز بنظام إدارى قوى.

- إن هناك الكثير من التطورات التى طرأت على المؤسسات، و من هذة التطورات الشائعة الإعتماد على مصادر التمويل المحلية بدلا من المصادر العالمية.

٣- الإنتاجية وبنية العمليات:

- وحدات البيع: تصمم وحدات البيع بحيث تلائم البنية التقليدية لهذا النوع من المؤسسات و تخضع لأشكال العمالة المعتادة.

- البنية الرئيسية: يجب على البنية الرئيسية أن تكون قادرة على توفير الخدمات و توفير نظام التحكم و الإدارة فى نفس الوقت، وبنفس الكفائة و التوازن.

- وحدات البيع يجب ان تركز على الوصول لدرجة عالية من الإنتاجية.: و بسبب إرتفاع الأجور و كونها أكبر بند للمصاريف ، فإن هذة الإنتاجية تعتمد على إنتاجية الفرد أكثر من إعتمادها على خفض التكلفة. حاليا،كل موظف يتولى بين ١١٥ - ٢٨٠ عميل فى كل وحدة بيع ، بالإضافة يمكنهم أيضا أن يتولوا مسؤلية العديد من عملاء الإدخار فى نفس الوقت.

- التكلفة بالنسبة لكمية رأس المال اتى تتعامل فيها المؤسسة يجب أن تقع بين ١٢ - ٢٥ ٪، هذة النسبة سوف تكون أعلى فى المؤسسات التى تدفع أجور أعلى. لهذا السبب فإن هذة المؤسسات تواجة ضغوطا شديدة لكى تزيد من حجم القروض لكى تقلل من النسبة المذكورة سابقا. و لكن فى هذة الحالة يبرز سؤالا هاما و هو. هل أن هذا الهدف يتفق مع الهدف الاساسي للمؤسسة؟

٤- تحاول و إستخدام المعلومات:

- تركز المؤسسات الناجحة على كل المستويات، تركز على عدد قليل من مؤشرات الأداء ، هذه المؤشرات مثل عدد القروض و نوعيتها تعتبر من أهم المعلومات للمؤسسات النامية الغير حكومية

- زيادة الإهتمام بمؤشرات الأرباح على مستوى الفروع و ذلك لزيادة الاهتمام بخفض التكاليف و التشجيع على ذيادة الإنتاج من داخل الفرع أو الوحدة المالية . إن الا هتمام بزيادة الإنتاج يجب أن
يصاحبة أيضا إهتمام بأنواع التمويل و حجم القروض.

- إن العقول الإلكترونية (الكمبيوتر) ليست هى المصدر الوحيد للمعلومات. إن الحصول على المعلومات الجيدة يمكن أن يتم بدون الكمبيوتر على مستوى الوحدات و الفروع ، الكمبيوترز يجب أن تعتبر وسيلة لزيادة الإنتاج فقط.

٥- المصادر البشرية:

- المؤسسات المالية الناجحة تقوم بتعيين شباب صغير السن و بدون خبرة، والذى لدية القابلية على و التعود على العمل فى جو غير تقليدى و فى مناخ المؤسسات .

- التدريب داخل المؤسسة يساعد على تمرير المعلومات الخاصة بالوظيفة من الموظفين القدامى إلى الموظفين حديثى التعيين. وهذة الطريقة تعتمد على التدريب الشفوى والعملى باإضافة للتعليم داخل الفصل للتاكيد.

- بعض المؤسسات الناجحة تقوم باستخدام عدة وسائل لرفع الإنتاج مثل التركيز و الإصرارعلى مهمات معينة و إنجازها، ترقية الموظفين المجتهدين لمراكز أعلى، تنظيم الوحدات كفريق متناسق، عرض أجور و إمتيازات مغرية ووضع برنامج للحوافز.

٦-حيوية المؤسسة:

- إن القيادة القوية للمؤسسات المالية الممولة للمشاريع الصغيرة، لا تقتصر فقط على أن تكون هذة القيادة محبوبة بين الموظفين و لكن يجب أن تتسم بالإخلاص و التفانى للمؤسسة من إجل ضمان الإستمرارية، بالإضافة إلي هذا فإن هذة القيادة يجب أن تكون لديها المهارات اللازمة لإدارة العمليات المختلفة و إدارة العلاقات الخارجية و أخيرا فإن هذة القيادات يجب أن يكون لديها القدرة لتحفيز الموظفين.

- مجلس إدارة نشط و فعال برئاسة أعضاء أكفاء فى غاية الأهمية لنجاح المؤسسة ، و خاصة عندما تحتاج المؤسسة إلى رئيس جديدة ليحل محل الرئيس المتقاعد .

- بعض المؤسسات إهتمت بالتوسع الأفقى عن طريق فتح فروع فى مناطق جديدة بصفة مستمرة و بنسبة ٢٠٪. أما بالنسبة للتوسع الرأسى فى المناطق ذاتها فقد ثبتت صعوبة تنفيذة لانة قد يسبب إختلال فى المعادلة التى أدت إلى نجاح الفرع.

- إن عنصر الإبتكار فى المؤسسات المالية يتطلب الإهتمام المستمر بثلاثة مراحل مختلفة: تحديدالالسوق و المنتج الملائم، كيفية توصيل الخدمات ، وأخيرا تطبيق المرحلتين السابقتين على مستوى الؤسسة. فى حالة توفير خدمات جديدة يجب على المؤسسة تراعى حجم الفروع و قدرتها على إستيعاب الخدمات الجديدة.

- من أهم عناصر نجاح المؤسسة قدرتها على التعامل مع الكوارث التى قد تواجهها ، حيث تتطلب إتخاذ قرارات حاذمة و سريعة لإنقاذ المؤسسة و التاقلم على الأوضاع الجديدة.

ملحق
وحدات البيع لمؤسسة تمويل خاصة بالمشاريع الصغرى

بنك جارمين
(فرع)

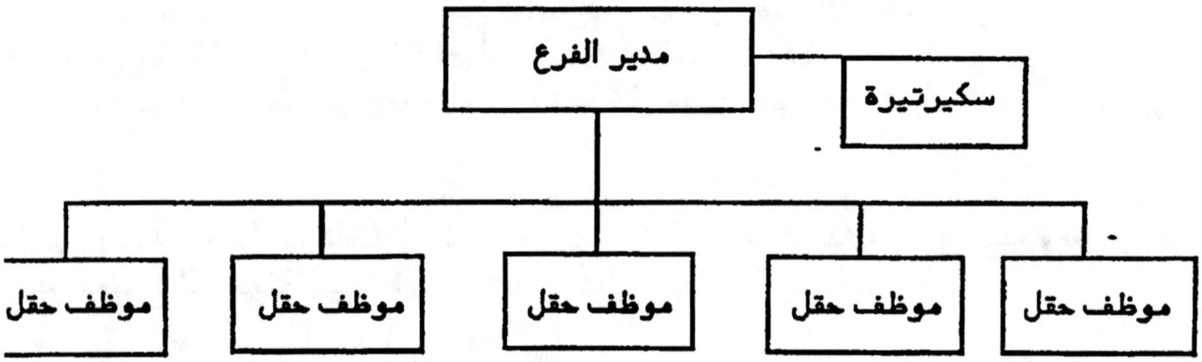

(لحد ٩ موظفين حقليين - بعض الفروع الكبيرة لديها مساعد مدير ايضا)

ب . ر. إ.
وحدة قروية

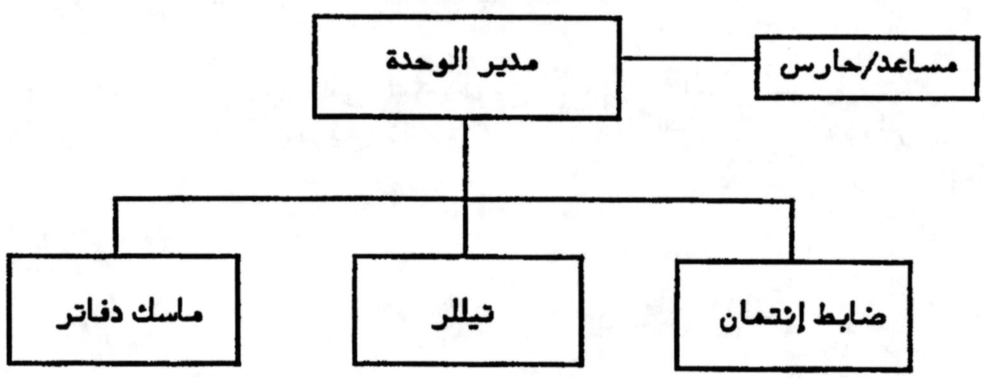

ملحق
وحدات البيع لمؤسسة تمويل خاصة بالمشاريع الصغيرة

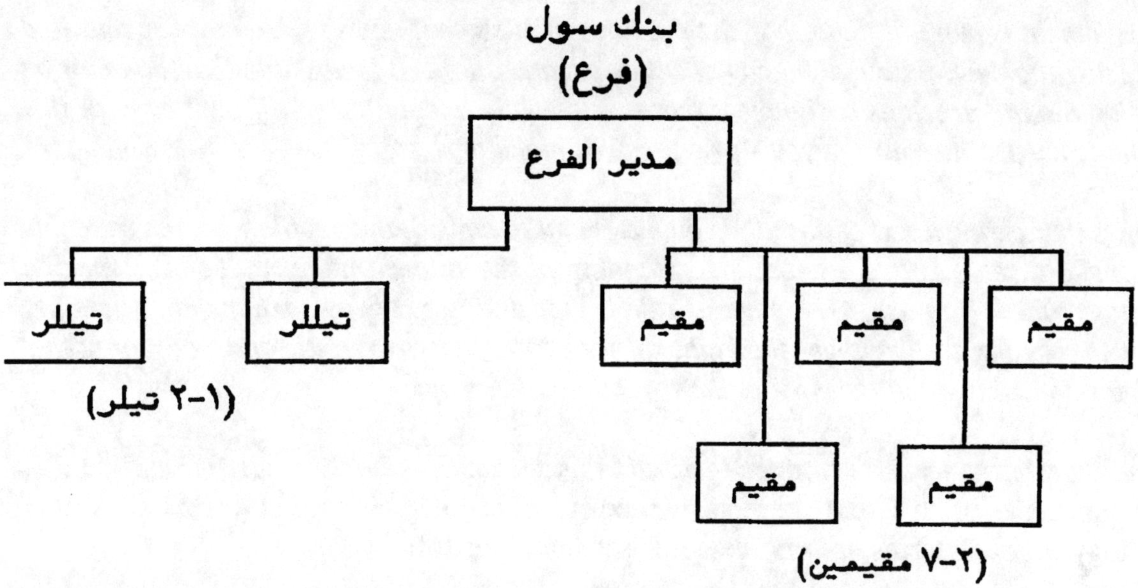

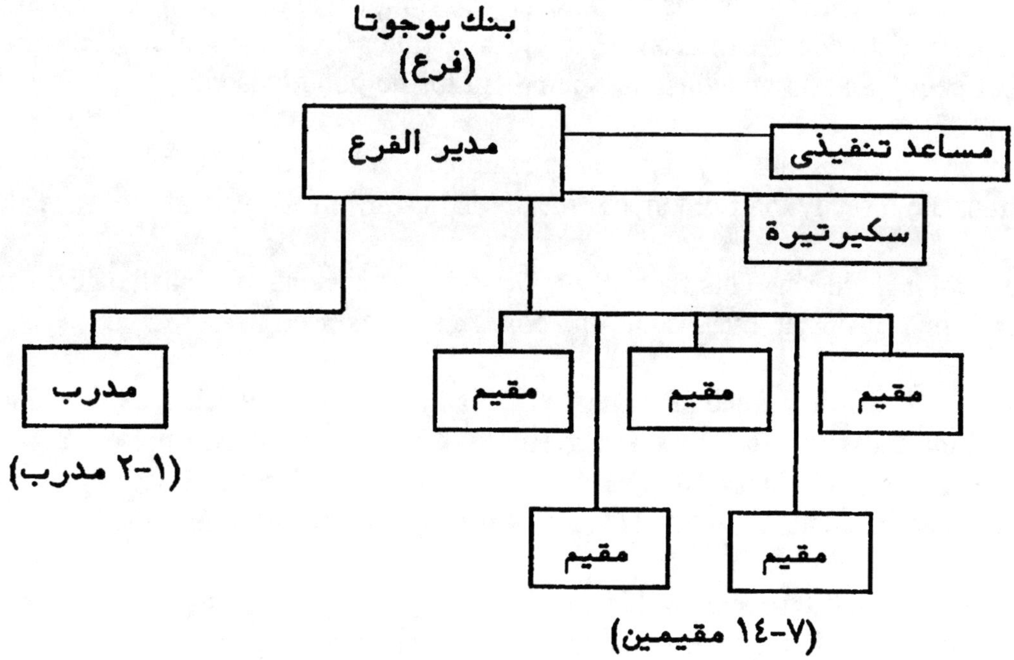

ASSIGNMENT 4 - NOTES

General Comments:

This assignment is more difficult than the previous one, since it deals with a more specialized business text, namely, financial management or organization. It is possible that one may be able to handle the previous assignment quite well, while encountering difficulties with this one. Don't let this discourage you - practice will make perfect.

Sometimes in tackling a text of this kind you may want to consult the people who generate this text, to make sure you have a good understanding of the subject-matter and of the specific terminology which they use. The general rule is that asking is always better than guessing, for even if you don't always get the right answers, at least you tried, and you cannot be blamed for something you have taken the trouble to check out.

The leading microenterprise finance institutions have achieved active portfolios (line 5) - The opening line of this text presents immediate questions of correct financial Arabic terminology for such terms as "microenterprise" and "portfolio."

10,000, 4 percent (lines 6 and 8) - The rendition of numbers is a tricky aspect of English-Arabic translation, and requires special care. The transposition of numbers and the positioning of symbols such as the percentage symbol also require special attention.
In the case of percentage, be consistent in using either the % symbol, or the word "percent" or "per cent," and don't switch between them for no good reason.

"charisma" (page 2, line 27) - Here is an example of a "borrowed" English word which does not translate directly, and requires some special effort on the part of the translator.

Organizational charts: This type of graphic material presents two challenges: first, the text needs to be translated, and second, the boxes and lines need to be drawn.

Very often you run into technical terms in a table or a chart which are not explained in the body of the text and, since they are given out of context, they may present a problem as to the actual meaning. There is no easy solution to this problem, and here again it may come down to communicating with the source of the original text if at all possible.

As for the formatting, here we have the advantage of line drawing and table creating in a DOS-based computer program, and even more sophisticated graphic programs in Windows in Microsoft Word or WordPerfect for Windows. One should take full advantage of these programs, since they make for a high quality translation product and enhance your reputation as a professional English-Arabic translator.

SECTION 4

WHERE DO I GO FROM HERE?

After you have completed all the assignments, or at least those you have chosen to do, you have to make a major decision. If you have never translated for profit before, you have to ask yourself if you are ready to try your hand at soliciting for-profit translation work. If the answer is yes, contact one or two of the enclosed work sources (Appendix E) and apply for a test or a short assignment. If you have translated for profit before in a specific area, such as legal documents, and you feel you are now ready to venture into another area, such as medical translation, first try out some short assignments in that field, until you become comfortable with it. it is important that you develop a relationship with one or more translation companies in your own geographical area. There is absolutely no reason in this day and age for a translator, say, in Wisconsin, not to develop a profitable relationship with a translation company in Florida, and in time you may indeed find out that a certain company on the other side of the continent is your best source of work. But as a beginner, there are many advantages to interfacing personally with the staff of a translation company close to home. They can give you a great deal of practical advice, help you with the hardware and the software, and share other kinds of experience with you. There is an old saying: "A good neighbor is better than a distant relative."

If, on the other hand, you feel you are not ready to take the plunge, you may want to consider a translation course or study program. Refer to Appendix 4 in the book, and see if there is a program close to home you can sign up for. Or you may decide to continue practicing on your own.

Whatever you decide to do, don't give up too easily. If you do enjoy the challenge of translation, continue to improve you skills. Remember: Translation can be a full-time career or a very fulfilling and profitable sideline. It is definitely the kind of expertise worth having, no matter what else you choose to do with your time.

APPENDIX A: REQUISITES FOR PROFESSIONAL TRANSLATORS

Any person who knows more than one language has the ability to explain a word or a sentence in what translators call "the source language" (the language you translate from) by using an equivalent word or sentence in what they call "the target language" (the language you translate into). This, in effect, is the beginning of translation. But it is only the beginning. It does not automatically turn a person into an accomplished translator. Along with the knowledge of the source and the target language, a translator must have an aptitude for translation. Some people are endowed with a talent for translation. It is not an acquired skill, like riding a bicycle. It is rather a talent, like playing the violin. Some people have it and some don't. It is not necessarily an indication of a lower or higher IQ. Nor is it an indication of how linguistically gifted one is. It is an inborn skill that enables a person to change a text from one language into another quickly and accurately, or, if you will, think in more than one language at the same time. If you possess this skill, then it behooves you to develop it and make use of it, because there is never an overabundance of good translators, and it is almost axiomatic that the good ones can always find either full-time or part-time work.

The **first** requisite for the working translator is a thorough knowledge of both the source and the target languages. There is no point in billing oneself as a translator if one is not fully familiar with both languages, or does not possess a vocabulary in both equal to that of a speaker of those languages who has a university education or its equivalent.

The **second** requisite is thorough "at-homeness" in both cultures. A language is a living phenomenon. It does not exist apart from the culture where it is spoken and written. It communicates not only the names of objects and different kinds of action, but also feelings, attitudes, beliefs, and so on. To be fully familiar with a language, one must also be familiar with the culture in which the language is used, indeed, with the people who use it, their ways, manners, beliefs and all that goes into making a culture.

Third, one must keep up with the growth and change of the language, and be up-to-date in all of its nuances and neologisms. Languages are in a constant state of flux, and words change meaning from year to year. A pejorative term can become laudatory, and a neutral term can become loaded with meaning. Thirty years ago the English word "gay" simply meant "joyous." Now it is used to define an entire segment of society. We once spoke of the "almighty dollar." Now as we travel abroad we may find out the dollar is not necessarily everyone's preferred currency.

Fourth, a distinction must be made between the languages one translates from and into. Generally speaking, one translates from another language into one's own native language. This is because one is usually intimately familiar with one's own language, while even years of study and experience do not necessarily enable one to be completely at home with an acquired language. The exceptions to this rule are usually those people who have lived in more than one culture, and have spoken more than one language on a regular basis. Those may be able to translate in both directions. There are also rare gifted individuals who have mastered another language to such a degree that they can go both ways. They are indeed extremely rare. Given all of this, one should allow for the fact that while the ability of the accomplished translator to write and speak in the target language (i.e., one's native tongue) may be flawless, that person may not necessarily be able to write excellent prose or give great speeches in the source language (i.e., the language from which one translates). Then again, it is not necessary to be able to write and speak well in the language one translates from, while it is to be expected that a good translator is also a good writer and speaker in his or her native language.

Fifth, a professional translator has to be able to translate in more than one area of knowledge. Most professional translators are called upon to translate in a variety of fields. It is not uncommon for a translator to cover as many as twenty or thirty fields of knowledge in one year, including such areas as political subjects, economics, law, medicine, communications and so on. Obviously, it would be hard to find a translator who is an economist, a lawyer, a medical doctor, and an engineer all wrapped into one. In fact, such a person probably does not exist. One does not have to be a lawyer to translate legal documents. Many a professional translator has been able to gain enough knowledge and acquire a vocabulary in a variety of technical fields to be able to produce perfectly accurate and well-written translations in those fields. This is not nearly as difficult as it may seem, since most technical fields utilize a well-defined number of terms which keep repeating themselves, and as one keeps translating the same subject, they become more and more familiar to the translator. One must, however, have a natural curiosity about many different areas of human knowledge and activity, and an interest in increasing one's vocabulary in a variety of related as well as unrelated fields.

Sixth, an effective translator must have a facility for writing or speaking (depending on whether the method used is writing, speaking, or dictation), and the ability to articulate quickly and accurately, either orally or in writing. Like a reporter, a translator must be able to transmit ideas in real time, and in good understandable language. Translation is a form of writing and speech-making, and a translator is, in a sense, a writer and an orator.

Seventh, a professional translator must develop a good speed of translation. There are two reasons for this: First, most clients wait until the last minute to assign a translation job. As a result, they turn to a translator or a translation service with what is perhaps the most typical question in this business: "How soon can you have this job ready for me?" The professional translator has to be prepared to accept that long job with the short turnaround time, or there will be no repeat business from that particular client or from most other clients, for that matter. Secondly, translation is generally paid by the word. The more words one can translate per hour, the more income one will generate. Translating 50 words per hour can land a translator in the poorhouse. Serious translation starts at 250 words per hour, and can reach as high as 1000 words per hour using word processing, and close to 3000 words per hour using dictation (the author actually knows such a translator). High volume translators are the ones who will be the most successful.

Eighth, a translator must develop research skills, and be able to acquire reference sources which are essential for producing high quality translation. Without such sources even the best of translators cannot hope to be able to handle a large variety of subjects in many unrelated fields. Dedicated translators are the ones who are always on the lookout for new reference sources, and over time develop a data bank which can be used in their work.

Ninth, today's translator cannot be a stranger to hardware, software, fax, modem, the Internet, and the latest developments in all those media. Translation has become completely dependent on electronic tools. Gone are the days of handwriting, the typewriter, and all the other "prehistoric" means of communication. The more one becomes involved in translation, the more one finds oneself caught up in the latest high-tech developments.

Tenth, a translator who wishes to be busy on a fairly regular basis doing translation work must carefully consider the fact that certain languages are in high demand, say, in Washington or in Los Angeles, while others are not. Thus, for example, there is high demand for Japanese, German, Spanish, French, Chinese, Arabic, Russian and Italian in both Washington and Los Angeles, but not nearly as much for Bulgarian, Farsi, Czech, or Afrikaans. If your language falls within the second group, it is extremely advisable to also have language expertise in one of the languages of the first group, or to seriously consider whether your particular language has enough of a demand to warrant a major investment of time and effort on your part. One should always check and see what kind of a potential one's language specialty has in a given geographic area.

The above ten points are the essential criteria for developing a translation career. There are many other considerations, but none as important as these. If you feel that you can meet all of the above criteria, then you should continue reading this handbook and putting it to good use.

The Well-Rounded Translator

The main division in the translation field is between literary and technical translation. Literary translation, which covers such areas as fiction, poetry, drama, and the humanities in general, is often done by writers of the same genre who actually author works of the same kind in the target language, or at least by translators with the required literary aptitude. For practical reasons, this handbook will not cover literary translation, but will instead focus on the other major area of translation, namely, technical translation. High quality literary translation has always been the domain of the few, and is hardly lucrative (don't even think of doing literary translation if your motive is money), while technical translation is done by a much greater number of practitioners, and is an ever-growing and expanding field with excellent earning opportunities. This chapter discusses the characteristics of the well-rounded technical translator.

The term "technical" is extremely broad. In the translation business it covers much more than technical subjects in the narrow sense of the word. In fact, there is an overlap between literary and technical translation when it comes to such areas as social sciences, political subjects, and many others.

One way of defining technical translation is by asking the question, does the subject being translated require a specialized vocabulary, or is the language non-specialized? If the text being translated includes specialized terms in a given field, then the translation is technical.

The more areas (and languages) a translator can cover, the greater the opportunity for developing a successful translation career. Furthermore, as one becomes proficient in several areas, it becomes easier to add more. Besides, many technical areas are interrelated, and proficiency in one increases proficiency in another. In addition, every area breaks down into many subareas, each with its own vocabulary and its own linguistic idiosyncrasies. Thus, for example, translating in Arabic does not make one an expert in all spoken Arabic dialects, yet a knowledge of several of those dialects is very beneficial for the professional Arabic translator.

How does one become a well-rounded translator? The answer can be summed up in one word—experience. The key to effective translation is practice. Since human knowledge grows day by day, and since language keeps growing and changing, the well-rounded translator must keep in touch with knowledge and language on a regular basis. The worst thing that can happen to a translator is to be out of touch with the source language for more than a couple of years. What the rusty translator may find out is that new words, new concepts and new ways of using those words and applying those concepts have come into being during that period of "hibernation," and one's old expertise is no longer reliable.

Translation, therefore, is a commitment one makes not for a limited period of time, but rather long-term. It is to be assumed that anyone who becomes a translator is the kind of person who loves words and loves the challenge of using words effectively and correctly. Such a person will not become an occasional translator, but will make translation a lifelong practice.

Good and Bad Translation Habits

The accomplished translator can develop good as well as bad habits. Starting with the bad, we have already pointed out one—losing touch with the source language for long periods of time. Another bad habit is taking illegitimate shortcuts while translating. There are several types of such shortcuts. The most typical is failing to look up a word one is really not sure how to translate. Being ninety percent sure of a word's meaning is not good enough in professional translation. If one is not sure of a word's meaning, even after all available means have been exhausted, then one must put in a translator's note to that effect, or make it known in some other way that there is a problem with translating that particular word. Anything less would be deceptive.

Another illegitimate shortcut is summarizing a paragraph instead of providing a *full* translation. There is such a thing as summary translation of a paragraph or a document. If a summary is called for, then this is precisely what the translator is expected to provide. But the most common form of translation is what's known in the business as a verbatim translation, which is a full and complete rendition of the source text. When verbatim translation is ordered, anything less than a full translation is an illegitimate shortcut. Unfortunately, some translators tend to overlook this from time to time, especially when they undertake more work than they can accomplish by a given deadline, and decide to summarize rather than miss that deadline.

Perhaps the worst habit for a translator is to decide at a certain point in time that his or her knowledge of either the source or the target language is so good that it cannot possibly stand any improvement. The moment one stops growing linguistically, one is no longer on the cutting edge of one's profession. The good translator is a perennial language student, always eager and willing to learn more and to keep up with the latest.

As for good habits, the most important, perhaps, are the ones we obtain by reversing the above-mentioned bad habits. But there are many more. One excellent habit is to read professional literature in the field one will be called upon to translate in with reasonable frequency. One good example is *Scientific American*, which can help anyone who translates subjects of science and technology to learn the style or styles used in scientific writing. People who work in the field of translating business documents should definitely read business periodicals, not the least of which is *The Wall Street Journal*. One does not have to be a scientist to translate scientific articles, or have a business degree to translate business documents, but a general understanding of the subject goes a long way towards providing an accurate translation of the subject.

Another excellent habit is to translate not only for profit but also for enjoyment and experience. Most people, unfortunately, are not so taken with their daily work that they would want to continue doing it after hours for fun or practice. But an accomplished translator is someone who will on occasion translate simply for the sake of sharpening his or her skill, or accept a very small fee because of personal commitment to the subject matter, or because of a personal interest. This writer, for example, enjoys translating poetry because of the challenge of doing what is perhaps the most difficult type of translation, and, quite simply, because of the enjoyment of poetry.

Yet another good habit is always to be on the lookout for dictionaries. Many dictionaries are hard to find, and are available in few places. This writer in all his travels across the United States and abroad always stops in bookstores to look for dictionaries. One can also order dictionaries from bookstores and from publishers, but then one has to know what to order and from whom.

The last good habit I would like to mention is the practice of compiling word lists and building a reference library. Dictionaries do not have all the words and terms a translator needs, nor do they contain all the information which specialized references may have. There are aids for translators put out by certain organizations, and there is professional literature in every field. In recent years there has been a growing awareness of the need for terminology management, and with the constant advances in computer technology databases have been proliferating, making the work of the translator much easier than ever before. Good references are worth their weight in gold when they are needed for a specific translation, and over time the experienced translator develops an extensive library of glossaries which become essential for any translation assignment.

APPENDIX B: TRANSLATION TECHNIQUES

Preliminary Considerations

You are given a text to translate. Before you commit yourself to doing any work on it, you must ask yourself a few preliminary questions. They are:

1. Is the text legible?
2. Am I familiar enough with the subject to tackle it?
3. Do I have the linguistic resources (dictionaries, human contacts) to decipher unfamiliar words?
4. Is the text complete, or are there any missing parts?
5. Can I do it within the requested timeframe?
6. Do I have a good reason for doing it (doing it as a learning experience, or because you enjoy it, or to help a friend, or because you are properly compensated for doing it)?

Once you have answered all the above questions to your own satisfaction, you are ready to proceed with the translation.

Effective Approaches

There is no single effective approach to translation, and over time translators develop personal techniques which enhance the quality and the speed of their translation. No one set of rules applies equally to everyone, but there are certain methods and means of translation which can help almost any translator achieve greater accuracy and output. The following is a review of some of the key techniques which are becoming almost universal among professional translators.

The first and foremost question a translator must deal with today is what kind of equipment to use in the process of translating. In the days of the pen and the typewriter this question was much less crucial. Today, however, translation has become almost totally dependent on computers, for several good reasons: (a) Word processing allows far greater flexibility in producing text than any other contemporary means. The output of most translators has been tripled and quadrupled through the use of computers; (b) Computers allow text to be stored on a disk and reprinted or modified later on, a function which is invaluable in the translation field; (c) Clients nowadays are getting used to asking for translation on disk, since it allows them to edit, reprint, modify and enhance the physical appearance of a document; (d) If more than one translator is involved in a given translation project, the text from the various translators can be entered by an editor on one disk and equalized or manipulated as necessary, without having to redo any particular portion thereof.

In addition, it is becoming more common every day to use electronic means such as a modem, fax or e-mail to transmit and receive text. These tools are no longer a luxury. Their cost has been coming down, and more and more translators are acquiring them. Many people today are saying they cannot imagine how translators were ever able to manage without them. The answer is very simple: manage we did, but it took us ten days to two weeks to do what we can now receive, translate and deliver in two or three days.

The next question when approaching a translation assignment is: Am I qualified to do this particular translation? Only an honest answer will do. If one is not sure, then chances are one should not tackle that particular task. One must feel confident about a particular assignment if the results are to be satisfactory. The exception to this rule is a case where a client cannot find anyone else to do that particular job, and for some good reason is either willing to take a chance or to receive less than a complete and fully accurate rendition. In such a case it should be made clear between translator and client that the translation is not legally binding.

Once the commitment is made to proceed with the job, the translator will spend some time going over the entire document even if it is book-length and do a realistic assessment of the following points:

a. How long will it take to translate the document?
b. What reference tools are needed to get it done?
c. What kind of preliminary steps are needed prior to the actual work of translating?
d. What special problems are related to the document, such as legibility of blurred or poorly copied text or difficult handwriting?
e. Does the document contain text in a language or languages other than the main source language, and, if so, can the translator handle that language?

Regarding the question of time, one can do a quick estimate of the length of the document by averaging words per line, times lines per page, times number of pages. An experienced translator has a pretty good idea of the number of words per hour he or she can translate. This is an essential feature of undertaking a professional translation job, since most clients have tight deadlines and tend to give repeat business to those translators known for keeping to their deadlines.

As for reference tools, if, for example, one is given a document about telecommunications, one should make use of one=s own resources in that field and/or borrow from other sources whatever one needs to accomplish the task.

Preliminary steps prior to actual translation can include a consultation with an expert in a specialized technical field regarding a difficult term, phrase, paragraph or concept which the translator does not feel comfortable with. Having access to such experts is one of the translator=s most cherished assets. It can make all the difference in the world between a correct and effective translation and one that misses the main point of the entire text. Another preliminary step is a trip to the local, regional or even specialized library to do some research on the subject.

The problem of legibility should be identified *before* one begins the task, not after. Sometimes the problem may start in the middle of the document and be so severe as to render the translation of the first part useless. In that case, the translator may have wasted a great deal of time. Sometimes the problem is minor, and does not affect the overall outcome of the translation. In other cases, the client may decide to proceed with the translation and simply put the designation [illegible] (between brackets rather than parentheses) wherever a word or part of the text cannot be deciphered.

Unbeknownst to client and translator, when a translation job is first assigned, there may be portions of text inside the source document in a language other than the main language of the document. This can happen in commercial, scientific and scholarly documents. It even happens in Tolstoy=s novel *War and Peace,* when the author starts using French instead of Russian. This too should be detected prior to commencing the translation work, and a decision has to be made as to: (a) Does that text need to be translated? (b) Can the translator handle it? (c) Is it necessary to assign it to another translator?

Once all this preliminary work has been done, one is ready to proceed with the actual translation work.

Depending on the particular text, one should either start translating at this point, or, in the case of a text containing highly specialized terminology which may send the translator on frequent trips to the dictionary, one should first go through the document and make a list of as many unknown or uncertain terms as possible, and then spend some time looking them up and making a word list. This technique saves a great deal of time, since once a list is completed it is much easier to sail through the text, and the time spent initially on making the list is very short compared to the time wasted on repeated interruptions to look up words. Moreover, by first mastering the more difficult terminology of the text, one gains a much better understanding of the subject and is certain to produce a better translation. From the very start, make it a habit to compile word lists and glossaries of subjectspecific terminologies, and keep it in a computer database program for future reference. In time, these lists will become your most valuable translation tool.

One should also follow good work habits. Some translators, particularly those engaged in freelance work, tend to overdo it, especially during their Abusy season,@ when they can generate a large income during a relatively short period of time. They will go for twelve or more hours a day, and before they know it they will start complaining of stiffness in the neck and shoulders, blurred vision, and fatigue. One should not translate more than eight hours a day. Six is ideal. Eight is tolerable, provided one takes a few short ten to fifteen minute breaks. Ten is pushing it. Over ten is definitely hazardous to your health.

Before you get ready to submit your translation go over it again, using the following checklist:

Omissions– did you fail to translate any particular word or phrase, or even paragraph?
Format– does your format follow the original (breaking into paragraphs, for instance)?
Mistranslations– did you mistranslate any particular word?
Unknown words Cwere there words you were not able to translate which you would like to explore further?
Meaning– did you miss the meaning of any phrase or sentence?
Spelling– did you misspell any word which the spell-check function on your computer did not catch?
Grammar– did you make any grammatical mistakes?
Punctuation– did you mispunctuate or miss any punctuation marks?
Clarity– did you fail to clearly convey the meaning of any particular part of the text?
Consistency– did you call something by one name and then by another without any good reason?
Sound-alike words– did you mistranslate a word because it looks or sounds like the word in your target language but in reality has a different meaning?
Style– are you satisfied with the way your translation reflects the style of the original text (for example, the original is written in a clear, direct style, while the translation sounds more complex and indirect?)

This checklist is by no means exhaustive, but it does cover the main areas a translator must pay attention to.

As was already explained, your personal computer is your best friend when it comes to translating, editing, and producing a final copy. One can learn a few basic commands, say, in WordPerfect or Microsoft Word, and start using the computer. But there is much more to software than entering, deleting and inserting text. The better acquainted with software you become, the more it will help you with translation. Learn how to do columns and tables, how to use special technical and scientific symbols, do graphic functions, use the spell-check and the thesaurus, create data bases for glossaries and for your own administrative records, and you will tackle a great variety of technical text in many fields at a speed that will amaze you. Remember: speed in translation is the most important thing next to language proficiency. Without it you will not be profitable, and you will be overrun by the competition. With an established record of fast accurate translation you can write your own ticket.

After a few years of using the computer you may want to consider dictation. Personally, I prefer a mix of PC and dictation. When I have an unusually long job and not enough time to do it in, I may revert to dictation. Otherwise, I prefer word-processing. One could argue that by dictating one gets more done and earns more, but there are other things to consider, such as the cost of transcription, the need to edit transcription, and the better control one has over writing than speaking. Some of us are natural speakers; others are writers.

One continues to develop translation techniques over time. One of the most wonderful things about translation, in my opinion, is the fact that your mind is never idle, never in a rut, but rather always being challenged by new tasks, new subjects, new knowledge, and the need to keep up with new developments in language, with different fields of human knowledge, and with the events of the world. As a translator in the Washington area since the late seventies, I have found myself in the middle of world events, beginning with the peace treaty between Egypt and Israel in 1979, when I met Begin, Sadat and Carter, and, more recently, in my daily dealings with events in post-Cold War Eastern Europe, with a strife-torn Middle East, the famine in Somalia, the new North American Free Trade Agreement (NAFTA) between the United States, Canada and Mexico, and the growing involvement of the U.S. space program with the space programs of other nations. Very few people cover as broad an area as a translator. Every day we in the translation business find new challenges, and have to solve new problems. As a result, we are always developing new techniques and finding new answers.

APPENDIX C: TRANSLATOR'S SELF-EVALUATION

The following criteria were developed some years ago by a U.S. Government agency for determining the skill level of a potential translator whom that agency might have liked to hire. You may want to read this chapter carefully to try to make an honest determination as to where on this scale you find yourself at this time. If you are below Level 2+, you need to keep practicing. If you are at Level 3 or higher, you can start doing some professional translating. After Level 4 you are ready for some serious translating, and at Level 5 you can start making a living as a translator.

Translator Skill Levels

Level 0

No functional ability to translate the language. Consistently misunderstanding or cannot comprehend at all.

Level 0+

Can translate all or some place names (i.e., street or city designations), corporate names, numbers and isolated words and phrases,
often translating these inaccurately.

In rendering translations, writes using only memorized material and set expressions. Spelling and representation of symbols (letters, syllables, characters) are frequently incorrect.

Level 1

Sufficient skill to translate the simplest connected written material in a form equivalent to usual printing or typescript. Can translate either representations of familiar formulaic verbal exchanges or simple language containing only the highest-frequency grammatical patterns and vocabulary items, including cognates when appropriate. Translated texts include simple narratives of routine behavior; concrete descriptions of persons, places and things; and explanations of geography and government such as those simplified for tourists. Mistranslations common.

In rendering translations, writes in simple sentences (or clauses), making continual errors in spelling, grammar and punctuation, but translation can be read and understood by a native reader used to dealing with foreigners attempting to translate his/her language.

Level 1+

Sufficient skill to translate simple discourse for informative social purposes in printed form. Can translate material such as announcements or public events, popular advertising notes containing biographical information or narration of events and straightforward newspaper headlines. Has some difficulty with the cohesive factors in discourse, such as matching pronouns with referents.

In rendering translations, writing shows good control of elementary vocabulary and some control of basic syntactic patterns, but major errors still occur when expressing more complex thoughts. Dictionary usage may still yield incorrect vocabulary of forms, although can use a dictionary to advantage to translate simple ideas. Translations, though faulty, are comprehensible to native readers used to dealing with foreigners.

Level 2

Sufficient skill to translate simple authentic written material in a form equivalent to usual printing. Can translate uncomplicated, but authentic prose on familiar subjects that are normally present in a predictable sequence, which aids the translator in his/her work. Texts may include description and narration in context, such as news items describing frequently occurring events, simple biographical information, social notices, formatted business letters and simple technical material written for the general reader. The prose is predominantly in familiar sentence patterns. Some mistranslations.

In rendering translations, has written vocabulary sufficient to perform simple translations with some circumlocutions. Still makes common errors in spelling and punctuation, but shows some control of the most common formats and punctuation conventions. Good control of morphology of language (in inflected languages) and of the most frequently used syntactic structures. Elementary constructions are usually handled quite accurately, and translations are understandable to a native reader *not* used to reading the translations of foreigners.

Level 2+

Sufficient skill to translate most factual material in nontechnical prose as well as some discussions on concrete topics related to special professional interests. Has begun to make sensible guesses about unfamiliar words by using linguistic context and prior knowledge. May react personally to material, but does not yet detect subjective attitudes, values or judgments in the material to be translated.

In rendering translations, often shows surprising fluency and ease of expression, but under time constraints and pressure language may be inaccurate and/or incomprehensible. Generally strong in either grammar or vocabulary, but not in both. Weaknesses or unevenness in one of the foregoing or in spelling results in occasional mistranslations. Areas of weakness range from simple constructions, such as plurals, articles, prepositions and negatives, to more complex structures, word order and relative clauses. Normally controls general vocabulary, with some misuse of everyday vocabulary still evident. Shows a limited ability to use circumlocutions. Uses dictionary to advantage to supply unknown words. Translations are understandable to native readers not used to dealing with foreigner's attempts to translate the language, though style is obviously foreign.

Level 3

Able to translate authentic prose on unfamiliar subjects. Translating ability is not dependent on subject matter knowledge. Texts will include news stories similar to wire service reports, routine correspondence, general reports and technical material in his/her professional field, all of which include hypothesis, argumentation and supported opinions. Such texts typically include grammatical patterns and vocabulary ordinarily encountered in professional reading. Mistranslations rare. Almost always able to correctly translate material, relate ideas and make inferences. Rarely has to pause over or reread general vocabulary. However, may experience some difficulty with unusually complex structures and low-frequency idioms.

In preparing translations, control of structure, spelling, and general vocabulary is adequate to convey his/her message accurately, but style may be obviously foreign. Errors virtually never interfere with comprehension and rarely disturb the native reader. Punctuation generally controlled. Employs a full range of structures. Control of grammar good, with only sporadic errors in basic structures, occasional errors in the most complex frequent structures and somewhat more frequent errors in low-frequency complex structures. Consistent control of compound and complex sentences. Relationship of ideas presented in original material is consistently clear.

Level 3+

Increased ability to translate a variety of styles and forms of language pertinent to professional needs. Rarely mistranslates such texts or rarely experiences difficulty relating ideas or making inferences. Ability to compprehend many sociolinguistic and cultural references. However, may miss some nuances and subtleties. Increased ability to translate unusually complex structures and low-frequency idioms; however, accuracy is not complete.

In rendering translations, able to write the language in a few prose styles pertinent to professional/educational needs. Not always able to tailor language to suit original material. Weaknesses may lie in poor control of low-frequency, complex structures, vocabulary or the ability to express subtleties and nuances.

Level 4

Able to translate fluently and accurately all styles and forms of the language pertinent to professional needs. Can translate more difficult prose and follow unpredictable turns of thought readily in any area directed to the general reader and all materials in his/her own special field, including official and professional documents and correspondence. Able to translate precise and extensive vocabulary, including nuances and subtleties, and recognize all professionally relevant vocabulary known to the educated nonprofessional native, although may have some difficulty with slang. Can translate reasonably legible handwriting without difficulty. Understands almost all sociolinguistic and cultural references.

In rendering translations, able to write the language precisely and accurately in a variety of prose styles pertinent to professional/ educational needs. Errors of grammar are rare, including those in low-frequency complex structures. Consistently able to tailor language to suit material and able to express subtleties and nuances.

Level 4+

Increased ability to translate extremely difficult or abstract prose. Increased ability to translate a variety of vocabulary, idioms, colloquialisms and slang. Strong sensitivity to sociolinguistic and cultural references. Increased ability to translate less than fully legible handwriting. Accuracy is close to that of an educated translator, but still not equivalent.

In rendering translations, able to write the language precisely and accurately, in a wide variety of prose styles pertinent to professional/educational needs.

Level 5

Can translate extremely difficult and abstract prose (i.e., legal, technical), as well as highly colloquial writings and the literary forms of the language. Translates a wide variety of vocabulary and idioms, colloquialisms, slang and pertinent cultural references. With varying degrees of difficulty, can translate all kinds of handwritten documents. Able to understand how natives think as they produce a text. Accuracy is equivalent to that of a well-educated translator.

In rendering translations, has writing proficiency equal to that of a well-educated native. Without nonnative errors of structure, spelling, style or vocabulary, can translate both formal and informal correspondence, official reports and documents and professional/educational articles, including writing for special purposes which might include legal, technical, educational, literary and colloquial writing.

APPENDIX D: ARABIC TECHNICAL DICTIONARIES

General Dictionaries
A Dictionary of Modern Written Arabic, Wehr, H. Wiesbaden: Otto Harrassowitz 1993 *This is one of the best general Arabic-English dictionaries around. Available in hardcover and paperback.*
Al-Mawrid, Baalbaki, M., International Book Centre 1998
Contains many modern words and idioms.
Arabic-English Lexicon, 2 vols., Ln., E. W., Cambridge: Islamic Texts Society 1984
The Oxford English-Arabic Dictionary of Current Usage, Doniach, N.S., Oxford: Oxford University Press 1985
Al-Fara'id al-Durriyah, Hava, G., Beirut: Dar al-Mashriq 1982
An Arabic-English Lexicon, 8 vols., Ln., E. W., Beirut: Librairie du Liban 1980
Al-Qamus al-'Asri, Elias, Elias A., Cairo: Modern Press 1960

Arabic: Dialects
NTC's Gulf Arabic-English Dictionary, Hamdi, A., Lincolnwood,IL: NTC Publishing Group 1999
A Dictionary of Post-Classical Yemeni Arabic, Piamenta, M., Leiden, Brill 1997.
al-Qamus al-Arabi al-Shabi al-Filastini, Barghuthi, A., al-Lahjah
al-Filastiniyah al-Darijah, Birah: Jamiyat Inash al-Usrah, Lajnat al-Abhath al-Ijitimaiyah
A Dictionary of Iraqi Arabic, Beene, W., Washington: Georgetown University Press 1991
Dictionary of Egyptian Arabic, Hinds, Martin, Beirut: Librairie du Liban 1987 *Egyptian terms.*
An Arabic-English Dictionary of the Colloquial Arabic of Egypt, Spiro, S., Beirut: Librairie du Liban 1980
A Dictionary of Moroccan Arabic: Moroccan-English, Harrell, R.S., Washington: Georgetown University Press 1986
A Dictionary of Syrian Arabic: English-Arabic, Harrell,R.S., Wash-ington: Georgetown University Press 1964

Arabic: Agriculture
Chihabi's Dictionary of Agriculture and Allied Terminology, Al-Khatib, A., 1978 *English-Arabic*

Arabic: Botany
Botany and Microbiology Dictionary: English-Arabic, Safat, Kuwait: Kuwait Foundation for the Advancement of Sciences 1985
Illustrated Polyglotic Dictionary of Plant Names, Bedevian, A., Cairo: Argus and Papazian Presses 1936

Arabic: Business and Related Fields
Glossary of Islamic Economics, Khan, M.A., London: Mansell 1990 *Arabic-English*
The Office Dictionary in English and Arabic, Compiled by Multi-Lingual International Publishers Ltd, London: Oxford University Press 1987
Management Dictionary (Arabic-Arabic-English), Ghattas, N., Brech, E. et al, Beirut: Librairie du Liban 1983
English-Arabic Dictionary of Accounting and Finance, Abdeen, A., Beirut: Librairie du Liban, John Wiley & Sons 1982
A Dictionary of Economics, Business & Finance: English-Arabic with an Arabic Glossary, Ghattas, N., Beirut: Librairie du Liban 1982
Banking and Financial Dictionary: English, French, Arabic, El Assiouty, M.N., Cairo: Distributor, Investment Trustee Department, National Bank of Egypt 1980
Dictionnaire des Termes Economiques et Commerciaux Hanni, M., Beirut: Librairie du Liban 1972 *English-French-Arabic*

Arabic: Chemistry
Unified Dictionary of Chemistry Terms: English, French, Arabic, Tunis: Arab League Educational, Cultural and Scientific Organization 1992
Kuwait Science Encyclopedia, Chemistry Dictionary, Kuwait: Book & Author Programme 1984
Illustrated Dictionary of Chemistry in English with English-Arabic & Arabic-English Glossaries, Godman, A., Beirut: Librairie du Liban 1982

Arabic: Civil Engineering
Arabic Dictionary of Civil Engineering, Kay, E., London: Routledge & Kegan Paul 1986

Arabic: Communications
A Dictionary of Audio-visual Technology: English-Arabic, Sieny, M.E., Beirut: Librairie du Liban 1987
Dictionary of Mass Communications: English-French-Arabic, Badawi, A.Z., Cairo: Dar al-Kitab al-Masri 1980

Arabic: Computers
Encyclopedic Dictionary of Computer Terms, El-Zohairy, N., International Book Center 1996
Encyclopedia of Computer Terms, Hammad, A.E., American Global Publishing 1994 *English-Arabic*
English Arabic Computer Dictionary, Kashou, R., Reading, Berkshire, UK: University of Reading & Sagar Computers Ltd 1992
An Illustrated Dictionary of Data Processing, Computing, and Office Automation: English-Arabic with English Index, Cusic, D., Beirut: Librairie du Liban 1988
Al-Kilani Dictionary of Computer Terminology, English-English-Arabic, Kilani, Taiseer, and Mazen, Beirut: Librairie du Liban 1987
A Dictionary of Data Processing and Computer Terms: English-French-Arabic, Haddad, E.W., Beirut: Librairie du Liban 1987
Illustrated Dictionary of Computing Science, Quentin, R.D., Beirut: Librairie du Liban 1987
Arabic Computer Dictionary, Ghanayem, M.F., Texas: International House Publications 1986 *Arabic-English*

Arabic: Geography
Dictionary of Arabic Topography and Place Names, Groom, N., London: Librairie du Liban 1983
Glossary of Arabic Place Names, Arabian American Oil Company, s.l.: ARAMCO 1978

Arabic: Journalism
al-Qamus al-Ilami: Arabi-Inkilizi, Najm, A., Baghdad: Wizarat al-Thaqafah wa-a;-Ilam 1982

Arabic: Law
Arabic-English Law Dictionary, Amin, S.H., Glasgow: Royston 1992
Faruqi's Law Dictionary, 5th rev. ed., Faruqi, H., Beirut: Librairie du Liban 1988 *English-Arabic*
Customs Dictionary: English-Arabic, Mahmoud, R., Cairo: published by author 1984
Faruqi's Law Dictionary, Faruqi, H., Beirut: Librairie du Liban 1997 *Arabic-English*
Law Dictionary: English-Arabic, al-Wahab, D.I.I., Beirut: Librairie du Liban 1972

Arabic: Medicine
Hitti's Medical Dictionary: English-Arabic, Hitti, Y.K., Beirut: Lib-rairie du Liban 1994 *Illustrated.*
A Modern Arabic Dictionary of Dental Terms: English-Arabic, Duyat, M., Amman: Dar al-Ibdaa 1990
Concise Medical Dictionary, Allah, J.& Fawzi, M., Cairo: University Book Centre 1986
Qamus Mustalahat Tibb al-Asnan, Mutayyam, K., s.n.: Matbaat al-Taqddum 1984
The New Medical-Pharmaceutical Dictionary, Oweida, A.M., Cairo: Dar al-Fikr al-Arabi 1970
Dictionary of Anatomy, Abadir, F.M., Princeton University Arabic Collection, Alexandria: Al Maaref Establishment 1968

Arabic: Military
Modern Military Dictionary, Kayyali, M.S., Arab Institute for Research and Publishing, Beirut, London: Third World Center for Research and Publishing 1991 *Arabic-English-Arabic*
Arabic Military Dictionary, Kay, E., London: Routledge & Kegan Paul 1986 *English-Arabic-English*
Pocket Book of Military Terms, 6th ed. Badran, C., Cairo: Greater Egypt Publishers 1982 *English-Arabic*
Al-Mu'jam al-'Askari al-Muwahhad, Committee for Standardizing Military Terminology for Arab Armies. 1971 *Arabic-English*
Al-Mu'jam al-'Askari al-Muwahhad, Committee for Standardizing Military Terminology for Arab Armies, Cairo: Dar al-Ma'arif 1970 *English-Arabic*

Arabic: Nautical
Elsevier's Maritime Dictionary, Bakr, M., Elsevier Science Ltd 1987 *English-French-Arabic*

Arabic: Oil
A New Dictionary of Petroleum and the Oil Industry, Al-Khatib, A., Beirut: Librairie du Liban 1990 *English-Arabic*

Arabic: Psychology and Psychiatry

Mujam Ilm al-Nafs wa-al Tibb al-Nafsi: Injilizi-Arabi, Jabir, J., Cairo: Dar al-Nahdah al-Arabiyah 1988
Mujam Ilm al-Nafs, Inkilizi-Faransi-Arabi, Aqil, F., Beirut: Dar al-Ilm lil-Malayin 1977
Dictionary of Psychology: English-Arabic, Illustrated, Zahran, H., Cairo: Al Shaab Print House 1972

Arabic: Science and Technology
Mustalahat al-Duru, Amman: al-Majma al-Lughah al-Arabiyah al-Urduni 1994 *Dictionary of explosives*
al-Mujam al-Muwahhad Li-Mustalahat al-Riyadiyat wa-al-Falak: Injilizi, Faransi, Arabi, Tunis: al-Munazzamah 1990
Unified Dictionary for Terminologies of General and Nuclear Physics: English, French, Arabic, Tunis: Arab League Educational, Cultural and Scientific Organization 1989
New Dictionary of Scientific and Technical Terms, Al-Khatib, A., Beirut: Libraire du Liban 1981 *English-Arabic*
Mujam al-Hayawan, Maluf, A., Beirut: Dar al-Raid al-Arabi 1980
Dictionary of Zoological Terms, Unified Dictionary of Scientific Terms for General Education Levels, No.4, s.l.: Iraqi Academy Press 1976
Dictionnaire des sciences de la nature, Ghaleb, E., Beirut: Imprimerie Catholique 1965 *Arabic-English-French*
Space Dictionary, al-Laqqani, M., Cairo: Dar El-Hana Press 1962

APPENDIX E: SOURCES OF TRANSLATION WORK

This book includes a CD (inside the front cover) with lists of translations companies and international corporations who do a large volume of translation in all languages.

If you choose freelance translation, you should consider yourself a one-person translation company. Your main concern will be where to find work. The need for freelance translation is greater than anyone can estimate, and is clearly growing at a rapid rate. Worldwide, translation is a multibillion dollar industry. But finding translation work on your own is easier said than done. The main problem is that translation is hardly ever a steady, ongoing function of any particular work source, such as an embassy, a company, a government agency, or even a publisher. None of those needs translation every day of the year. Each of them may need a great deal of translation all at once (more than any one person can handle within the given time-frame), and then none for a long time. And, if any one of them needs translation on an ongoing basis, chances are a decision will be made to hire an in-house translator rather than farm out the work.

The fact remains, however, that a well-rounded freelancer can earn well over $50,000 a year, and, in the case of highly specialized technical translators in major languages like Spanish, German, Japanese or Russian, even $100,000 or more. The secret to all of this is establishing for yourself a good clientele. There are two ways of doing this. The first, and by far the hardest, is finding your own clients and working with them directly. You may want to contact embassies, law firms, publishers, government agencies and so on, and solicit work directly from them. If you are fortunate enough to find some good steady clients on your own, you will be doing quite well. But the problem often lies in the word "steady." What seems to be a steady client today may not be so steady tomorrow.

This brings us to the second, and by far the safer option, which is translation agencies. There are hundreds of them in the United States, and they handle huge amounts of translation business every year. In this chapter we will discuss translation agencies, as well as direct sources of translation available to the freelancer.

Translation Agencies

Translation agencies, also known as translation companies, or translation bureaus, are for the most part privately owned commercial establishments ranging in size from one or two employees to ten or more, but hardly ever larger than ten. Some are divisions of larger companies, such as Berlitz, which is primarily a language school and publisher, offering translation as a secondary function. Some specialize in one language only, such as Spanish, German, or Japanese. Most offer several languages, and quite a few bill themselves as offering "all languages." This last type is somewhat pretentious, since there are more languages in the world than any one person can identify. But what they really mean is that they will make the effort to find a translator in almost any language they may be called upon to translate.

As a general rule, translation agencies employ relatively few in-house translators, since the flow of work in any given language is usually uneven. Instead, they rely on the services of a network of hundreds of freelancers who can handle a great variety of subjects. Those freelancers are located all over the United States and even abroad. The ones who are most reliable and professional get the major share of the work, and some of them earn the above-quoted figures.

As a freelancer, you need to cultivate at least one such agency, preferably two or three. The problem in working with only one is that, with few exceptions, there may not be a steady flow of work coming out of any given agency in any given language, in subjects you are equipped to handle. Two or three will give you better coverage, and assure a better flow. On the other hand, you may find yourself in a situation where all three ask you to do something at the same time, and you may not be able to do it. You need to establish an understanding with your agencies that would make an allowance for such a scenario, so that you don't spoil your relationship with any one of them.

The worst thing you can do as a freelancer working with translation agencies is to overcommit yourself. Your most important personal asset is your reliability. Once you fail to meet deadlines (keep in mind—the agency stands to lose a client if deadlines are not met), your reliability becomes questionable, and if you do it once too often, you may soon find out that those phone calls from the agency offering you work assignments stop coming.

Where do you look for translation agencies? Below you will find a listing of hundreds of such agencies. You can find more in the Yellow Pages, or through the ATA (American Translators Association), which has local chapters around the country. My suggestion is to start with those close to home. In this day and age of international electronic communications, distance has little meaning. But then again, close to home still works, because you can meet the people there, befriend them, and in some instances even avail yourself of their dictionaries and other resources.

Keep in mind that a translation company has overhead, and also needs to make some profit to stay in business. They do the hard work of finding translation assignments, and therefore share with you the profit from the job. You can usually make more money by going directly to the client, and if you have enough of your own clients you don't need a translation company to send work your way. But most freelance translators do need those companies, which invariably provide a more steady flow of work than what a freelancer can get on his or her own.

The two things all translation companies appreciate and reward in a freelancer are honesty and loyalty. If you agree to a deadline, stick to it. Don't renege on it at the last minute. That's a sure prescription to spoil your association with your company. Equally important is not to go behind the company's back and try to solicit its own clients directly. Some companies will make you sign an agreement to this effect. Others will rely on the honor system. Don't abuse their trust. It usually doesn't pay off.

Direct Sources of Work

Working with translation agencies usually does not stop you from finding your own clients, as long as there is no conflict of interest with the agency's clients. It would be impossible to list here all the potential sources of direct translation work, since they include practically the entire human race (everyone needs a document translated at some point). But there are some major sources which ought to be mentioned, and here are some of the more important ones.

Law Firms

Law firms are a major source of translation work. Some of the larger firms hire full-time translators or staff members who are bilingual, especially if they do business on a regular basis with a foreign entity. Most firms use translators on an as-needed basis. Legal translation is a specialized field in which you need to acquire experience working with legal documents. There are several legal specialties, such as patent law, international law, immigration, and so on. Each specialty has its own style and terminology, which a translator needs to become acquainted with. As a freelancer, adding legal translation to your list of specialties is an excellent idea. You will find out that your volume of translation will increase considerably by doing so.

Quite often, a law firm needs both document translation and interpretation. Keep in mind that interpretation is a discipline separate from translation, and that there is a big difference between one-on-one consecutive interpreting and simultaneous conference interpreting. If asked by a law firm to do both text translation and interpreting, be sure to find out first exactly what the assignments consist of.

Industry

Corporations doing business in other countries have to deal with documents originated in the languages of those countries or English documents that need to be translated into those languages. Here again we find the two approaches of either hiring translators or farming out work to freelancers and to translation services (or a combination of both). This field is perhaps the fastest growing source of translation in the closing years of the twentieth century. More and more major American companies are turning to international business as a way to offset the decline of business at home and to gain a share of the world market. Their need for translation is growing every day, and even those who have in-house translators are finding themselves using freelancers because of their volume of translation work.

If you are fortunate enough to form a relationship with a major company doing business overseas, you may find yourself in the enviable position of dealing with a major, steady source of translation.
How does one get work with major corporations? If you have a special expertise in their field of work, say you are a telecommunications expert and you would like to translate for Sprint, find out who handles outside vendors or services, and give them a call or drop them a note. It also helps to know someone in the company, who can do some of the legwork for you and put you in touch with the right people. As a general rule, this is not easy to do. But persistence does pay off some of the time, and even if only a few respond, it is worth the effort.

The U.S. Government

For several decades following World War Two, translation in the federal government enjoyed a boom. The onset of the Cold War resulted in wide-scale translation activities on the part of the U.S. Department of Defense (DoD), all the branches of the service (particularly the Army, Navy, and Air Force), and the Central Intelligence Agency (CIA). In addition, such multilingual organizations as the Voice of America (which started broadcasting in 1942 in 40 languages), sprang into being. These and other organizations employed a host of translators, and farmed out millions of words every year to be translated. Looking back, those were the feast years of government translation. During the nineties, however, a major shift has been taking place. Since 1992, there has been a sharp decline in government translations, and those translation agencies and freelancers who were dependent on government work for their bread and butter, are hurting. This is not to say that the U.S. Government is no longer a source of employment for translators. There are still many opportunities for translation in the government, offered by such bodies as the Language Services division of the U.S. Department of State (for in-house as well as freelance translators and interpreters), the Library of Congress, the U.S. Patent and Trademark Office, and so on (see list of U.S. Government Agencies, Appendix 4).

My translation company, Schreiber Translations, Inc. (STI), started out in life as a full-service translation company for the federal government. This was in the early eighties, when the boom was still on. We provided translation from and into over 50 languages and dialects, as well as interpreting, transcription, voice-over, graphics, and editing. Luckily for us, we realized early on that, as the world was changing, we were better off not being locked into government work, and we were able to develop a lucrative practice in the nongovernmental sectors. Today, government work makes up less than 50% of our total translation work.

What does all of this mean to linguists seeking translation work in the closing years of the twentieth century? There is no one simple answer. The government has been known to swing like a fast-moving pendulum. This author believes that before long the federal government will be launching new major translation projects, in such sectors as world trade and international relations. American interaction with other cultures and languages is far from diminishing. If anything, it is increasing day by day. One good example is the American space program, conducted by the National Aeronautics and Space Administration (NASA). Back in the sixties, there were two major space programs in the world—the Soviet and the American. Today, many countries in Western Europe and Asia have an active space program, and many of them are involved in cooperative efforts. NASA is actively involved in this new international space scene, and the need for translation in this particular organization should not be underestimated. But all of this, of course, is speculative. The federal government is making a historical effort to reduce its enormous deficit, and since the lawmakers of our land are not necessarily attuned to the critical importance of translation, translation may well be a casualty of the budget wars. Translators would be well advised not to write off doing translation for the government, since it is, and will continue to be, the single biggest employer around. But they should put at least as much, if not more, effort into finding translation work outside the government, where indeed the field is all but limitless.

What are the pros and cons of translating for the government? For many linguists over the years, the government has offered job security. I know some fine translators who have worked for the government for many years and had interesting and fulfilling careers. On the other hand, career translators in the government are not paid exceptionally high salaries. Quite a few freelance on the side in an effort to supplement their income. As for freelancers who contract with the government, here we have mixed results. Some have found themselves a cozy niche and are kept busy on a fairly regular basis. Others go through the "feast and famine" syndrome. Some have been frustrated by spending a long time hunting for government assignments, with little result. To freelance effectively for the government, one should, in most instances, work in one of the top five languages the U.S. Government is interested in (Spanish, Russian, German, French and Japanese). Any other language, even Chinese or Arabic, may not offer enough of a flow. One should also make many contacts. On the downside, government agencies, with few exceptions, are notorious for not paying on time. A few years ago, the government passed a "prompt payment" act, which mandates 30-day net payment, with interest accruing thereafter. The problem is, more than a few agencies take at least another 30 days to process an invoice, claiming that it takes that long to get your invoice "into the system." Others take even longer, and simply neglect to add interest. If you try to get it, you may soon find out you waste more time going after it than it's worth. In some extreme cases—which are by no means rare—it can take six to twelve months to get paid. Your invoice simply gets lost in the system. Your remedy is to contact your congressperson, who will call that particular government office to make sure you get paid. The problem is, those folks in the finance office often resent being put on the spot in this manner, and while they will expedite your payment, you may not get work next time. It all sounds shocking, but having been there, it is my civic duty to let you know.

Another drawback of government freelancing is the incredible amount of paperwork you are asked to fill out in doing some of those jobs. I have done five and ten dollar jobs that required three detailed forms filled out, plus an invoice in six copies, mailed to three different offices (finance, procurement, and contract). It took me longer to do the paperwork than to translate, and clearly the whole thing was not worth my while. If you do a fair amount of freelancing for the government, you learn to overlook these excesses. Otherwise, you may have to decide whether it's all worth it.

A third major drawback to doing government work is the fact that quite often the translation standards of a particular agency may be quite low. As a result, you run the risk of developing poor translation habits, lack of attention to details, lack of sufficient editing and proofing, and so on. What that means in a practical sense is that when a more demanding job comes along, especially in the private sector, you may find out your performance is not satisfactory, and you may lose your client.

Having said all this, it behooves me to add that during the last seventeen years I have interacted with hundreds of government employees and dozens of agencies, and many of those have been a delight to work with, and overall I have been very fortunate to have this unique opportunity to take part in many historical events, including the peace treaty between Israel and Egypt, the Gulf War, the disarmament agreement with the former Soviet Union, the Bosnian peace agreement, and many more. Thus, working with the government as a linguist is by no means a dull experience, and if you learn how to take some of the problems in your stride, you can do quite well.

State and Local Government

Government at all levels, from the municipal to the federal, needs translation. At the local level we find more and more city and county government translating their pamphlets, brochures and other documents into the languages of their immigrant populations, notably Asian languages and Spanish. In addition, local government has an ongoing need for interpreters, mostly for the court system, but also for social services, hospitals, and other local institutions. At this time of tight budgets, this may not be the most lucrative field, but it is definitely worth exploring, since it is local, and mostly uses local linguists.

Major Organizations

Among the largest organizations that use a great deal of translation one should mention the United Nations, The World Bank, the World Health Organization, the Organization of American States, to cite only some of the better-known ones here in the U.S. Surely there are more in Europe, such as the World Court, the European Community, NATO, and many more. Most of these organizations use in-house linguists, and do not farm out translation work if they can help it. But quite often they have more documents to translate than they can handle in-house, and they look for outside help.

Publishers

Book publishers use freelance translators in many different ways. This is not an easy field to break into, particularly for the beginner. Many publishers turn to academia for translators, and if you are in academia and can translate from or into another language in your field of expertise, there is a chance you can get the work. Others turn to established translators with name recognition. But it is certainly worth trying, to query publishers and find out if they need your services.

Software Localization Companies

A fast-growing area of translation is software localization, or translation of software-related text into other languages and adapting the text to the target culture. Software localization companies specialize in computer subjects and in English-into-foreign language translation. They employ in-house translators, but they also use freelancers from time to time. Their work encompasses everything from computer manuals to localization of web-sites.

Networking

An excellent source of work for freelance translators is personal contacts with other translators. The ATA's local chapters are one place where translators meet and get to know each other. The annual conference of the ATA holds a networking session, which is very valuable. One also meets translators through personal contacts in the translation field.

The latest way to meet translators is on the Internet. Entities such as the Foreign Language Forum on CompuServe bring together translators from all over the world. All you need to do is post a message on one of those programs, and before you know it you get a response from someone in your own town or half way around the world.

Keeping in touch with other translators is a prime means of finding out about work sources and assignments. There are clearly many advantages to networking in the translation field, and the more contacts one has the better.

The following is a list of translation companies who use freelance translators. The companies are not rated. It is up to you to find out which are best suited to your needs.

-A-

A L Madrid & Associates, 165 Ponce de Leon Boulevard , Coral Gables, FL 33134 Phone: (305)448-8985 Fax: (305)448-7519 e-mail: info@almadrid,com Web site: www.amlogos.com Contact: Alberto Lares Member: ATA

A & M Logos International, Inc., 40 Rector Street, Ste. 1504, New York, NY 10006 Phone: (212)233-7061 Fax: (212)233-7167 e-mail: trans@amlogos.com Web site: www.amlogos.com
Contact: Elena Gapeeva Member: ATA

A Perfect Translation, 3415 Waterview Trail, Rockwall, TX 75087 e-mail: aptrans@msn.com
Contact:Rianne Sanchez Member: ATA

AAA Worldwide Translation Services, 4820 Minnetonka Blvd., St. Louis Park, MN 55416 Phone: (612)922-7446 Fax: (612)922-2001 e-mail: aaawwide2@aol.com
Contact: Danny Freier Member: ATA

ABC Worldwide Translations & Interpretations, 8306 Wilshire Boulevard, Ste. 200, Beverly Hills, CA 90211 Phone: (310)260-7700 Fax: (310)260-7705 e-mail: info@wordexpress.com
Web site:www.wordexpress.net Contact: Muriel Redoute Member: ATA

ABS Translation & Interpreting Service, 1685 Hampton Road, Abington, PA 19001 Phone: (215)886-2219 Fax: (215)886-7671 e-mail: ABStrans@aol.com Contact: Aram Sarkisian Member: ATA

A.C.E. InfoTech Group, 1450 114th Ave SE, Ste. 1-230, Seattle, WA 98004 Phone: (425)453-4444 Fax: (425)453-0188 Web site: www.aceinfotech.comContact: Maya Vengadasalam Member: ATA

AE Inc. Translations, 15995 N. Barkers Landing, Ste. 111, Houston, TX 77079 Phone: (281)870-0677 Fax: (281)556-9737 e-mail: translations@aetrans.com Web site: www.aetrans.com
Contact: Stephen D. Ross, President Member: ATA

ABLE International, Inc., 8 Wright Acres Road, Bedford, NH 03110
Phone: (603)625-2253 Fax: (603)625-0950 Web site: www.ableint.com Member: ATA

Academy of Languages Translation & Interpretation Services, 216 First Ave. South, Ste. 330, Seattle, WA 98104
Phone: (206)521-8601 Fax: (206)521-8605
e-mail: trasnalte@wal.org Web site: www.wal.org Contact: Mercedes Creelman Member: ATA

Academy of Legal and Technical Translation, Three Continental Towers, 1701 Golf Road, Ste. 604, Rolling Meadows, IL 60008
Phone: (847)364-7700 Fax: (847)364-7883
e-mail: info@transexpert.com Web site: www.transexpert.com
Contact: Hema Desai Member: ATA

Academy Translations, P.O. Box 357, East Berlin, CT 06023
Phone: (860)828-9615 Fax: (860)828-3965
e-mail: acadtran@pobox.com
Contact: David J. Marsh, Director of Operations
Founded 1996. Member: ATA, NAJIT. Translates all languages, both from and into English. Emphasis on all areas of translation, with specialties in Business and Finance, Insurance and Banking, Manufacturing, Immigration and

Naturalization and Broadcast and Print Journalism. Prospective translators should demonstrate proficiency in their languages, and be able to verify their education and experience. ATA or other accreditation is preferred. Resumes are evaluated, and if qualified, translators are sent a letter with a subcontractual agreement. Maintains a pool of over 1800 translators.

Accent on Language, 160 East 56th St., 5th Fl., New York, NY 10022 Phone: (212)486-6790 Fax: (212)486-2439
e-mail: info@accentonlanguage.com Web site: www.accentonlanguage. com
Contact: Brian E. McDermott Member: ATA

Accent Typography & Translation, 1086 Rainberry Court, Neenah, WI 54956 Phone: (920)751-8260 Fax: (920)729-5843
e-mail: accent@athenet.net
Contact: Kimberlee A. Heier, President Member: ATA

Accento, The Language Company, 5527 Dyer St., Dallas, TX 75206 Phone: (214)363-5353 Fax: (214)363-0067
e-mail: accento@accento.net Web site: www.accento.net Contact: James Mahler Member: ATA

Access Transport & Translation Services, Inc., 528 S North Lake Boulevard, Ste. 1000, Altamonte Springs, FL 32701
Phone: (888)748-7575 Fax: (407)330-7959 e-mail: gengelman@accessontime.com Web site: www.accessontime.com
Contact: Stacey L. Whidden Member: ATA

Accomplished Translation Services, 305 Broadway, Ste. 408, New York, NY 10007 Phone: (212)227-7440 Fax: (212)227-7524 e-mail: kungarsohn@hotmail.com Web site: www.accomplishedtranstion.com
Contact: Ken ungarsohn Member: ATA

Accu Trans, Inc., 4517 Minnetonka Boulevard, Ste. 200, Minneapolis, MN 55416 Phone: (612)823-1231 Fax: (952)925-4772 e-mail: attranslation@yahoo.com Contact: Ken ungarsohn Member: ATA

Accura International Translations 12862 Cherry Way, Thornton, CO 80241 Phone: (303)280-1292 Fax: (303)280-1489
e-mail: accutrans.com Contact: Tanja M. Tombaugh Member: ATA

Accurapid Translation Services, Inc., 806 Main St., Poughkeepsie, NY 12603 Phone:(845)473-4550 Fax: (845)473-4554
Web site: accurapid.com Contact: Gabe Bokor
Founded 1978. Member: ATA. Translates German, Spanish, French, Hungarian and Japanese both from and into English, and Portuguese and Russian from English. Emphasis on Engineering, Patents, Law, Business and Finance trans-lation. Prospective translators should demonstrate competence and a professional attitude. Resumes are filed for future reference. The company pioneered the use of technological tools in the industry. The company counts freelance translators from Europe, Asia and the Americas in its professional pool. Maintains a pool of 600 translators.

Accurate Spanish Translations by Spanish Business Services, Inc., P.O. Box 720519, Dallas, TX 75372
Phone:(214)821-2050 Fax: (214)821-7065 e-mail: sbscorp@swbell.net Web site: www.spanishbusiness.com
Contact: Robert H. Brandao Member: ATA

ACCUWORLD, LLC, 200 West Madison St., Ste. 230, Chicago, IL 60606
Phone:(312)641-0441 Fax:(312)641-7370 e-mail: ts@inlinguachi.com Contact: Human Resources Department
Founded 1968. Member: ATA. Translates all languages, both from and into English. Covers all areas, with specialties in foreign language voice-overs and technical manual translation. Resumes are compiled in a database according to area of expertise. The company, headquartered in Bern, Switzerland, has over 300 worldwide locations. It provides language training, cultural training, translation/interpretation services, and foreign language typesetting and voiceovers. Maintains a pool of 800+ translators.

Acentos, Marketing & Advertising & Translations, 400 E. Lake St., Minneapolis, MN 55408 Phone: (612)824-6109 Fax: (612)825-1729 e-mail: acentos@compuserve.com Contact: Franklin Curbelo Member: ATA

AD-EX WORLDWIDE, 525 Middlefield Rd., Ste. 150, Menlo Park, CA 9402 Phone: (800)223-7753 Fax: (650)325-8428 e-mail: ADEXTRAN@compuserve.com Web site:www.ad-ex.net Contact: Robert Addis
Founded 1957. Member: ATA. Translates in all major languages, in all industrial fields, especially in the power and aerospace industries. Prospective translators must have demonstrable years of experience and written evidence of

competence, including resumes and work samples. Resumes are responded to with a request for samples which are then thoroughly examined. The company is always glad to hear from veteran professional translators. Their client base is worldwide. Maintains a pool of "hundreds" of translators.

Adams Translation Services, 10435 Burnet Rd., Ste. 125, Austin, TX 78758 Phone:(512)821-1818 Fax:(512)821-1888 e-mail: mdavila@adamstrans.com Web site: adamstrans.com Contact: Martha Davila
Founded 1982. Member: ATA, AATIA, AITA. Translates all European as well as Asian languages, including Arabic and Hebrew. Emphasis on Hardware, Software, Legal, and Engineering translations. Prospective translators should be native speakers with college/graduate degree in their language/s and training or experience in specialized technical area/s and be familiar with C.A.T. tools. Resumes are entered in a database and called as possible jobs come up. The company also has desktop publishing and hypertext services. Maintains a pool of 1000+ translators.

Adaptive Language Resources, Inc., 45 Mount Auburn St., Watertown, MA 02139 Phone: (617)924-0554 Fax:(617)924-0280 Web site: www.adaptivelanguage.com Contact: Adrian Spidle Member: ATA

Advance Language Studios, 500 N. Michigan Ave., Chicago, IL 60611 Phone:(312)782-8123 Fax:(312)782-8356
Contact: Patrick Schoorlemmer
Founded 1963. Member: ATA. Translates from English into Spanish, French, German, Italian, Portuguese, Dutch, Japanese, Korean, Mandarin, Russian, and Polish. Emphasis on Technical, Advertising, Financial, Legal, and Commercial translations. Prospective translators should be born and raised in country of target language. Resumes are entered in a database. Company services include Translation, Interpreting, Desktop Pub-lishing, Video dubbing in in-house studio. Maintains a pool of 1000+ translators.

Advanced Communication and Translation, Inc., 6404 Stratford Rd., Chevy Chase, MD 20815 Phone: (301)654-2890 Fax: (301)654-2891 e-mail: act@act-translate.comWeb site: www.at-translate.com
Contact: Monique-Paule Tubb Member: ATA

Advanced Global Services, Inc., P.O. Box 965, Chesterton, IN 46304 Phone: (219)921-1733 Fax: (219)921-0640 e-mail: fruslcs@gte.net Web site: www.FR-USA.COM Contact: Sylvie Prudhomme Member: ATA

Advanced Language Translation, 564 E Ridge Road, Ste. 105, Rochester, NY 14621
Phone: (716)342-1250 Fax: (716)342-1270 e-mail: info@advancedlanguage.com Web site: www.advancedlangauge.com
Contact: Scott Bass Member: ATA

Affinity Language Services, 101 S. Fairview Ave., Wind Gap, PA 18091 Phone: (610)863-3955 Fax: (610)863-8571 e-mail: info@affinity-languages.com Web site: www.affinitylanguages.com Contact: Michelle Zuccarini
Founded 1998. Member: ATA. Works in Spanish, German, French, Italian, and Dutch. Also in Japanese. Main areas: Technical, sci-tech, legal, medical, and business. Also provides interpretation, editing, proofreading, transcription, and copywriting. Uses translators worldwide.

Agnew Tech-II, 741 Lakefield Rd., Ste. C, Westlake Village, CA 91361 Phone: (805)494-3999 Fax: (805)494-1749 e-mail: agnewi @agnew.com Web site: agnew.com Contact: Irene Agnew
Founded 1986. Member: ATA, NAWBO, WITI. Translates Spanish, Chinese, French, German, Japanese, Russian, Vietnamese, etc. from English. Also scripts and voiceover. Covers all technical areas. Prospective translators should have a B.A. degree or higher and 2-3 years experience. Resumes received via e-mail, reviewed, graded and scheduled for a translation test. The company is a full-service translation bureau, as well as providing desktop publishing, web page design, multimedia, and audiovisual services. Maintains a pool of 300-400 translators.

AimTrans, Inc., 14752 Beach Blvd, Ste. 201, La Mirada, CA 90638 Phone: (714)522-8200 Fax: (714)522-7773 Web site: www.aimtrans.com Contact: Irene Agnew member: ATA

Airspeed Translations, 4200 Westheimer Road, Ste. 201, Houston, TX 77027
Phone: (713)586-2577 e-mail: rknauth@att.net
Web site: www.airspeedtranslations.com Contact: Rick Knauth

Alanguage Bank, Inc., 150 Lafayette St., 5th Floor, New York, NY 10013 Phone: (212)213-3336 Fax:(212)685-7263 e-mail: peiwens@alanguagebank.comWeb site: www.alanguagebank.com

Contact: Pei Wen Shih Member: ATA

Albanian Translation Services, 11880 Barclay Dr., Moreno Valley, CA 92557 Phone: (909)275-9278 Fax:(909)684-3134 e-mail: tirana@email.msn.com Contact: Mirela S. Kuhn Member: ATA

Albors and Associates, Inc., P.O. Box 5516 Winter Park, FL 32793 Phone: (800)785-8634Fax: (407)657-7004
e-mail: rene@albors.com Web site: www.albors.com
Contact: René A. Albors, President
Founded 1996. Member: ATA, NAJIT, Hispanic Chamber of Commerce, Orlando Chamber of Commerce. Translates Spanish, French, Portuguese, Japan-ese, German, Chinese, Russian, Polish, Arabic and Italian, both from and into English. Emphasis on Legal, Medical and Business translations. Prospective translators should be experienced, expert with terminology, and prompt in their delivery of finished work. Accepts unsolicited resumes for translation and inter-pretation. Resumes are computer-filed, and a letter of thanks is sent to acknowledge receipt. Maintains a pool of 5300 translators.

Alexandria Translations, 8827 Fort Hunt Rd., Alexandria, VA 22308 Phone:(703)799-7606 Fax:(703)799-7607 e-mail: 102554.3407 @compu-serve.com Contact: Lidia Terziotti Member: ATA
Translates and edits documents in a variety of languages.

All-Language Services, 545 Fifth Ave., New York, NY 10017 Phone: (212)986-1688 Fax: (212)986-3396
e-mail: alsny@idt.com Web site: all-language.com Contact: Miriam Edgelow, Personnel
Founded 1959. Uses freelance translators and interpreters. Accepts unsolicited resumes. If interested, asks for work sample, and offers a small initial assignment. Applicant must be a professional translator. Main languages (both ways) are Spanish, French, Italian, German, Portuguese, Chinese, Korean, Japanese, Dutch, and Russian. In total, some 59 languages. Main subjects are finance, law, advertising, banking, including brochures, annual reports, and manuals. Uses 80 translators in house, and some 1000 on call.

All Language Translations, 656 Lansing St., Schenectady, NY 12303 Phone: (518)372-6804 Fax: (518)374-6174 e-mail: cezary@netcom.com Contact: Cezary Drzymalski Member: ATA

Allegro Translations, 4513 Vernon Blvd., Madison, WI 53705 Phone: (608)233-3208 Fax: (608)233-3511 e-mail: info@allegro.com Web site: www.allegro-translation.com Contact: Yaël Bratzlavsky
Founded 1993. Member: ATA. Translates English into Spanish, German, French, Japanese, Chinese, Russian, Italian, Brazilian Portuguese, Hmong and Laotian. Technical manuals, user manuals, employee handbooks, and marketing. Has over 100 translators.

Allen Translation Service, Box 1529, Morristown, NJ 07962
Phone: (973)292-2737 Fax: (973)292-3954 Contact: Jeanette C. Fredericks Member: ATA

Allslavic Translation Services, 4930 NW 84th Ave., Ft. Lauderdale, FL 33351
Phone: (800)775-5504 Fax: (954)741-3898 e-mail: info@slavprom.com Web site: www.slavpromc.com
Contact: Stanka Moskov Member: ATA

ALLSPEAK Interpreting Services, P. 0. Box 1606, Glendale, CA 91209
Phone: (818)246-1515 Fax: (818)246-4211 e-mail: allspeakint@aol.com Contact: Tatiana E. Vorobieff Member: ATA

Allworld Language Consultants, Inc., P.O. Box 2128, Rockville, MD 20847
Phone: (301)881-8884 Fax: (301)881-6877 Web site: www.alcinc.com
Contact: Carlos Scandiffio Member: ATA

ALTA Language Services, 3355 Lennox Rd. NE, Ste. 510, Atlanta, GA 30326 Phone: (404)240-1810 Fax: (404)239-9516
e-mail: robert@altalang.com
Contact: Robert Jones
Company founded 1982. Member: ATA, AAIT. Uses freelance translators and interpreters. Accepts unsolicited resumes. Resumes are filed by language. Requires outstanding translation skills. Main languages (both ways) are Spanish, German, French, Japanese, Portuguese, Dutch, Italian, Chinese, Korean, and Russian. Main subjects are legal, medical, and general. Does multilingual typesetting in addition to translation and interpretation. Engages around 300 translators.

ALTCO Translations, 1426 Ridgeview Rd., Columbus, OH 43221 Phone: (614)486-2014 Fax: (614)486-6940 e-mail: trudypeters@ compuserve.com Contact: Trudy E. Peters, Owner.
Founded 1982. Member: ATA. Uses freelancers for translation and inter-pretation. Accepts resumes, and enters the more promising ones into a database. Applicants must be experienced. Main languages (both ways) are Spanish, French, German, Russian, and Japanese. Also translates into other languages, notably Italian. Main subjects are patents, business documents, manuals, certificates, brochures. Uses dozens of translators.

Always Ready Translation Services, 11026 Ventura Blvd., Room 10, Studio City, CA 91604 Phone: (800)240-6601 Fax: (818)755-8959 e-mail: language@worldnet.att.net Contact: Dan Prescott, President
Founded 1985. Accepts resumes. Translates Spanish, Asian languages, Russian, Armenian, and other European languages.

Ambassador Translating, Inc., 442 Route 202-206 N., #PMB200, Bedminster, NJ 07921 Phone: (908)429-0200 Fax: (908)429-0333 e-mail: rosa@am-translating.com Web site: www.am-translating.com
Contact: Rosa A. Stevenson Member: ATA

America Translating Services, P.O. Box 800272, Santa Clarita, CA 91380 Phone: (800)535-0555 Fax: (800)316-2230 e-mail: rstevenson@aol.com Web site: am-translating.com Contact: Rosa A. Steventon, Coordinator Member: ATA
Founded 1984. Member: ATA, CCIA. Translates all languages, both from and into English. Emphasis on Legal, Technical and Medical translation. Prospective translators should provide sample translations, reference list. Resumes are listed in a database. Specializes in voiceover work. Maintains a pool of over 1,000 translators.

American Bureau of Professional Translators, 8401 Westheimer Rd., Ste. 115, Houston, TX 77063
Phone: (713)789-2500 Fax: (713)789-8920 e-mail: abpt@abpt.com Web site: www.abpt.com Contact: Ms. Lu Waterhouse Member: ATA

American Business Concepts, LLC, P.O. Box 212942, Columbia, SC 29221
Phone: (803)749-2060 Fax: (803)407-3010 e-mail: abctranslation@aol.com Contact: Taeko T. Kerr Member: ATA

American Education Research Corp., Box 996, West Covina, CA 91793
Phone: (626)339-4404 Fax: (626)339-9081e-mail: aerc@cyberg8t.com
Web site: www.credencialsevaluation.comContact: John A. Sheety Member: ATA

American Translation Partners, 839 Albany St., Boston, MA 02119
Phone: (617)989-9989 Fax: (617)989-9919 e-mail: info@americantranslationpartners.com
Web site: www.americantranslationpartners.com Contact: Scott Crystal
Founded 1998. Member: ATA, NAJIT, NETA, MMIA, LPDAM, FIT, TTI, LISA, AIIC. Accepts resumes. Requires language proficiency and experience as well as computer proficiency. Translates Spanish, Portuguese, French, German, Italian, Japanese, Chinese, Korean, Vietnamese, Haitian Creole, Afrikaans, and all Indian dialects. Works in government, legal, medical, insurance, technical, financial, software subjects in more than 200 language pairs. Has 1500 translators in New England and 3500 worldwide.

Amway Corporation, 7575 East Fulton Rd., Ada, MI 49355 Phone:(616)787-7372 Fax:(616)787-7956
e-mail: tieu_o'brien@alticor.com Contact: Tieu O'Brien
Company founded 1959. Member: ATA. Translates Spanish, French, German, Italian, Dutch, Japanese, Chinese, Korean, Portuguese, Hindi, Polish, Hungarian, Czech, Slovak, Slovene, Turkish, Indonesian, Vietnamese, Malay, and Russian both from and into English. Bulk of work in Spanish and French. Emphasis on Marketing literature, Legal documentation, Product-related materials (Labels, brochures), Technical documentation (chemical and biological topics). Prospective translators should have at least 3-5 years full-time experience as a translator and/or interpreter. ATA accreditation preferred. Resumes are placed in a database. Maintains a pool of 200-300 translators.

ANDALEX International, Inc., 10101 SW Barbur Blvd, Ste. 101, Portland, OR 97219
Phone:(503)241-9756 Fax:(503)243-6815 e-mail: info@andalexintl.com Web site: www.andalexint.com
Contact: Andrei Lupenko Member: ATA

Antiquariat Literary Services, Inc., 12042 Trumbull Way, Reston, VA 20190
Phone:(703)707-8531 Fax:(703)707-8532
e-mail: alstranslation.com Web site: www.alstranslation.net Contact: Rebecca Marie Hindrichs Member: ATA

Antler Translation Services, 48 Woodport Rd., Sparta, NJ 07871 Phone: (201)729-8465 Fax:(201)729-9389

e-mail: antler@sparta.csnet.net Web site: www.quikpage.com Contact: Patrick W. Clevenger
Founded 1988. Translates in all languages. Emphasis on Technical, Medical, and Chemical translation. Prospective translators should provide evidence of competence and experience. Resumes are added to a database. Maintains a pool of 100 translators.

APS International Ltd, 7800 Glenroy Rd., Minneapolis, MN 55439 Phone: (612)831-7776 Fax: (612)831-8150 e-mail: trans@aps-now.com Contact: Ann Mickow Member: ATA

Arab American Translators, 5827 Columbia Pike, #415, Falls Church, VA 22041
Phone: (703)820-5612 Fax: (703)820-1318 e-mail: info@translatearabic.com Web site: www.translatearabic.com
Contact: Radwan Hakim Member: ATA

ArchiText Inc., 240 Pleasant St., Methuen, MA 01844
Phone: (978)688-7200 Fax: (978)688-7222 e-mail: hansf@architext-usa.com Web site: www.architext-usa.com
Contact: Hans Fenstermacher Member: ATA

Argo Translation, Inc., 3747 S. Howell Ave., Milwaukee WI 53207 Phone: (414)615-6000 Fax: (414)615-6005 e-mail: sales@argotrans.com Web site: www.argotrans.com Contact: Jacqueline LaCarelli
Founded 1995. Member: ATA. Uses freelance translators and interpreters. Accepts unsolicited resumes. Works in all languages and subjects, viz., medical, technical, legal, commercial. Always on the lookout for professional translators. Has 575 translators.

Around The World, Inc., 12281 Butterfield Drive NW, Pickerington, OH 43147
Phone: (614)575-2424 Fax: (614)575-2423 e-mail:atw@nls.com Web site: www.atwtranslation.com
Contact: Gary West Member: ATA
Founded 1998. Member: ATA, BBB. Translates all languages, mainly technical, advertising, business and legal. Has satellite offices in Kansas City, Columbus, Brussels (Belgium), and Paris (France). Translates and typesets for private and business sectors. Utilizes over 5000 translators.

ASET International Services Corporation, 2009 North 14th St., Ste. 214, Arlington, VA 22201 Phone:(703) 516-9266 Fax:(703)516-9269 e-mail: Khendzel@asetquality.com Web site: asetquality.com
Contact: Kevin S. Hendzel, Director of Language Services
Founded 1987. Member: ATA. Translates in over 100 languages, both from and into English. Emphasis on Equipment Manuals, Pharmaceuticals and Medical Equipment, Software Localization, Nuclear, Chemical, Industrial and Structural Engineering, Law and Legislation, Regulations and Codes, Education and Consumer Goods translation. Prospective translators are required to have 10 years professional translating experience and formal technical training in a specialty area. Resumes are archived in database and assignments given when appropriate match arises. Resumes *must be faxed or submitted by e-mail.* The company also works with engineering drawings and specifications and possesses full AutoCad and full-color printing capabilities. They provide interpreting services and are an authorized Master Distributor for the Philips interpreting equipment series. Welcomes voice-over talent. Maintains a pool of 1000 translators.

Asian Link Corp., 1108 W Valley Blvd., Ste. 4, Alhambra, CA 91803
Phone: (626)300-9191 Fax: (626)300-8955 e-mail:sophia@asialink.com Contact: Sophia N. Yang Member: ATA

Asian Translation Service, 7393 S. Locust St., Midvale, UT 84047
Phone: (801)565-8281 Fax: (801)565-0320 e-mail:ats@asiantranslation.com Web site: www.asiantranslation.com
Contact: Steve Stevens
Founded 1992. Member: ATA. Translates English into Hmong, Vietnamese, Cambodian, Thai, Korean, Japanese, Chinese, Tagalog, Malay, and Indonesian, mainly health-related, business, personal documents, and product catalogues. Provides full range of translation and interpretation. Uses about 30 translators.

Asian Translations, Inc., 3702 E. Lake St., Ste. 102, Minneapolis, MN 55406
Phone: (612)712-5432 Fax: (612)721-5778 e-mail: atrans@asiantranslations.com
Web site: www.asiantranslations.com Contact: Sokunthea (Sue) Hendry Member: ATA

ASIST Translation Services, 4663 Executive Drive, Ste. 11, Columbus, OH 43220 Phone: (614)451-6744 Fax: (614)451-1349
e-mail: asist@asisttranslations.com Contact: Elena Tsinman, President
Founded 1983. Member: ATA. Uses freelance translators and inter-preters. Accepts unsolicited resumes. All resumes are

entered in a database. If qualified, translator is Contacted immediately. Applicant must be experienced, native speaker, and have a university degree. Main languages are English into French, Spanish, Chinese, Japanese, Russian, Arabic, German, Somali, Portuguese and Italian. Additional languages are Dutch, Swedish and Danish. Does 2-3 million words a year. Does also typesetting, Web site translation, software translation, localization, audio-visual productions, and desktop publishing. Maintains pool of 2000 translators.

ATL Ultrasound, P.O. Box 3003, Bothell, WA 98041
e-mail: tony.messent@philips.com Contact: Tony Messent, MS 264 Member: ATA

Atlantic International, Translators, Inc., 4956 Vermack Rd., Atlanta, GA 30338
Phone: (770)350-9050 Fax: (770)350-9051 e-mail: atlanticit@aol.com Web site: www.atlanticitinc.com
Contact: Rogelio Cipriano Member: ATA

Atlas Translation Services, 336 North Central Ave., Ste. 6, Glendale, CA 91203 Phone: (818)242-2400 Fax: (818)242-2475 e-mail: atlas @atlaspvs.com Contact: Sorina Kalili
Founded 1993. Uses freelancers for translation. Accepts unsolicited resumes. Main languages (both ways) are Farsi, German, Spanish, French, Arabic, Chin-ese, and Japanese. Main subjects are legal, business, and scripts. Also does legal interpretation.

Audio To Go, Inc., 42 West 89th St., New York, NY 10024
Phone: (212)721-1183 Fax: (212)721-1273 e-mail: info@a2g.com Web site: www.a2g.com Contact: Gayle Goldfarb
Founded 1991. Member: NYCT. Accepts resumes. Requires certification, experience, native speakers in target language. Translates all languages. Translates audio and video programs with narrators in their native language.

Avant Page, 1138 Villaverde Lane, Davis, CA 95616
Phone: (530)750-2060 Fax: (530)750-2024 e-mail: luis@avantpage.com Web site: www.avantpage.com
Contact: Luis Miguel, President
Founded 1996. Member: ATA. Accepts resumes. Requires 3 years exp., certification/accreditation where available. Translates English into Spanish, Japanese, Chinese (simplified and traditional), Korean, French, German, Vietnamese, Arabic, Hebrew, Italian, and Portuguese. Also Farsi, Thai, and Tagalog. Main areas are business, hi tech, biotechnology, and government documents. Does multilingual desktop publishing. Does over one million words per year. Utilizes over 200 translators.

Avantext, 614 Grand Avenue, Ste. 203, Oakland, CA 94610
Phone: (510)832-1608 Fax: (510)832-1617 e-mail: info@avantext-usa.com Web site: www.avantext-usa.com

-B-

BBC Multilingual Translations, 1231 Somerset Drive, McLean, VA 22101 Phone: (703)448-0893 Fax: (703)448-8077
e-mail: mansourf@aol.com

Babel Tower, Inc., P.O. Box 491023, Ft. Lauderdale, FL 33349
Phone: (954)731-9180 Fax: (954)731-1366 e-mail: babeltower@aol.com Web site: www.babeltowerinc.com
Contact: Sandra Fernandez Founded 1996. Member: ATA. Translates all languages.

Barinas Translation Consultants, Inc., 1100 NW Loop 410, Ste. 700, San Antonio, TX 78213 Phone: (210)545-0019
Fax: (210)545-4731 160424 E-mail: info@barinas.com Web site: www.barinas.comContact: Sonia Barinas, President
Company founded 1980. Member: MPI, AAHA, TSHE, SATC, San Antonio Chamber of Commerce, GSHMA, ISMP, THMA. Uses freelance translators and interpreters. Accepts unsolicited resumes. Resumes are checked for quality and experience, then filed by language and areas of expertise. Please submit sample with resume, and indicate degree in translation and/or interpretation. Degree in law, medicine etc. is a plus. Main language pairs are Spanish/English, French/ English, French/Spanish, Portuguese/English, German/English, Chinese/English, Japanese/English. Main subjects are legal, medical, technical, telecom. Specializes in simultaneous interpretation for meetings and conventions. Does about 350 projects a year. Uses hundreds of freelancers.

Berkeley Scientific Translation Service, Inc., P.O.Box 150, Berkeley CA 94701 Phone:(510)548-4665 Fax: (510)548-4666 e-mail: marlo@berksci.com Web site: www.berksci.comContact: Dr. Marlo R. Martin
Founded 1974. Member: ATA, NCTA. Translates Japan-ese, Korean, Chinese, and other major European and Asian languages, both from and into English. Emphasis on Mechanical, Automotive, Chemical and Chemical Engineering, Computers and Software, Electronics, Biotechnology, Pharma-ceuticals, Physics and Patent translations. Prospective translators should be able to produce autho-

ritative translations into their native language within a specialized area. Resumes are screened for educational background and subject expertise as related to translation experience. The company was founded by a physicist and engineer and seeks translators with similar qualifications. Maintains a pool of 70-100 translators.

Berlitz GlobalNet, 132 W. 31st St., New York, NY 10001
Phone: (917)339-4890 e-mail: james.keller@nyc.berlitz.com Web site: www.berlitz.com Contact: Beatriz Almonte
Founded 1882. Member: ATA. **Berlitz** is an international organization of language schools which offer translation services as a sideline. Most of its branches use the services of freelance trans-lators. Berlitz is very active in the localization of software. Prospective translators should definitely consider Contacting this company. Check out its Web site at: www.berlitz.com.

Betmar Languages, 6260 Highway 65 NE, Ste. 308, Minneapolis, MN 55432 Phone: (612)572-9711 Fax: (612)571-3467 e-mail: best@betmar.com Contact: Elizabeth A. Loo Member: ATA

Bilingual Services, 9707 Chapel Down, Austin, TX 78729 Phone: (512) 258-1932 Fax:(512)258-2131
email: 71754.2717@compuserve.com Contact: Vivian Carmona-Agosto, President
Member: ATA, AATIA. Translates Spanish, French, German, Vietnamese, Russian, Chinese (Taiwanese & Mandarin/Cantonese), Italian, and Portuguese, both from and into English. Emphasis on advertising, PR, merchandising, computer, health, social services and petroleum. Prospective translators should have ATA or other accreditation or license. Resumes are filed according to language, and, within languages, according to equipment. Translators must have computer/fax/modem/etc. Resumes are also welcome from Texas-based interpreters. Uses professionals whose work will reflect well on both the company and its clients.

BioMedical Translators, 3477 Kenneth Drive, Palo Alto, CA 94303 Phone:(650)494-1317 Fax:(650)494-1394
e-mail: biomed@biomedical.com Contact: Monique Vazire
Founded 1992. Member: ATA, NCTA. Main languages translated are French, German, Italian, Spanish, Dutch, Swedish, Portuguese, Danish, Japanese, and Chinese. Emphasis is on Medical and Biological translation, including equipment, studies and software. Prospective translators should possess at least one year experience, have knowledge of the medical field, and have access to medical dictionaries. Their equipment should include a PC and modem or e-mail; software should include Word and WordPerfect. Resumes are reviewed by the recruiting department and responded to with a test translation, which is then evaluated. The company specializes exclusively in the medical field and its peripherals. Their services also include desktop publishing. Maintains a pool of 500+ translators.

Bloomberg L.P., 100 Business Park Drive, P.O. Box 888, Princeton, NJ 08542 Phone:(609)279-4955
Contact: Elsa Shilling

Bowne Translation Services, 345 Hudson St., New York, NY 10014 Phone: (212)924-5500 Fax: (212)229-3410
e-mail: lisa.dimeglio@bowne.com Web site: www.bowne.com Contact: Lisa Di Meglio
Company founded 1989. Member: ATA. Uses freelance translators and interpreters. Accepts unsolicited resumes. Applicants sign a confidentiality agreement and are sent a test. If successful, they are given small assignments at first, leading to larger ones. Main language pairs are English into Spanish, Ger-man, French, Chinese, Japanese, and Portuguese, and Spanish, French, German, and Japanese into English. Additional languages are Italian, Dutch, Swedish, Danish, Norwegian, Greek, Polish, Hungarian, Czech, Bulgarian, and Tagalog. Main subjects are financial, legal, corporate, and industrial, as well as documents related to IPO/mergers and acquistions. Keeps about 400-500 translators in its pool.

BRADSON Corporation, 1735 Jefferson Davis Highway, Ste. 705, Arlington, VA 22202 Phone: (703)413-3050
Fax: (703)413-3056 Contact: John S. Horner

BRIDGE-LINGUATEC LANGUAGE SERVICES, 915 South Colorado Blvd., Denver, CO 80246 Phone: (303)777-7783 Fax:(303)777-7246
e-mail: translators@bridgeschool.com
Web site: www.bridge-linguatec.com
Contact: Michelle Duvall
Founded 1981. Translates mainly Spanish, French, German, Arabic, Dutch, Russian and Portuguese. Emphasis on legal and medical. Prospective translators should, by preference, be native speakers. Resumes are filed by language and translators Contacted by need.. The company also provides ESL training for executives, foreign language instruction, and interpretation services. Maintains a pool of 150-200 translators

The Bridge-World Language Center, Inc., 110 2nd Street S, Ste. 213, Waite Park, MN 56387 Phone: (320)259-9239
Fax:(320)654-1698 e-mail: co@bridgelanguage.com Web site: www.bridgelanguage.com
Contact: Francisco Almarza Member: ATA

Brigham and Women's Hospital, 75 Francis St., Boston, MA 02115 Phone: (617)732-6640 Fax: (617)975-0813 e-mail: igarcia@partners.org Contact: Ileana Jimenez Garcia Member: ATA

Bromberg & Associates, 28475 Ranchwood Drive, Southfield, MI 48076
Phone: (248)827-7164 Fax: (248)827-3621 e-mail: jinny@linguacity.com Web site: www.linguacity.com
Contact: Jinny Bromberg Member: ATA

Bruce International, Inc., 10550 SW Allen Blvd., Ste. 123, Beaverton, OR 97005
Phone: (503)643-8448 Fax: (503)643-7174 e-mail: info@bruceinternational.com
Web site: www.bruce international.com Contact: Oscar Andrino Member: ATA

Bureau of Translation Services, 30 Washington Ave., Haddonfield, NJ 08033 Phone: (609)795-8669 Fax: (609)795-8737 e-mail: wschrieks@btsinc.com Web site: btsinc.com Contact: Wim Schrieks Member: ATA

Burg Translation Bureau, Inc., 29 South LaSalle, Ste. 936, Chicago, IL 60603 Phone:(312)263-3379 Fax:(312)263-4325 e-mail: burg@interaccess.com Web site: www.burgtranslations.com Contact: Lodovico Passalacqua, President Founded 1936. Member: ATA. Emphasis on technical translation. Prospected translators are "evaluated." Provides translation and typesetting services.

-C-

CC Scientific. Ltd., Rancho Las Palmas Office Park, 42-600 Bob Hope Drive, Ste. 404, Rancho Mirage, CA 92270
Phone: (760)341-7544 Fax: (760)341-7514 e-mail: CCSLtd@aol.com Contact: Jaime R. Carlo-Casellas Member: ATA

C.P. Language Institute, 225 West 57th St., Ste. 404, New York, NY 10019 Phone: (212)246-2054 Fax: (212)247-2258
e-mail: info@cpli.com Web site: www.cpli.com Contact: Yuki Saito
Founded 1980. Member: ATA. Translates Chinese, Japanese, Korean, Spanish, Arabic, Russian, French, German, Hebrew, Hindi, Urdu, Vietnamese, Italian, Portuguese, Thai, Khmer, Tagalog and Indonesian, both from and into English. Emphasis on Advertising, Technical, Patent, Financial, Medical, Legal, Personal Document and Textbook translation. Prospective translators should show pro-ficiency in English and the target language and should be experienced. Resumes are responded to with a call-in or an e-mailed test translation in order to assess the candidate's ability. The company has two departments - programs and services. Programs is a language school providing small group and private language instruction. Services comprise translation, typesetting, formatting, interpretation, voiceovers and subtitling. Maintains a pool of 300 translators.

CTS Language Link TM, 911 Main St., Ste. 300, Vancouver, WA 98660
Phone: (360)693-7100 Fax: (360)693-9292 e-mail: jennyt@ctsll.com Contact: Jenny Tallis-Grow Member: ATA

Calvin International Communications, Inc., 869 Plymouth Rock Drive, St. Louis, MO 63131 Phone: (314)821-5033 Fax: (314)821-5035 e-mail: calvinint@cs.com Contact: Beatriz E. Arauco-Calvin Member: ATA

Carolina Polyglot, Inc., PO Box 36334, Charlotte, NC 28236
Phone:(704)366-5781 Fax:(704)364-2998 e-mail: wdepaula@carolinapolyglot.com
Web site: www.carolinapolyglot.com Contact: Dr. William DePaula
Company founded 1971. Member: ATA, CATI. Accepts unsolicited resumes. Resumes are filed by language pair. E-mail and fax filed electronically. Require-ments for applicants include academic degree, previous experience, professional affiliation/accreditation, references. Main languages (both ways) are French, Spanish, Italian, Portuguese, Romanian, German, Dutch, Arabic, Chinese, Vietnamese, and Japanese. Also translates Turkish, Farsi, Africaans, Hindi, Danish, Norwegian, Swedish, and Finnish. Main subjects are immigration, education, law, business, medicine, insurance, theology, ecology, literature, and computers. Uses over 30 translators.

Caterpillar, Inc., Dealer Capability Dept., Corp Translation, 501 SW Jefferson Ave., Peoria, IL 61630
Phone: (309)494-5216 e-mail: opherk_jorg@CAT.com Contact: Dr. Jorg Opherk Member: ATA

CDNOW, Inc., 1005 Virginia Drive, Fort Washington, PA 19034
Phone: (215)619-9696 Fax: (215)619-9559 e-mail: emcpartland@cdnow.com Web site: www.cdnow.com
Contact: Erica A. McPartland Member: ATA

Certified Interpreters & Translators (CIT), PO Box 390006, San Diego, CA 92149 Phone: (619)475-8586 Fax: (619)472-2157
Company founded 1983. Uses freelance translators and interpreters. Accepts unsolicited resumes. Resumes are filed by language and geographical area. Interpreters have to be certified. Main language pair is English-Spanish, followed by English into German and Tagalog, Russian, Arabic, and Japanese into English. Also Portuguese, Polish, and Vietnamese into English. Main subjects are legal, medical, technical, literary, commercial, as well as manuals. Does conference interpreting. Also does translator and interpreter training.

Certified Languages International, 4700 SW Macadam Ave., #200, Portland, OR 97201
Phone: (503)525-9601 Fax: (503)525-9607 e-mail: bill@clilang.com Web site: www.clilang.com
Contact: William Graeper Member: ATA

Certified Translation Services, One Harbison Way, Ste. 105, Columbia, SC 29212
Phone: (800)730-9970 Fax: (803)781-5052 e-mail and web site: certifiedtranslationservices.com Contact: Ed Crosby
Member: ATA

Cherry Creek Language Centre, Inc., 1071 Jersey St., Denver, CO 80220
Phone: (303)756-2520 Fax: (303)782-5686 e-mail: ignacio@translationlinks.com Web site: www.translationlinks.com
Contact: Ignacio Jimenez

Chicago Multi-Lingua Graphics, Inc., 960 Grove St., Evanston, IL 60201 Phone: (847)864-3230 Fax: (847)864-3202
e-mail: infor@multimedia.com Web site: www.multilingua.com Contact: Yi Han Member: ATA

Choice Translating & Interpreting, 8701 Mallard Creek Rd., Charlotte, NC 28262 Phone: (704)717-0043 Fax: (704)717-0046 -mail: hr@choicetranslating.com Web site: www.choicetranslating.com
Contact: Sophie David-Gunn Member: ATA

CinciLingua, Inc., 322 East Fourth St., Cincinnati, OH 45202 Phone: (513)721-8782 Fax:(513)721-8819
email: translat@cincilingua.com Web site: www.cincilingua.com Contact: Michael Sum
Founded 1972. Member: ATA, ASME. Translates in Spanish, French, German, Chinese, Japanese, etc., both from and into English. Prospective translators should have college degree, professional experience in a technical specialty, and references. Should have a computer. Resumes are reviewed by the Project Manager and entered in a database. Qualified candidates may be asked to translate a short sample for additional information.

CITI Translation Center, Inc., 1000 Quayside Terrace, PH8, Miami Beach FL 33138 Phone: (305)868-1746 Fax: (305)868-1748 e-mail: info@cititran.com Web site: www.cititran.com Contact: Fernando Velez-Pardo
Founded 1987. Member: ATA, FLATA. Translates German, Russian, Japanese, Chinese, French, Italian and Spanish, both from and into English. Emphasis on Technical, Communication Manuals, Medical, Business and Personal Documents translation. Prospective translators should be experienced, preferably with accre-ditation and/or certification. Resumes are reviewed and the applicant Contacted if there is a specific need for that language or specialty area. The company supports markets in the Americas, Europe and the Pacific Rim. Maintains a pool of 60 translators.

CME Corporation, 2945 Three Leaves Drive, Mount Pleasant, MI 48858
Phone: (517)773-0377 Fax: (517)773-1105 Contact: Fumiko Lobert Member: ATA

Columbia Language Services, 11818 SE Mill Plain Blvd., #307, Vancouver, WA 98684
Phone: (360)896-3881 Fax: (360)896-4074 e-mail: mail@columbia-language.com
Web site: www.columbia-language.com Contact: Sveltana Linchuk Member: ATA

CommGap International Comm Services. 5369 S Baker St., Murray, UT 84107
Phone: (801)262-8984 Fax: (801)262-8996 e-mail: info@commgap.com Web site: www.commgap.com
Contact: Lelani P. Craig Member: ATA

Community Interpreter Services, Catholic Charities/Greater Boston, 270 Washington St., Somerville, MA 02143 Phone: (617)629-5767 Fax: (617)629-5768 e-mail: inna_persitsgimelberg@ccab.com Web site: www.ccab.org
Contact: Inna P. Gimelberg, Program Manager
Founded in 1986. Member: ATA, MMIA, NETA. Accepts resumes. Translates Haitian Creole, Spanish, Cape Verdean Creole, Vietnamese, Russian, Khmer, Portuguese, Cantonese-Chinese, Vietnamese, Polish, Farsi, Bosnian and Albanian. Also Somali, Swahili, Italian, French, Arabic, Khmer and Laotian. Emphasis on Personal Document translation. Prospective translators should live in Massachusetts or a bordering state, and possess at least a Bachelor's degree, past

translating experience, and fluency in at least two languages. Mostly certificates and correspondence. Qualified resumes are responded to with an interview appointment. They are a nonprofit service operated by Catholic Charities. Maintains a pool of 200 translators and interpreters.

ComNet International, 31255 Cedar Valley, Ste. 212, Westlake Village, CA 91362 Phone:(818)991-1277 Fax:(818)991-1699 Web site: comnetint.com Contact: Dr. Elias Agel
Founded 1989. Member: ATA. Translates all languages, in all subjects. Pro-spective translators should have extensive experience and should provide references. Resumes are reviewed and entered into a database. The company also provides desktop publishing, art production and printing services. It also does voice-overs and dubbing. Specialties include Middle East consulting services, electronic update filing and interagency network cooperation. Maintains a pool of 600 translators.

Comprehensive Language Center, 4200 Wilson Blvd., Ste. 950, Arlington VA 22203 Phone: (703)247-0700 Fax: (703)247-4295 e-mail: kjdresen@comlang.com Web site: www.comlang.com Contact: Kelly Jones Dresen
Company founded 1980 as CACI. Member: ATA. uses freelance translators and interpreters. Accepted unsolicited resumes, but not unsolicited phone calls. Quali-fied applicants are sent a database form which is processed and are called upon when needed in their area of expertise. Requirements include college degree, 2 years professional experience as linguist, or appropriate certification/specialized degree. Over 100 languages. Main areas are technical, legal, promotional, busi-ness. Company also does training, transcription, software and web page local-ization, and video narration.

Contact International Inc., 717 Light St., Baltimore, MD 21230 Phone: (800)333-3812 Fax:(800)333-5637 e-mail: Contact@cicenter.com Web site: www.cicenter.com Contact: Greg Bathon Member: ATA

Continental Book Company, 625 E. 70th Ave. #5, Denver, CO 80229 Phone: (303)289-1761 Fax:(303)289-1764 e-mail: cbc@continentalbook.com Web site: www.continentalbook.com Contact: Karen A. Manville Member: ATA

Continental Communications Agency, 5775 East Los Angeles Ave., #226, Simi Valley, CA 93063 Phone:(805)527-4446 Fax:(805)527-4460 e-mail: cca_inc@ix.netcom.com Contact: Peter Charbonneau Member: ATA

Continental Interpreting Services, Inc., 3111 N. Tustin Ave., Ste. 235, Orange, CA 92865 Phone:(800)201-7121 Fax:(714)283-9045 e-mail: info@wespeakyourlanguage.com
Web site: www.wespeakyourlanguage.com Contact: Kevin McQuire Member: ATA

Copper Translation Service, 530 Franklin St., Ste. 207, Schenectady, NY 12305 Phone: (518)372-8940 Fax: (518)372-8952 -mail: angelos@coppertranslation.com Web site: www.coppertranslation.com Contact: Angelos G. Tzelepis
Company founded 1971. Member: ATA. Uses freelance translators and inter-preters. Accepts unsolicited resumes. Applicant must be native speaker of target language. Main areas are legal, medical, and business. Over 700 translators in pool.

Corporate Translations, Inc., 1300 Aviation Blvd., Redondo Beach, CA 90278 Phone: (310)376-1400 Fax: (310)376-1394 e-mail: translators@corporatetranslations.com Web site: www.corporatetranslations.com
Contact: Toni Andrews
Founded 1995. Member: ATA, SCATIA. Accepts resumes. Requires experience, ATA accreditation and references. Translates all languages.

Corporate Translations, 1300 Aviation Blvd., Redondo Beach, CA 90278
Phone: (860)450-0405 Fax: (860)450-0409 e-mail:ctoomey@corptrans.inc.com Web site: www.orptrans.inc.com
Contact: Carolyn Toomey Founded 1995. Member: ATA

Cosmopolitan Business Communication, 8025 Marshall Circle, Arvada, CO 80003 Phone: (303)422-6702 Contact: Maya León Meis

Cosmopolitan Translation Bureau, 53 West Jackson Blvd., Ste. 1260, Chicago, IL 60604 Phone: (312) 726-2610 Fax: (312)427-8591 Contact: Emanuel H. Steen Member: ATA

Coto Interpreting, Translating & Graphics, 447 Burchett St., 2nd Floor, Glendale, CA 91203
Phone: (818)551-4545 Fax: (818)551-1123 Contact: Melanie Coto-Trevor Member: ATA

Course Crafters, 44 Merrimac St., Newburyport, MA 01950 Phone: (978)465-2040 Fax: (978)465-5027

e-mail:lise@coursecrafters.com Web site: www.coursecrafters.com Contact: Lise B. Ragan Member: ATA

Creo International, 520 Marquette Ave., Ste. 700, Minneapolis, MN 55402
Phone: (612)342-9800 Fax: (612)342-9745 e-mail:cthudson@creo-works.com Web site: www.creo-works.com
Contact: Christa Tiefenbacher Member: ATA

Counterpoint Language Consultants, Inc., PO Box 6184 Bridgewater, NJ 08807 Phone: (908)231-0991 Fax: (908)231-8266 e-mail: ctpt@ctpt.com Web site: www.counterpoint Language.com Contact: Dr. Lynne R. Judd
Founded 1979. Member: ATA. Company uses freelance translators and interpreters. Accepts unsolicited resumes. Main languages (both ways) are French, German, Spanish, Chinese, Japanese, Portuguese, Russian, Greek, Hindi and Italian. Also Thai, Swahili, Gujarati, Czech and Slovak. Main areas are pharma-ceuticals, telecom, and lega. Provides worldwide business language training. Uses over about 110 translators.

Crimson Language Services, Inc., 258 Harvard St., Ste. 305, Brookline, MA 02146 Phone: (617)731-6920 Fax: (617)731-5244 e-mail: crimson@tiac.net Contact: John Connors
Founded 1992. Member: ATA. Resumes are responded to with calls and/or tests on an as-needed basis.

Cross Cultural Comm Systems, Inc., 50 Cross St., P.O. Box 860, Winchester, MA 01890
Phone: (781)729-3736 Fax: (781)729-1217 e-mail:cccs@icnt.comContact: Zarita Araujo Member: ATA

Crossword Translation Services, 16350 Park Ten Place, Ste. 201, Houston, TX 77084 Phone: (281)578-1300 Fax: (281)578-1334 e-mail:language@crosswordtranslation.com Contact: Office Staff
Founded 1997. Member: ATA. Accepts resumes. Translates and interpretrs most languages in all fields. Uses many translators and interpreters.

Cybertec USA, Inc., 153 West Westfield Ave., Roselle Park, NJ 07204-1816 Phone:(908)245-3305 Fax:(908)245-5434 e-mail: cybertec_inc @compuserve.com Web site: www.cybertecusa.com Contact: Joseph Nunes
Founded 1990. Member: ATA, NYCT. Uses freelance translators and interpreters. Accepts unsolicited resumes. Resumes are filed by language and specialty. Translators are required to be experienced professional translators. Accreditation and/or diploma preferred. Translates mainly Portuguese, Spanish, French, Italian, and German. Also Chinese, Japanese and Korean, technical, industrial, business and legal. Does over 5 million words per year. Over 100 translators in company's pool.

CyraCom International Inc., 7332 N Oracle Rd., Tucson, AZ 85704
Phone: (520)745-9447 Fax: (520)745-9022 Web site: www.cyracom.com Contact: Paul Burns
Company founded 1997. Member: ATA. Provides telephonic inter-pretation services on demand 24 hours a day, 7 days a week in about 150 languages. Has a secure system that provides rapid access to interpreters.

-D-

DFP Translating Service, 42 Frederick Place, Bergenfield, NJ 07621 Phone: (201)343-2258 Fax: (201)343-4155 e-mail: info@ translationservices.netWeb site: www.translationservices.net Contact: Doris Pacheco

DTS Language Services, Inc., 308 W. Rosemary St., Ste. 210, Chapel Hill, NC 27516 Phone: (800)524-0722 Fax: (919)942-0686 e-mail: sales@dtstrans.com Web site: www.dtstrans.com Contact: Lucia Apollo Shaw
Founded 1972. Member: ATA, DIA, STC. Accepts resumes only electronically. Requires 5 years min. professional technical translation experience with related degree. Translates mainly Portuguese, French, Spanish, German, Italian, Czech, Vietnamese, Japanese, and Korean. Also Dutch, Finnish, Norwegian, Swedish. Mainly technical, medical, marketing, patents.

Detroit Translation Bureau, 30800 Telegraph Rd., Ste.1930, Bingham Farms, MI 48025 Phone: (248)593-6710 Fax: (248)593-6720 e-mail: info@dtbonline.com Web site: www.dtbonline.com
Founded 1946. Member: ATA, LISA, SAW. Accepts resumes. Translates mainly Spanish (Mexico, Spain), Canadian French, German, Japanese, Italian, Norwegian, Dutch, Finnish and Korean. Mainly automotive – technical, training and marketing. Uses hundreds of translators.

Digital Publishing, Inc., 1805 Hicks Rd., Rolling Meadows, IL 60008
Phone: (847)776-0200 Fax: (847)776-0249e-mail: translation@digitalpub.com Web site: www.digital pub.com
Contact: Debbie Shulman

Digitek International, Inc./SAKHR, 7631 Leesburg Pike, Ste. B, Fall Church, VA 22043 Phone: (703)883-0134 Fax: (Contact: Youb Benyoucef

Diplomatic Language Services, 1901 N. 19th St., Ste. 600, Arlington, VA 22209 Phone:(703)243-4856 Fax:(703)358-9189 e-mail: resume@dls-inc.com Web site: www.dls-inc.com
Founded 1985. Member: ATA, NCATA, NAJIT. Accepts resumes. Requires 5 years professional experience. Translates all languages. Provides all translation and interpretation services as well as language training.

DocuTrans, Inc., 4712 S. 2675 W, Roy, UT 84067 Phone: (801)776-6510 Fax: (801)776-4027 e-mail: translate@docutrans.com Web site: www.docutrans.com Contact: Gabariele H. Johnson Member: ATA

Dragon Crest Associates, Inc., 11026 Ventura Blvd., Ste. 10, Studio City, CA 91604 Phone: (800)240-6601 Fax: (818)755-8959 e-mail: language@worldnet.att.com Contact: Dan Prescott Member: ATA

DrTango.com, Inc., 20 Mansell Court East, Ste. 100, Roswell, GA 30076d Phone: (770)649-0298 Fax: (770)649-0299 e-mail:cecilia@drtango.com Web site: www.drtango.com Contact: Cecilia Santamarina Member: ATA

Dynamic Language Center, Ltd., 15215 52nd Ave. S., Ste. 100, Seattle, WA 98188 Phone:(206)244-6709 Fax:(206)243-3795 e-mail: dynamic@d-l-c.com Web site: www.d-l-c.com Contact: Ricardo Antezana
Founded 1985. Member: ATA, SOMI (Society of Medical Interpreters), WITS, NOTIS. Translates Spanish, French, German, Italian, Chinese, Japanese, Russian, Korean, Arabic, and Vietnamese both from and into English.Total of over 85 languages. Emphasis on Technical Manuals, Industrial Project Specifications, Contracts and Patents, Legal Documentation, Commercial Correspondence, Promotional Brochures, Technical Presentations, Software Support Materials, Business Cards and Credentials translation. Prospective translators should be ATA accredited, have college-level education in both source and target languages, native speaker in target language. New translators must do a test translation. Not all resumes will receive a response. The company also provides text and graphics conversion, composition and layout, design and illustration, phototypesetting, scanning and HTML publishing services. They also do foreign language tape transcription and foreign language voiceovers. The company additionally provides interpreting and instructional services. Maintains a pool of over 600 translators.

-E-

800-Translate, 865 United Nations Plaza, New York, NY 10017 Phone: (800)872-6752 Fax: (888)872-6752 Web site: Contact: Ken Clark

East West Institute, 110 North Berendo St., Los Angeles, CA 90004 Phone: (213)389-7944 Fax: (213)382-0757 e-mail: ewincc@mindspring.com Web site: www.ewincc.com Contact: Danny Ree, Personnel Manager
Company founded 1989. Uses freelance translators and interpreters. Accepts unsolicited resumes. Translates all languages, both from and into English. Mainly Korean, Spanish, Japanese, Cheinese, Vietnamese. Prospective translators should be U.S. residents. Resumes are kept and applicants called if necessary. Interpreters provided only in Southern California.

echo international, Three Gateway Center, Floor 14 W, Pittsburgh, PA 15222 Phone: (412) 261-1101 Fax: (412) 261-1159 e-mail: dutka@echotrans.com Contact: Leslie A. Dutka

Echo Translation, P.O. Box 15301, Minneapolis, MN 55415 Phone: (612) 822-3473 Fax: (612) 371-9398 e-mail: echobea@aol.com Contact: Bea Cabrera

Eiber Translations 65-11 174th St., Fresh Meadows, NY 11365
Phone: (718) 463-2900 Fax: (718) 359-4073 e-mail: ibertrans@aol.com Contact: Edna H. Eiber

El Andar Translations, P.O. Box 7745, Santa Cruz, CA 95061
Phone: (831) 457-8353 Fax: (831) 457-8354 e-mail: translations@elandar.com Web site: www.elandar.com
Contact: Marga Vaquer

Elance.com, 820A Kifer Rd., Sunnyvale, CA 94086 Phone: (408) 524-759 Fax: (408) 524-4814 e-mail: Daniel@elancc.com Web site: www.elance.com Contact: Daniel L. Shapiro

Elocale, Inc., 815 Park Blvd., Ste. 255, Boise, ID 83712

Phone: (208)336-5530 Fax: (208)343-1336 info@elocale.com Web site: www.elocale.com
Contact: Cary Clark

Encompass Globalization, 4040 Lake Washington Blvd. NE, Ste. 205, Kirkland, WA 98019 Phone: (425)828-2079 Fax: (425)828-2088 e-mail: nataliez@encompglobal.com Web site: www.encompglobal.com
Contact: Nathalie H. Zimmerman

Eriksen Translations Inc., 32 Court St., 20th Fl., Brooklyn, NY 11201 Phone: (718)802-9010 Fax: (718)802-0041 e-mail: info@ erikseninc.com Web site: eriksenInc.com Contact: Leah Riggiero
Founded 1986. Member: ATA, NYCT, STC. Translates mainly Spanish, French, Portuguese, Japanese, Chinese, German, Danish, Finnish, Norwegian and Swedish. Emphasis on Legal, Financial, Advertising, Medical and Computers. Translators are encouraged to register on web site . The company also provides editing and typesetting services and Web site development. Maintains a pool of 2000 translators.

eTranslations, 222 Milwaukee St., Ste. 302, Denver, CO 80206 Phone: (303)388-4488 Fax: (303)388-2255 e-mail: info@etranslations.com Web site: www.etranslations.com Contact: Stephen Blum

Eurasia International, 16530 Ventura Blvd., Ste. 206, Encino, CA 91436 Phone: (818)907-9718 Fax; (818)907-9763 e-mail: VMordukhay@worldnet.att.net Web site: www.eurasia-usa.com Contact: Violetta Mordukhay
Founded 1993. Member: ATA. Accepts resumes. Translates mainly Spanish, German, Hebrew, Russian, French, Arabic, Farsi and Indonesian. Also Romanina, Slovak, Malay, Japanese, Polish, Czech and Chinese. Mostly immigration, legal, and book publishing. Pool of over 200 translators.

Eureka-Foreign College Evaluators & Translators, 5308 West Lawrence, Chicago, IL 60630 Phone:(773)545-1700 Fax:(773)545-1716 e-mail: eureka@interaccess.com Web site: www.polishtranslations.com
Contact: Maria Drewicz, Executive Director
Founded 1992. Member: The Translators and Interpreters Guild. Translates Polish, both from and into English, and German and Spanish into English. Emphasis on University Admission Documents, Immigration & Naturalization, Business, Technical, Medical and Legal translation. Prospective translators should have IBM-compatible PC, Word Perfect 5.1 DOS or Windows, minimum Bachelor's Degree. Resumes are reviewed, and qualified persons Contacted. The company specializes in credential evaluation and Polish-American consulting services for business cooperation, cultural and marketing advisement, and is currently looking for Polish translators and interpreters. Maintains a pool of 10 translators.

EuroNet Language Services, 295 Madison Ave., 45th Fl., New York, NY 10017 Phone:(212)271-0401 Fax:(212)271-0404 e-mail: euronet@mindspring.com Contact: Anouk, HRM
Founded 1989. Member: NYCT, ATA. Uses freelance translators and interpreters. Accepts unsolicited resumes. Translates Spanish, French, Portuguese, Italian, Dutch, German, Swedish, and other Euro-pean languages, both from and into English. Translates all subjects. Prospective translators must be native speakers with bilingual capacity in English and possess a university degree. Resumes are reviewed and added to a database. Maintains a pool of 300 translators.

Excel Translations, Inc., 564 Market St., Ste. 705, San Francisco, CA 94104 Phone: (415)434-4224 Fax: (415)434-4221 e-mail: info@xltrans. com Web site: www.xltrans.com Contact: Hervé Rodriguez
Founded 1995. Member: ATA, NCTA, TAALS, STC, HTML Guild, SPA. Translates French, Spanish, German, Japanese, Portuguese, Italian, Chinese and Dutch, all from English. Emphasis on Software Localization and Legal and Medical translation. Prospective translators should have three years' translation experience and a specialty field. They should be native speakers and have access to the Internet. Resumes are screened and entered into a data base if passed. Applicants are notified by postcard. The company works with both freelancers and in-house translators and provides full DTP services. Maintains a pool of 500 translators.

Executive Linguist Agency, Inc., 500 S. Sepulveda Blvd., Ste. 300, Manhattan Beach, CA 90266 Phone: (310)376-1409 Fax; (310)376-9285 e-mail: executivelinguist@earthlink.net Contact: Ronald R. Randolph

Expert Language Services, Inc., 745 Kirkton Court, Rochester Hills, MI 48307 Phone: (810)656-4220 Fax: (810)656-2733 e-mail:els@rust.net Contact: Lori Ann Elzerman

-F-

FLS, Inc., 3609 A-5 Memorial Parkway SW, Huntsville AL 35801 Phone: (205)881-1120 Fax: (205)880-1112 e-mail: mail@flstranslation.com Web site: www.flstranslation.com Contact: Judith H. Smith
Company founded 1979. Member: ATA. Uses freelance translators and interpreters. Unsolicited resumes accepted. Translates over 60 languages, mainly Japanese, Spanish, French, Chinese, Korean, German and East European languages. Mostly technical and legal. Over

200 translators.

Federal News Service, 620 National Press Building NW, Washington, DC 20045 Phone: (202)347-1400 Fax: (202)626-2630 e-mail: info@fednews.com Web site: www.fednews.com Contact: Marina Makanova
Founded 1987. Accepts resumes. Requires college degree. Translates mainly Spanish, French, Russian, Chinese, and Arabic. Uses 63 translators. The company is a news wire that provides government transcripts, online newsclipping, news monitoring services, and translations in almost any language.

First Translation Services, 3072 Brighton, 1st St., Brooklyn, NY 11235
Phone: (718)372-7723 Fax: (718)265-6653 Contact: Jack Kleyman Member: ATA

Foreign Exchange Translations, Inc., One Richmond Square, Providence, RI 02906 Phone: (401)454-0787 Fax: (401)454-0789 e-mail: adnresh@fxtrans.com Web site: www.fxtrans.com Contact: Andres Heuberger Member: ATA

Foreign Ink, Ltd., 5735 Washburn Ave. S, Minneapolis MN 55410 Phone: (612)920-4884 Fax: (612)924-9075 e-mail: greg@fornink.com Web site: fornink.com Contact: Gregory Stricherz Member: ATA

-G-

GES Translation Services, 836 Manhattan Ave., Brooklyn, NY 11222
Phone: (718)389-8453 Fax: (718)389-4442 e-mail:ges@flashcom.net Contact: Richard Rzeznik

Garcia-Shilling International, 1402 Corinth, L.B. 139, Dallas, TX 75215 Phone: (214)428-4428 Fax: (214)428-4458 e-mail: acento@swbell.net Web site: www.garciashillinginternational.com Contact: Luis A. Garcia, Sr.

Gateway Direct, 45 W. 34th St., Ste. 203, New York, NY 10001 Phone: (202)695-5394 Fax: (202)695-5106 e-mail: gatewaydirect@earthlink.com Contact: Sergiy Orlov

Gene Mayer Associates, 9 Depot St., 2nd Fl., Milford, CT 06460 Phone: (203)882-5990 Fax: (203)882-5995 e-mail: info@design4language.com
Founded 1985. Member: ATA, AIGA, Design Management Institute, National Investor Relations Institute, CT Art Directors Club. Provides graphic design, translation and production of complex printed material used by global corporations. Emphasis on business (employee information, annual reports, marketing brochures, corporate policy manuals). The firms handles translation, design, book layout and production in 30 languages. Prefers to work with agencies or with translators with a qualified track record with large corporate clients.

The Geo Group, 6 Odana Court, Ste. 205, Madison, WI 53719 Phone: (608)230-1000 Fax: (608)230-1010 e-mail: translation@thegeogroup.com Web site: www.thegeogroup.com Contact: Translation Manager
Founded 1991. Accepts resumes. Requires min. 3 years translation/inter-preting experience. Main languages are French, German, Hmong, Italian, Portuguese, Spanish, Japanese, Chinese and Dutch. Also other European languages. Main subjects are medical, automotive, marketing, computers, dairy equipment, legal and audio/video. Uses a pool of over 500 translators.

Geotext Translations, 352 7th Ave., New York, NY 10001
Phone: (202)631-7432 Fax: (202)631-7407 -mail: translations@geotext.com Web site: www.geotext.com
Contact: Joseph Duncan

German Language Services, 2658 48th Ave., SW, Seattle, WA 98116 Phone: (206)938-3600 Fax: (206)938-8308 e-mail: GermanLanguage@GermanLanguageServices.comWeb site: www.GermanLanguageServices.com
Contact: Maia Costa
Founded 1979. Member: ATA, NOTIS, GALL. Accepts resumes only in electronic form. Requires formal training in translation or interpretation and 5 years experience. Only translates German.

Global Advanced Translation Services, Inc., 501 S. Fairfax Ave., #212, Los Angeles, CA 90036
Phone: (323)937-1525 Fax: (323)937-6568 e-mail: mteper@aol.com Contact: Marina Teper Member: ATA

Global Impact Inc., 13570 Grove Drive, #212, Maple Grove, MN 55311 Phone: (763)424-7449 Fax: (763)424-7407 e-mail: info@global-impactinc.com Web site: www.global-impactinc.com Contact: Kathi Winger Member: ATA

The Global Institute of Languages and Culture, Inc., 7301 NW 4th st., Ste. 110, Plantation, FL 33317 Phone: (954)327-1662 Fax: (955)327-8116 e-mail: globalin@gate.net Web site: www.globalinstitute.com
Contact: Antonieta Mercado
Member: ATA. Translates Spanish, Portuguese, Italian, French, Ger-man, etc., both from and into English. Emphasis on General, Computer, Medical and Legal translation. Prospective translators should have a college degree, experience, and should be native speakers of the target language. Resumes are responded to based on the applicant's qualifications and the company's needs. Maintains a pool of 20 translators.

Global Languages & Cultures, Inc., 680 N. Lake Shore Drive, Ste. 919, Chicago, IL 60611 Phone: (312)981-4444 Fax: (312)981-4445 -mail: yozturk@e-translation.com Web site: www.e-translation.com Contact: Sedef Olcer

Global Language Solutions/The Russian Word, Inc., 19800 MacArthur Blvd., Ste. 520, Irvine, CA 92612 e-mail: info@globallanguages.com Web site: www.globallanguages.com Contact: Inna Kassatkina

Global Software Solutions, 210 SW Morrison St., Ste. 300, Portland, OR 97204 Phone: (503)827-0787 Fax: (503)827-0790 e-mail: kirsteens@g11n.com Web site: www.G11N.com Contact: Kirsteen Scott

Global Translation Systems Inc., 910 Airport Rd., Chapel Hill, NC 27514 Phone:(919)967-2010 Fax:(919)929-1333 e-mail: mike@globaltranslation.com Web site: www.globaltranslation.com Contact: Michael Collins Member: ATA

Global Visions LLC, 4820 Eastwind Rd., Virginia Beach, VA 23464
Phone: (757)495-3719 Fax: (757)495-6398 e-mail: globalvisions60@hotmail.com Contact: Kristi B. Emerson
Member: ATA

The Global Word, Inc., 63 Grand Ave., River Edge, NJ 07661 hone: (201)343-0015 Fax: (201)343-4155 e-mail: info@globalword.com Web site: www.globalword.com Contact: Michael Fundaro Member: ATA

Global Works.Com, 129 W. 27th St., New York, NY 10001 Phone; (212)414-1300 Fax: (212)414-8700 e-mail: emantello@globalworks.com Web site: www.globalworks.com Contact: Elisabeth Mantello Member: ATA

GlobalDoc Inc., 1800 Peachtree St., Ste. 370, Atlanta, GA 30309 Phone:(404)350-6740 Fax:(404)350-6747 e-mail: mail@globaldoc.com Web site: www.globaldoc.com Contact: Michael W. Cooper
Founded 1990. Member: ATA, STC. Translates all Major European languages plus Japanese, both from and into English. Emphasis on Technical, Telecommunication, Hardware/Software, and Office Products translation. Prospective translators should be ATA member, possess translation experience, and have modern word-processing capabilities, fax and modem. Candidates should have high levels of technical knowledge and be reliable, accessible, and able to work quickly. Resumes are entered into a database with notes regarding qualifications.

Go Global Translations, Inc., 19515 Rosedale Ave., Excelsior, MN 55331 Phone: (952)474-6413 Fax: (952)474-3756 e-mail:TeresaGoGlobal@cs.com Web site: www.goglobalranslations.com Contact: Teresa A. Crespo
Member: ATA

The Golf Channel, Inc., 7580 Commerce Center Drive, Orlando, FL 32819 Phone: (407)248-3344 Fax: (407)248-1344 e-mail: jkrisand@tgcinc.com Contact: James R. Krisanda Member: ATA

Grammaton, LLC, 137 Cambridge St., Ste. 100, Burlington, MA 01803 Phone: (781)365-4000 Fax: (781)365-1000 e-mail:wally.rodriguez@grammaton.com \Web site: www.grammaton.com Contact: Walter A. Rodriguez

Groupe Mistral, 522 Brewers Mill Rd., Harrodsburg, KY 40330 Phone: (859)366-4211 Fax:(630)477-0438 e-mail: mistral@groupmistral.com Web site: www.groupmistral.com Contact: Sylvie Gadness
Founded 1996. Accepts resumes. Translates French, Spanish, German, Haitian Creole, Italian, Oromo, Chinese, Japanese, Korean and Farsi, as well as all Indian languages and dialects and more. Emphasis on Engineering, Financial, Medical and Advertising translation. The company does not work with freelance translators; it is rather a consortium of in-house personnel. Prospective translators should be local, within driving distance, and should have translation experience. Specializes in French Computer translation. Maintains a pool of 120 translators.

-H-

HG Translations, P.O. Box 31372, Seattle, WA 98103 Phone: (206)374-2403 Fax: (206)374-2403

e-mail: admin@hgtranslation.com Web site: www.hgtranslations,com Contact: Gary M. Gilligan Member: ATA

H&K Translations, LLC, 701 Brickell Ave., Suite 3000, Miami, FL 33131 Phone: (305)789-7521 Fax: (305)789-7799 Contact: Maury M. Scharrer Member: ATA

Health Outcomes Group, 435 Middlefield Rd., Palo Alto, CA 94301 Phone: (650)321-4336 Fax: (650)321-4510 e-mail: hog_usa@compuserve.com Contact: David Himmelberger Member: ATA

Hernandez & Garcia, LLC, 7360 N. Lincoln Ave., Ste. 100, Lincolnwood, IL 60712 Phone: (847)676-4445 Fax: (847)676-1420 e-mail: mhernandez@hernandezgarcia.com Contact: Maritza Hernandez Member: ATA

Hightech Passport Limited, 1590 Oakland Rd., Ste. B202, San Jose, CA 95131 Phone: (408)453-6303 Fax: (408)453-9434 e-mail: magdalena@htpassport.com Web site: www.htpassport.com
Contact: Magdalena Enea, VP of Market Development
Founded 1992. Member: ATA, NCTA. Translates French, German, Spanish, Italian, Portuguese, Swedish, Dutch, Russian, Japanese, Chinese, and all Scan-dinavian from English. Emphasis on Computer Software, Documentation (both printed and online), Marketing Materials, Tapes, and Computer Training Literature translations. Complete range of internationalization and localization services, mainly to IT and medical industry. The company also provides software localization and testing, videotape localization, and desktop printing services. Maintains a pool of 150 translators.

Honda R&D North America, Inc., 21001 State Route 739, Raymond, OH 43067 Phone: (513)645-6164 Fax: (513)645-6341 e-mail: knason@oh.hra.com Contact: Kay T. Nason

-I-

IDEM Translation, 614 Greer Rd., Palo Alto, CA 94303 Phone: (415)329-0170 Fax: (41)329-0266 e-mail: idem@compuserve.com Contact: Mariam Nayiny Member: ATA

IRU Language & Translation Services, 2909 Hillcroft Ave., Ste. 538, Houston, TX 77057 Phone: (713)266-0020 Fax: (713)266-1716 e-mail: iru@aol.com Web site: www.iru-services.com Contact: Dagmar Beck
Founded 1989. Member: ATA, HITA. Translates mainly German, Spanish, Portuguese, French, Arabic, Russian, Japanese, Dutch, Bosnian and Italian, as well as all other languages. Emphasis on commercial, financial, technical and business. Prospective translators should have prior experience and excellent computer literacy, as well as the ability to deliver in a timely manner. Resumes are reviewed and entered into a data base by language. The company also provides language classes, chaperon services and cross-cultural seminars, with emphasis on Spanish and German. Maintains a pool of over 60 translators.

ISI, 3501 Market St., Philadelphia, PA 19104 Phone: (215)386-0100 Fax: (215)243-2208 e-mail: ellen.boyar@isinet.com Web site: www.isinet.com Contact: Ellen A. Boyar

ISI (Interpreting Services International Inc.), 6180 Laurel Canyon Blvd., #245, N. Hollywood, CA 91606 Phone: (818)753-9181 Fax: (818)753-9617 e-mail: info@isitrans.com Contact: Cathi Rimalower

INAWORD, 811 W. 7th St., Ste. 204, Los Angeles, CA 90017 hone: (213)688-6200 Fax: (800)805-7994 e-mail: info@inaword.net Web site: www.inaword.net Contact: Stella Fridman Member: ATA

Information Builders, Inc., Two Penn Plaza, New York, NY 10121
Phone: (212)736-4433 Fax: (212)967-6404 Web site: www.ibi.com Contact: Georgina Channer Member: ATA

The Information Foundry at Robert Bently, Inc., 1734 Massachusetts Ave., Cambridge, MA 02138
Phone: (617)528-4043 Fax: (617)876-9235 e-mail: john.harthborne@infofoundry.com
Web site: www.infofoundry.com Contact: John Harthborne Member : ATA

Inline Translation Services. Inc., 100 W. Broadway, Ste. 250, Glendale, CA 91210 Phone: (818)547-4995 Fax: (818)547-4013 e-mail: inlinela@inlinela.com Web site: www.inlinela.com Contact: Richard S. Paegelow Member: ATA

Inlingua, Inc., 171 East Ridgewood Ave., Ridgewood, NJ 07450 Phone: (201)444-9500 Fax: (201)444-0116 e-mail: ridgewood@inlingua.com Web site: www.inlingua.com Contact: Sandra Stern, Translation Services Coordinator

Founded 1977. Member: ATA. Accepts resumes from translators and interpreters.. Requires ATA accreditation. Main languages are Spanish, French, Portuguese, German, Italian, Chinese, Japanese, Russian, and Arabic. Also Hindi, Hungarian, Polish, Romanian and Dutch. Mainly legal, pharmaceutical, financial. Uses some 150 translators.

Inlingua Language & Intercultural Services, 4500 Park Glen Rd., Ste. 120, Saint Louis Park, MN 55416 Phone: (952)929-9155 Fax: (952)929-0020 e-mail: info@inlingua-mn.com Web site: www.inlingua.com/minneapolis.htm Cosntact: Carolyn W. Leavenworth Member: ATA

Inlingua Language Service Center, 1901 N. Moore St., Arlington, VA 22209 Phone: (703)527-8666 Fax: (703)527-8693 e-mail: intpschool@inlinguadc.com Web site: www.inlinguadc.com Contact: Harry Obst Member: ATA

Inlingua Translation Service, 95 Summit Ave., Summit, NJ 07901 Phone: (908)522-0622 Fax: (908)522-1433 e-mail: summit@inlingua.com Contact: Becky Miller
Founded 1968. Uses freelance translators and interpreters. Accepts unsolicited resumes. Resumes are kept on file for future jobs. Applicants must have computer, fax, and modem. Ten top languages are Spanish, French, Italian, Port-uguese, Russian, German, Chinese, Japanese, Danish, and Polish. Also translates Korean and Romanian. Main areas are lincenses, birth certificates, and transcripts. Has pool of some 30 translators. Operates as language school with translation services.

Inlingua Translation Service, 230 S. Broad St., 7th Fl., Philadelphia, PA 19102 Phone:(215)735-7646 Fax:(215)735-4188 e-mail: acassidy@inlingua.com Web site: www.inlingualv.com Contact: Angela Cassidy Member: ATA
Translates French, German, Japanese, Chinese, both from and into English. Emphasis on Legal and Pharmaceutical translation. Prospective translators should be ATA certified, with at least 3-5 years experience. Resumes are responded to with a letter of receipt. Maintains a pool of 200 translators.

Intela Services, 19146 Stare St., Northridge, CA 91324 Phone: (800)209-1663 Fax: (818)998-3993 e-mail: david@intela.com Web site: www.intela.com Contact: David Deaussin Member: ATA

Interclub, 4200 N. Central Ave., Chicago, IL 60634 Phone: (773)777-ABCD Fax: (773)202-0012 e-mail: Contact@interclubabdc.com Web site: www.translationsusa.com Member: ATA

Intermark Language Services Coporation, 2555 Cumberland Pkwy, Ste. 295, Atlanta, GA 30339 Phone: (770)444-3055 Fax: (770)444-3002 e-mail: info@intermark-languages.com Web site: www.intermark-languages.com Contact: Tom West
Founded 1995. Member: ATA. Accepts resumes. Interested in translators with with a law or business degree. Translates mainly French, Spanish, German, Portuguese and Swedish. Emphasis is on Law and Business translation. Prospective translators *must* provide a sample translation in every combination they wish to translate; ATA accreditation is preferred.

InterNation, Inc., 299 Broadway, Ste. 1400, New York, NY 10007 Phone:(212)619-5545 e-mail: info@internationinc.com Web site: www.internationinc.com
Founded 1990. Member: ATA, NYCT, BBB. Uses freelance translators and interpreters. Accepts unsolicited resumes. Prospective translators should have experience, adequate hardware and software. Resumes are reviewed, and a questionnaire mailed with a request for samples. The samples are then reviewed. Translates Spanish, French, German, Japanese, Chinese, Russian, Italian, and other major languages, both from and into English. Emphasis on Commercial Document, Legal Document, Video voice-over and subtitling, Advertising Copy, Scientific Material, Medical and Pharmaceutical translation. Specialties in Foreign Language Voiceovers and Subtitling. The company specializes in voiceovers for corporate sales, training and safety videos. It does post-production in over 25 languages. Also employs narrators and character actors in the New York City area. Maintains a pool of some 5000 translators.

International Bureau of Translations, Inc, 10291 North Meridian St., Ste. 350, Indianapolis, IN 46290 Phone: ((317)581-0060 Fax: (317) 581-1160 e-mail: ibtinc@ibtworld.com Web site: www.ibtworld.com Contact: Christian Gecewicz
Founded 1976. Member: OTIAQ, Indianapolis Chamber of Commerce, IUPUI, Indian University. Translates French, Spanish, German, Portuguese, Dutch, Italian, Japanese, Chinese, Korean and Russian, both from and into English, as well as various Slavic, Scandinavian, Eastern European and Asian languages. Emphasis on Business Correspondence, Medical, Technical, Legal and Personal Document translation. Prospective translators should be native speakers with access to a computer, modem, or fax. They should send a rate chart with their resume. Resumes are filed and the translator Contacted as the need arises. The company does foreign videos, court interpretation, cultural presentations, and conducts language classes. They research the cultural acceptability of company names, product names and slogans, and are the official translators for the International Violin Competition. Maintains a pool of 150 translators.

International Communication by Design, Inc., 1726 North First St., Milwaukee, WI 53212 Phone:(414)265-2171 Fax:(212)265-2101 -mail: info@icdtranslation.com Web site: www.icdtranslation.com Contact: Jennifer Marquardt,

Office Manager
Founded 1991. Member: ATA, Wisconsin World Trade Center, STC. Translates mainly Italian, Spanish, French, German, Portuguese, Dutch, Arabic, Greek, Japanese and Chinese. Also Korean, Russian and Swedish. Emphasis on Technical Manuals, medical and Legal translation. Also web site localization. Prospective translators should be native speakers and ATA accredited, with a specific area of expertise and must be able to send projects in via CompuServe. Resumes are filed and used as a resource for new translators, interpreters and typesetters. It is a translation service company with a wide range of clients, from large corporations to smaller cottage industries. The company is actively community involved. Maintains a pool of over 60 translators.

International Contact, Inc., 351 15th St., Oakland, CA 94612 Phone:(510)836-1180 Fax:(510)835-1314 e-mail: info@intl Contact.com Web site: www.intl Contact.com Contact: Accounting Member: ATA

International Effectiveness Centers, 690 Market St., Ste. 700, San Francisco, CA 94104 Phone:(415)788-4149 Fax:(415)788-4829 e-mail: iec@ie-center.com Web site: www.ie-center.com Contact: Taryk Rouchdy
Founded 1972. Member: ATA, NCTA. Translates Spanish, Chinese, Russian, and Portuguese, both from and into English, French and Vietnamese from English, and Japanese into English. Emphasis on Legal, Technical and Children's Book translation. Uses freelance translators and interpreters. Accept unsolicited resu-mes. Prospective translators must have at least 3 years experience and be tested unless they hold current ATA accreditation. Resumes are screened for qualifications and appropriate equipment and, if qualified, entered into a data base The company also does desktop publishing in all languages, as well as voiceovers, dubbing, promotional work, crosscultural and language training, and international business consulting. Maintains a pool of 7000 translators in its data base, 170 of whom are used regularly.

International Institute of Wisconsin, 1110 N. Old World 3rd St., Milwaukee, WI 83203 Phone: (414)225-6220 Fax: (414)225-6235 e-mail: iiw@excpc.com Web site: www.iiwisconsin.org Contact: Alexander P. Durtka, Jr.

International Language Center, 1416 S. Big Bend Blvd., St. Louis, MO 63117 Phone: (314)647-8888 Fax: (314)647-8889 e-mail: ilc@ilcworldwide.com Web site: www.ilcworldwide.com Contact: Dede S. Brunetti

International Language Service. Inc., 1221 S. Shepherd, Ste. 200, Houston, TX 77019 Phone: (713)783-3800 Fax: (713)529-7717 e-mail: i4@houston.rr.com Web site: www.eworld-link.com Contact: Kimberly K. Silverman

International Language Services, Inc., 5810 Baker Rd., Ste. 250, Minnetonka, MN 55345 Phone: (612)672-9600 Fax: (612)672-9400 e-mail: info@ilstranslations.com Web site: www.ilstraslations.com Contact: Phyllis Beatty
Founded 1982. Translates Spanish, French, German, Italian, Portuguese, Japanese, Swedish, Dutch, Danish, Chinese and most other languages from English. Emphasis on Medical, Technical, Business and Legal translation. Prospective translators should have ATA accreditation, references, a minimum 3-5 years experience, and be native speakers of the target language. Resumes are read and filed by language. Their primary focus is on biomedical instrumentation. Maintains a pool of over 300 translators.

International Language Source, Inc., P.O. Box 338, Holland, OH 43528 Phone:(419)865-4374 Fax:(419)865-7725 e-mail: ilsource @att.net Web site: www.ilsource.com Contact: Ryan Stevens, Account Manager
Founded 1981. Member: TAITA, ATA. Uses freelance translators and interpreters. Accepts unsolicited resumes. Prospective translators should have a specialty area and the appropriate resources for projects in that area. Resumes are kept for 6 months in an active database.

Contact may involve the paid translation of a short sample. Translates mainly French, Spanish, German, Italian and Chinese. Also Japanese, Portuguese and Hebrew. Emphasis on Glass Manufacturing and Retail, Automotive OEM and Aftermarket, Furniture, Legal, Industrial and Healthcare translation. In addition to translation services, the company provides video and interactive CD-ROM translation and voiceovers. The company is willing to consider internships and cooperative projects with other translation companies.

International Translating & Typesetting Company, 2730 Stemmons Freeway, Ste. 302, Dallas, TX 75207-2248 Phone:(214)630-0840 Fax: (214)630-6482 e-mail: 102462.161@compuserve.com Contact: Javier Galdeano, Translation Manager
Founded 1969. Member: Greater Dallas Chamber of Commerce. Translates Spanish, Chinese, French, German, Arabic, Russian, Japanese, Portuguese, Kore-an, Vietnamese, Bulgarian, Cambodian, Serbo-Croatian, Czech, Danish, Dutch, Farsi, Finnish, Greek, Gujarati, Hebrew, Hindi, Indonesian, Kurdish, Latin, Norwegian, Polish, Punjabi, Romanian, Hungarian, Swedish, Tagalog, Thai, Turkish, Ukrainian, and Urdu, both from and into English. Emphasis on Petro-leum, Electronics, Legal, Business, Advertising, Food Export, Chemical, and Civil Engineering translations. Prospective translators must accept work *only* from translation companies, and *never directly from end users*. They must have either IBM or Macintosh computers, a modem and a fax. Resumes are filed until a need arises. In addition to translation, the company also provides high-resolution typesetting in most languages. Maintains a pool of 200 translators.

International Translating Bureau, 16125 West 12 Mile Rd., South-field, MI 48076-2912 Phone:(248)559-1677 Fax:(248)559-1679 e-mail: itbinc @itbtranslations.com Contact: Mariano Pallarés, President

Founded 1977. Translates all language pairs. Emphasis on Automotive, Engineer-ing, Machine Tool, Legal, Medical, and Public Relations translation. Prospective translators should be native speakers of the target language, have at least 5 years residence in the source-language country, and have academic training or on-job experience in a specialized field. Candidates must have computer, fax and current software, particularly WordPerfect and Word for Windows for PC or Mac. Re-sumes are scanned for qualifications in which the company is interested and filed for future use. The company offers accurate, native-like translations. Maintains a pool of 250 translators.

International Translation Service, P.O. Box 188331, Sacramento, CA 95818 Phone: (530)753-7482 Fax: (530)753-7482 e-mail: its@yolo.com Web site: www.geocities.com/its worldwide Contact: Garry Pratt
Founded 1970. Uses freelance translators and interpreters. Accepts unsolicited resumes. Prospective translators must be experienced in both their languages and specialty fields, and should possess a variety of means of communications, includ-ing phone, fax and e-mail; they should have computers with the appropriate language fonts. Resumes are filed by language and the summiteers Contacted. Translates mainly Scandinavian, German, Spanish, and French, and also Estonian, Irish, Italian, Russian, Finnish, Portuguese, Polish, Dutch and more. Translates mainly legal, scientific, commercial, and medical. Maintains a pool of some 80 translators.

International Translation Services, P.O. Box 1707, Taos, NM 87571
Phone: (505)758-3444 Fax: (505)737-5484 e-mail: its2leslie@compuserve.com Contact: Leslie G. Haynes

International Translation Solutions, 10 S. 5th St., Ste. 320, Minnea-polis, MN 55402 Phone: (612)339-4660 e-mail: translate@intransol.com Web site: www.intransol.com Contact: Cary Rothschild
Founded 1987. Member: ATA, STC, NADTP, GBCC. Translates Spanish, French and German, both from and into English, and Portuguese, Korean, Japanese, Chinese, Arabic, Indonesian and Eastern European languages, from English. Emphasis on Commercial, Legal, Technical and Medical translations. Prospective translators should have professional experience, subject specialties, and possess computer, fax, modem, e-mail and other technologies. Resumes are reviewed and replied to with an application form requesting additional information. The company also provides multilingual typesetting and desktop publishing, graphic design, and audio and video production services. Maintains a pool of over 3,000 translators.

Interpretations, Inc., 8665 W. 96th St., Ste. 201, Overland Park, KS 66212 Phone: (913)338-2434 Fax: (913)338-2636 e-mail: interp@accessus.net Web site: www.exactwords.com Contact: Gloria J. Donohue
Founded 1991. Member: ATA, MICATA, International Trade Club, International Relations Council, Women's Resources Network. Translates mainly Spanish, French, German, Portuguese, Russian, Dutch, Swedish and Italian. Also Danish, Finnish and Korean. Emphasis on Instructional and Technical, Legal, Advertising, Video Script and Educational Materials translation. Prospective translators must be native speakers and have five years' experience; ATA accreditation is a must. They should be up-to-date on hardware and software. Resumes are reviewed and filed; a select number are asked to provide samples of their work and/or translate short paragraphs. The company also provides interpreters for meetings, conferences and telephone conferencing. Maintains a pool of about 100 translators.

Interpreters' Index.com, P.O. Box 880872, San Diego, CA 92168 hone: (619)850-8279 Fax: (619)334-9473 e-mail: info@interpretersindex.com Web site: www.interpretersindex.com Contact: Juana Esther Blanco Member: ATA

Interpreters International & Translations, 123-40 83rd Ave., Ste. 9D, Kew Gardens, NY 11415-3431 Phone: (718)544-0224 Fax:(718)261-3864 e-mail: mzinola@nyct.net Contact: Maria Zinola
Founded 1986. Member: ATA. Accepts resumes with college degree and 5 years experience. Translates mainly Arabic, Chinese, French, German, Hebrew, Japanese, Korean, Portuguese, Russian and Spanish. Also Czech, Dutch, Farsi, Greek, Haitian Creole, Hindi, Hugarian, Italian, Polish, Romanian, Serbian, Croatian, Turkish, Vietnamese and Yiddish. Mostly business, insurance, legal, marketing, medical and technical. Uses some 55 translators.

InterSol, Inc.,Three Point Drive, Ste. 301, Brea, CA 92821 Phone: (714)671-9180 Fax: (714)671-9188 email: solutions@intersolinc.com Web site: intersolinc.com Contact: Susana Turbitt
Founded 1996. Member: ATA. Accepts resumes. Translates mainly French, Italian, German, Spanish, Portuguese, Japanese, Chinese, Danish, Swedish and Finnish. Mostly medical, electronics, computers, automotive, general business, travel and sports. Also software localization. Uses some 30 translators.

Interspeak Translations, Inc., 114 East 32nd St., New York, NY 10016 Phone: (212)679-4772 Fax: (212)679-5084 Contact: Silvia Zehn Member: ATA

Intertech Translations, Ltd., 671 S. Gulph Rd., King of Prussia, PA 19406 Phone: (610)265-7776 Fax: (610)337-4994 e-mail: intertechltd@compuserve.com Contact: Carole K. Kenney Member: ATA

IRCO/International Language Bank,10301 NE Glisan St., Portland, OR 97220 Phone: (503)234-0068 Fax: (503)233-4724 e-mail: translation@mail.irco.com Web site: www.irco.org Contact: Translation Services Supervisor
Founded 1976. Member: ATA, NOTIS. Uses freelance translators. Accepts unsolicited resumes. Applicants should own PC or Mac, fax machine and e-mail, and have experience with the Internet and desktop publishing. Resumes are sorted by language and applicant's last

name and filed for future use. Translates Spanish, Russian, Romanian, Serbo-Croatian Vietnamese, Cambodian, Laotian, Mien, Hmong, Chinese, Japanese, Amharic, Tigrigna, Creole and Thai, all from English. Emphasis on community translation projects, such as government forms, employee manuals, social service literature, and translation for refugee and immigrant communities in the U.S. They specialize in refugee-related documents and languages. IRCO is the Immigrant and Refugee Community Organization and is a nonprofit agency. ILB has grown from providing language services to refugee communities to a full-service translation and interpreting agency. Maintains a pool of over 100 translators.

Italian Language Connection, Inc., 5225 Pooks Hill Rd. Ste. 504-S, Bethesda, MD 20814 Phone: (301)897-3728 Fax: (301)897-0872 e-mail: ItaTranslations@cs.com Contact: Mark L. Pisoni
Founded 1991. Member: ATA. Accepts resumes. Only translates Italian. Main subjects are economics and finance, legal, business, marketing and medical. Uses 15 translators.

Iverson Language Associates, Inc., P.O. Box 511759, Milwaukee, WI 53203 Phone:(414)271-1144 Fax:(414)271-0144 e-mail: steve@iversonlang.com Web site: www.iversonlang.com Contact: Steven P. Iverson, President
Founded 1986. Member: ATA, STC, ASTD. Translates French, Spanish, Japanese, Italian, Arabic, Dutch, and Korean from English, and Portuguese, German, Polish, Chinese and all other languages, both from and into English. Emphasis on Technical Manuals (large machines), Medical Operators' Manuals, Spec Sheets, Financial, Software, Advertising Packaging, and Legal translations. Prospective translators should have computer, fax, current software, e-mail. Must be native speakers in the target language, with a technical background and formal training in a specific field of concentration. Three years experience in the industry and good writing skills are preferred. Resumes are reviewed internally for the required criteria. If so, they are sent a Translator Profile to fill out, and the completed form made available to project managers for use on new projects. The company provides translation, interpretation, typesetting and video narration services in most major languages, as well as technical writing and illustration. Typesetting capabilities include Chinese and Japanese. Maintains a pool of 600 translators.

-J-

JBT Translations & Localization, 115 U. St., Salt Lake City, UT 84103 Phone: (801)355-0518 Fax: (801)355-1873 e-mail: juttabrandt@compuserve.com Contact: Jutta Brandt Member: ATA

J. D. Edwards, One Technology Way, Denver, CO 80237 Phone: (303)334-1638 Fax: (303)334-1679 e-mail: loy_searle@jdedwards.com Contact: LoyAnne Searle Member: ATA

JLS Language Corporation, 135 Willow Rd., Menlo Park, CA 94025 Phone: (415)321-9832 Fax: (415)329-9864 e-mail: info@jls.com Web site: jls.com Contact: Ms. Rikko Field, President
Founded 1977. Member: ATA. Translates Japanese, Chinese, German, French and Spanish, both from and into English, with other languages on request. Emphasis on High Tech translation. Prospective translators should have ATA accreditation, education and industry experience. Resumes are screened and filed, and the promising applicants tested. In addition to High Tech, the company also does Agribusiness, Biomedical and Patent translations, and provides Chinese and Japanese desktop publishing. Maintains a pool of "hundreds" of translators.

JTG, Inc., 105 N. Washington St., Ste. 300, Alexandria, VA 22314 hone: (703)548-7570 Fax: (703)548-8223 e-mail: hr@jtg-inc.com Web site: www.jtg-inc.com Contact: Muriel Jérôme-O'Keeffe Member: ATA

Japan-America Management, Ltd., 2020 Hogback Rd., Ste. 17, Ann Arbor, MI 48105 Phone: (734)973-6101 Fax: (734)973-1847 e-mail: jamltdmi@ameritech.net Contact: Landon Bartley Member: ATA

Japan Communication Consultants, 236 E. 47th St., 28th Fl., New York, NY 10017 Phone: (212)759-2033 Fax: (212)759-2149 e-mail: jcc@japancc.com Web site: www.japancc.com Contact: Mariko N. O'Hare Member: ATA

Japan Pacific Publications, Inc., 419 Occidental Ave. S. #509, Seattle, WA 98104 Phone: (206)622-7443 Fax: (206)621-1786 -mail: andrewt@japanpacific.com Web site: www.japanpacific.com Contact: Andrew Taylor, President
Founded 1983. Member: ATA. Uses freelance translators and interpreters. Accepts unsolicited resumes. Resumes are entered into database and evaluated for skills and experience. Main language is Japanese. Also translates Chinese and Korean. Main areas are agriculture, business, bio-med, tourism, marketing, software and wood products. Maintains pool of 35 translators. Translation, DTP, pre-press, image setting.

John Benjamins Publishing Company, P.O. Box 27519, Philadelphia PA 19118-0519 Phone: (215)836-1200 Fax: (215)836-1204 email: paul@ benjamins.com Contact: Paul Peranteau Member: ATA

Josef Silny & Associates, Inc., 1320 South Dixie Highway, Ste. 775, Coral Gables, FL 33146 Phone: (305)273-1616 Fax: (305)83601204 e-mail: translation@jsilny.com Web site: www.jsilny.com Contact: Josef Silny Member: ATA

-K-

K19.Com, P.O. Box 91927, Austin, TX 78709 Phone: (512)301-6623 Fax: (512)301-6624
e-mail: info@k19.com Web site: www.k19.com Contact: Albert Kadosh Member: ATA

The Kaiser Permanente Medical Group, 2241 Geary Blvd., Rm. 146, San Francisco, CA 94115
Phone: (415)202-2888 Fax: (415)202-3829 -mail: gayle.tang@kp.org Contact: Gayle Tang Member: ATA

Kern Corporation, 230 Park Ave., Ste. 925, New York, NY 10169 Phone: (212)953-2070 Contact: Eric Schloss

Kotru Direct, 1001 Avenue of the Americas, #1214, New York, NY 10018 Phone: (212)840-2300 Fax: (212)840-0004
e-mail: kdiny@aol.com Contact: Ravi Kotru Member: ATA

Kramer Translation, 893 Massasso St., Merced, CA 95340 Phone: (209)385-0425 Fax: (209)385-3747
e-mail: keith@thailinguist.com Web site: www.thailinguist.com Contact: Keith & Marisa Ensminger Member: ATA

-L-

LRA Interpreters, Inc., 5150 Wilshire Blvd., #506, Los Angeles, CA 90036 Phone: (323)933-1006 Fax: (323)933-1153
e-mail: lra2@flash.net Web site: www. Flash.net/˜lratrsln Contact: Abel Plockier Member: ATA

LangTech International, 5625 SW 170th Ave., Aloha, OR 97007 Phone: (503)646-2478 (to fax, call first)
e-mail: LangTech@oregonvos.net Web site: www.oregonvos.com Contact: Douglas Foran, Owner
Founded 1994. Member: Latin American Trade Council of Oregon. Does not accept resumes. Translates French (European and Canadian), Spanish, Italian and Portuguese (Brazilian and Lusitanian), both from and into English. Emphasis on Scientific/ Technical, Mechanical, Electronics, Automotive, Agricultural, Legal, Health Care/Medical and Employee Relations translation. Also interpretation and audio/visual narration.

Langua Translations, Inc., 30150 Telegraph Rd., Ste. 339, Bingham Farms, MI 48025 Phone: (810)645-6663 Fax: (810)645-5376 e-mail: rneely@languatutor.com Web site: www.languatutor.com Contact: R.P. Neely

Language Associates, 4924 N. Miller, Oklahoma City, OK 73112 Phone: (405)946-1624 Fax: (405)946-1302 e-mail: cessyevans@aol.com Contact: Cecilia Evans, General Manager
Founded 1980. Member: ATA, NAJIT. Uses freelance translators and interpreters. Accepts unsolicited resumes. Resumes are entered in the system for future reference. Main languages (both ways) are Spanish, French, German, Russian, Japanese, and Korean. Also translates Chinese, Italian, Portuguese, Arabic, and more.

The Language Bank, 875 O'Farrell St., Ste. 105, San Francisco, CA 94109 Phone: (415)885-0827 Fax: (415)885-1304
Contact: Yen Nguyen-le, Manager
Founded 1987. Uses freelance translators and interpreters. Accepts unsolicited resumes. Resumes are screened for qualifications. Main languages are Spanish, Chinese, Vietnamese, Russian, Tagalog, Thai, Laotian, Cambodian, and French. Emphasis on social services. Pool of more than 100 translators.

The Language Bank, Inc., 1323 Lancaster Drive, Orlando, FL 32806
Phone: (407)894-3300 Fax: (407)894-7825
e-mail: info@languagae-bank.com Web site: www.language-bank.com
Contact:Dennis Ray Merritt

The Language Center, 144 Tices Ln., E. Brunswick, NJ 08816
Phone: (732)613-4554 Fax: (732)238-7659
e-mail: tlc@thelanguagectr.com Web site: www.thelanguagectr.com
Contact: Mary Majkowski
Founded 1967. Member:ATA, TCD. Accepts resumes. Translates all languages. Main areas are health care, pharmaceutical, medical equipment and technical manuals.

The Language Center Inc., 7 Gilliam Ln., Riverside, CT 06878-0520 Phone: (203)698-1907 Fax:(203)698-2043

e-mail: thelanguagecenterinc@worldnet.att.net
Contact: Siri Ostensen, President
Founded 1978. Translates (both ways) Spanish, French, German, Portuguese, all Scandinavian languages, Italian, Japanese, Chinese, and Russian. Emphasis on Technical, Commercial and Legal translation. Prospective translators should provide sample translations. Resumes are entered into a data base. Maintains a pool of 30 translators.

The Language Company, PO Box 42376, Houston, TX 77242 Phone: (713)952-6704 Fax:(713)952-5513
e-mail: language@pdq.net Contact: Danielle Y. Pung, President
Founded 1981. Member: ATA, AATIA, HITA. Uses freelance translators and interpreters. Accepts unsolicited resumes. Translates French, Spanish, Russian, German, Portuguese, etc., both from and into English. Emphasis on Technical, Patent and Legal translation. Potential translators should have word processing and transmission capabilities. Resumes are reviewed and filed.

Language Company Translations, L.C., P.O. Box 721507, Norman, OK 73070 Phone: (405)321-5380 Fax: (405)366-7242 e-mail: 71564.2044 @compuserve.com Contact: Nancy T. Hancock, Director
Founded 1982. Member: ATA. Translates all languages in all technical dis-ciplines. Potential translators should have experience and total fluency. They should be able to produce translations on disk if needed. Resumes are acknowledged and filed. Freelancers are Contacted when appropriate work comes in. The company can take materials through final printing, working with commercial printers and supervising production. They also accept resumes from freelance interpreters. Maintains a pool of 40 translators.

The Language Connection, PO Box 1962, Laguna Beach, CA 92652 Phone: (949)497-9393 Fax: (949)497-7515
e-mail: languageconnection @compuserve.com Web site: www.languageconnection.com Contact: J. Arturo Valdivia, President Member: ATA

Language Direct, 9801 Westheimber, Ste. 302, Houston, TX 77042 Phone: (713)917-6870 Fax: (713)917-6806
e-mail: jylan@langdirect.com Web site: www.langdirect.com Contact: Jylan Saleh-Maloy Member: ATA

Language Doctors, 410 11th St. NE, #21, Washington, DC 20002 Phone: (202)544-2942 Fax: (202)547-2311
e-mail: languagedr@aol.com Contact: Stuart Bennett Member: ATA

Language Dynamics, 931 Howe Ave. #107, Sacramento, CA 95825 Phone: (916)920-4062 Fax: (916)920-3594
e-mail: juanvallej@aol.com Contact: Rhody Vallejo
Founded 1979. Translates Spanish, French, Italian, Russian and Chinese and Hmong. All subject areas are translated. Prospective translators should be of high quality. Resumes are read and kept on file for Contact on an as-needed basis.

The Language Exchange, Inc., P.O. Box 750, Burlington, WA 98233 Phone: (360)755-9910 Fax: (360)755-9919
e-mail: Langex@langex.com Web site: www.langex.com Contact: Jaye Stover Member: ATA

Language for Industry Worldwide, Inc., 186 South St., Boston, MA 02111 Phone: (617)451-1233 Fax: (617)451-2247 e-mail: smeek@lfiww.com Web site: www.lfiww.com Contact: Sherri Meek Member: ATA

The Language Group, 2421 Bowland Pkwy, Ste. 104-B, Virginia Beach, VA 23454 Phone: (757)431-9004 Fax: (75)431-0447 e-mail: info@thelanguagegroup.com Web site: www.thelanguagegroup.com Contact: Evelin Schuyler
Founded 1999. Member: ATA, TCD, NAJIT, ASTM, NCMA, ABWA, NCATA. Accepts resumes via e-mail. Translates mainly Chinese, Croatian, Czech, French, German, Italian, Japanese, Norwegian, Polish and Spanish. Mostly technical, engineering, finance and marketing. Uses some 150 translators.

Language Innovations, LLC, 1225 I St. NW, Ste. 500, Washington, DC 20005 Phone: (202)682-4737 Fax: (202)682-3114 e-mail: Translate@languageinnovations,com Web site: www.Language.qpg.com Contact: Brian S. Friedman Member: ATA

Language Intelligence, Ltd., 16 North Goodman St., Rochester, NY 14607 Phone: (716)244-5578 Fax: (716)244-7880
e-mail: mail@languageintelligence.com Contact: Irene White
Founded 1988. Member: ATA, STC. Accepts resumes. Main languages are French, Italian, German, Spanish, Dutch, Swedish, Danish, Japanese, Chinese and Portuguese. Emphasis on life sciences, web and CBT, marketing, pharmaceutical-medical, patents and software.

The Language Lab, 211 East 43rd St., #1904, New York, NY 10017 Phone: (212)697-2020 Fax: (212)697-2891
e-mail: info@thelanguagelab.com Web site: www.thelanguagelab.com Contact: Nicole Cee Member: ATA

Language Learning Enterprises (LLE), 1100 17th St. NW, Ste. 900, Washington, DC 20036 Phone: (202)775-0444 Fax: (202)785-5584 e-mail: hlacy@lle-inc.com Web site: www.lle-inc.com Contact: Heidi G. Lacy
Founded 1979. Resumes are carefully screened; prospective translators and interpreters are then interviewed over phone, references checked, and then tried out on a small project first. Requires minimum 2 years experience. Translates all languages "from Arabic to Zulu," both from and into English. Emphasis in all technical areas, with a specialty in medical interpretation. The company is the creator of LLE-Link, a 24-hour-a-day, 365 days-a-year telephone interpretation service using conference calling. Maintains a pool of 12 full-time people with 1000 linguists on call.

Language Line Services, 1 Lower Ragdale Drive, Bldg. 2, Monterey, CA 93940 Phone: (831)648-5819 Fax: (800)752-0073 e-mail: danyune@languageline.com Web site: www.languageline.com Contact: Daynune Geertsen

Language Link Corporation, 3100 Broadway, Ste. 110, Kansas City, MO 64111 Phone: (816)753-3122 Fax: (816)753-3262 e-mail: translation@languagelinkcorp.com Web site: www.languagelinkcorp.com Contact: Carrie Hewitt
Founded 1989. Member: ATA, ACTFL, MICATA, ASTM. Uses freelance translators and interpreters. Accpts unsolicited resumes. Main languages are Spanish, Russian, Chinese, Vietnamese, Arabic, Croatian, Japanese, Somali, Korean and Farsi.

Language Matters, 1445 Pearl St., Ste. 215, Boulder, CO 80302 hone: (303)442-3471 Fax: (303)442-5805 e-mail: info@languagematters.com Web site: www.languagematters.com Contact: Rosangela Fiori
Founded 1992. Member: ATA. TCA. Accepts resumes. Translates mainly French, German, Italian, Spanish, Russian, Japanese, Chinese, Swedish, Greek and Dutch. Mostly technical, legal and advertisement. Has a pool of 800 translators.

The Language Network, Inc., 5151 Belt Line Rd., Ste. 452, Dallas, TX, 75240 Phone: (972)960-9980 Fax: (972)960-9904 -mail: Language@flash.net Contact: Christine J. Finck Member: ATA

Language One, 2305 Calverty St. NW, Washington DC 20008 Phone: (202)328-0099 Fax: (202)328-1610 e-mail: translations@languageone.com Web site: www.languageone.com Contact: Lorraine B. Smith Member: ATA

Language Plus,4110 Rio Bravo, Ste. 202, El Paso TX 79902 hone: (915)544-8600 Fax: (915) 544-8640 e-mail: langplus@aol.com Web site: www.languageplus.com Contact: Connie Gyenis Member: ATA

The Language Service, Inc., 806 Main St., Poughkeepsie, NY 12603 Phone: (845)473-4303 Fax:(845)473-4467 e-mail: info@tlsmedtrans.com Web site: www.tlsmedtrans.com Contact: Jeanne De Tar
Founded 1950. Member: ATA, FIT. Uses freelance translators and interpreters. Accepts unsolicited resumes. Qualified linguists are filed for future reference. Main languages (both ways) are German, French, Spanish, Italian, and Portuguese, and Japanese into English. Also Dutch and Swedish into English. Main areas are medical, pharmaceutical, chemical and environmental. Does about one million words a year. Works with various translators, but mainly with a steady group of about ten. Owner is co-founder and former president of the ATA.

Language Services Associates, Inc., 607 North Easton, C, PO Box 205, Willow Grove, PA 19090 Phone: (215)657-6571 Fax: (215)659-7210 e-mail: lschriver@lsaweb.com Web site: www.lsaweb.com Contact: Laura T. Schriver
Founded 1991. Member: ATA, DVTA, NAJIT, CHICATA, NOTA. Uses freelance translators and interpreters. Accepts unsolicited resumes. Resumes are acknowledged, kept, and used when needed. Applicants should have ATA accreditation. Main languages (both ways) are Spanish, German, French, Chinese, Japanese, Korean, Vietnamese, Russian, Hindi, Italian, and Tamil. Also Cambodian, Arabic, Farsi, Hebrew, Dutch and more. Emphasis on Legal and corporate translation. Maintains a pool of 745 translators.

Language Services Consultants, Inc., P.O. Box 412, Ardmore, PA 19003 Phone: (610)617-8962 Fax: (610)617-9108 e-mail: ruth.karpeles@verizon.net Contact: Ruth S. Karpeles
Founded 1992. Member: ATA, DVTA. Accepts resumes. Translates mainly Spanish, Vietnamese, Cambodian, Russian, Chinese, Korean, French, Portuguese, Greek, Dutch and Albanian. Mostly medical, education and social services. Uses some 150 translators.

Language Solution, Inc. The, 1700 North Dixie Highway, #114, Boca Raton, FL 33432 Phone: (561)395-5098 Fax:(561)393-6893 e-mail: jgo @languagesolution.com Web site: languagesolution.com Jean Giles Ordóñez, President Contact: Derya Guven, Manager
Founded 1991. Member: Women in International Trade, Greater Miami Chamber of Commerce, World Trade Center-Ft. Lauderdale, SEFAC. Uses freelance translators and interpreters. Accepts unsolicited resumes. Resumes are entered in database, and applicants are sent forms to fill out. They should have experience, computer, and e-mail capabilities. Resumes are reviewed, and if appropriate, entered into a database. No responses are sent. Translates (both ways) Spanish, Portuguese, and Korean, and English into German, French, Japanese, and Greek. Emphasis on marketing and training material, web site translations, manuals for products, and legal contracts. It uses both PCs and Mac, PageMaker, and Quark Express. It has a voice-over studio, does sound edits, produces CD-ROM masters for web courses and training programs. Maintains an active pool of 30-40 translators.

Language Source, 2208 N. 72nd St., Wauwatosa, WI 53213 Phone: (414)607-8766 Fax: (414)607-8767 e-mail: langsource@aol.com Contact: Elizabeth Brudele-Baran

Languages International, Inc., 2849 Michigan St., NE #100, Grand Rapids, MI 49506 Phone: (616)285-0005 Fax: (616)285-0004 e-mail: dbertoni@iserv.net Web site: www.lang-int.com Contact: Delia L. Bertoni Member: ATA

The Languageworks, Inc.,1123 Broadway, Ste. 201, New York, NY 10010 Phone: (212)447-6060 Fax: (212)447-6257 e-mail: talwood@languageworks.com Web site: www.anguageworks.com Contact: Thomas Alwood Member: ATA

Latin American Business Services, 16127 Bridge Hampton Club Dr., Charlotte, NC 28277 Phone: (704)543-0657 Fax: (704)543-4076 e-mail: letellez@cs.com Web site: www.cs.com Contact: Luis E. Tellez Member: ATA

Latin American Translators Network, Inc.,1970 Cliff Valley Way NE, Ste. 208, Atlanta, GA 30329 Phone: (404)634-2635 Fax: (404)634-9683 e-mail: latn@latninc.com Web site: www.latninc.com Contact: Ann-Marie Bumbalo Member: ATA

Lazar & Associates, 2444 Wilshire Blvd., Ste. 411, Santa Monica, CA 90403 Phone: (310)453-3302 Fax: (310)453-6002 e-mail: languages@lazar.com Web site: www.lazar.com Contact: Elaine Lazar
Founded 1995. Member: ATA. Accepts resumes occasionally.Main languages are Spanish, French, Chinese, Japanese and German. Mostly medical, pharmaceutical, IT, business, legal and technical equipment manuals. Has a pool of over 3000 translators.

Le Chateau Enterprises Group, Inc. Phone: (941)574-5600 Fax: (941)574-3273 e-mail: info@letspeak.com Web site: www.letspeak.com Contact: Allendy Doxy Member: ATA

Legal Interpreting Services, Inc., 21-50 44th Drive, Long Island City, NY 11101 Phone: (718)786-7890 Fax: (718)786-8034 e-mail: accutran@aol.com Web site: www.accuratetranslation.com Contact: Alexandra Gerenburg Member: ATA

Leggett & Platt, Inc., Leggett Rd., #1, Carthage, MO 64836 Phone: (417)358-8131 Fax: (417)358-5840 Web site: www.leggett.com Contact: Tomasita Hernandez Member: ATA

Lemoine International, Inc., 339 E. 600 N., American Fork, UT 84003 Phone: (801)763-5644 Fax: (801)763-5660 e-mail: brigittem@lemoine-international.com Web site: www.lemoine-international.com Contact: Brigitte L. Morales Member: ATA

LEXFUSION, 16855 W. Bernardo Drive, San Diego, CA 92127 Phone: (858)860-1000 Fax: (858)860-1001 e-mail: bobc@lexfusion.com Web site: www.lexfusion.com Contact: Bob Cocchia Member: ATA

Liaison Language Center, 3500 Oak Lawn Ave., Ste. 110 LB 32, Dallas, TX 75219 Phone: (214)528-2731 Fax: (214)522-7167 e-mail: liaison@liaisonlanguage.com Web site: www.liaisonlanguage.com Contact: Gerda Stendell
Founded 1978. Member: ATA. Uses freelance translators and interpreters.. Translated mainly Spanish, Portuguese, German, French, Italian, Korean, Japanese, Chinese (Madarin and Cantonese) and Vietnamese. Mostly legal, oil, insurance. Has a pool of around 100 active translators and interpreters.

Liaison Multilingual Services, 3261 Cherryridge Rd., Englewood, CO 80110 Phone: (303)762-0997 Fax: (303)762-0999 e-mail: liaison@ecentral.com Web site:eMultilingual.com Contact: Suzanne Robinson Member: ATA

Lingo Systems, 15115 SW Sequoia Pkwy, #200, Portland, OR 97224 Phone: (503)419-4856 Fax: (503)419-4876 e-mail: info@lingosys.com Web site: www.lingosys.com Contact: Maja Bailey
Founded 1992. Member: ATA. LISA, SAO. Accepts resumes. Requires 5 years experience and knowledge of CAT tools. Translates mainly French, German, Italian, Spanish, Japanese, Chinese, Korean, Dutch, Scandinavian languages and Eastern European. Also Asian. Mostly IT, computer hardware and software, web sites, marketing and training materials. Maintains some 500 translators.

Lingua Communications Translation Services, 9321 Lavergne, Ste. 101, Skokie, IL 60077 Phone:(847)673-1607 Fax:(847)673-1669 Con-tact: Alex Babich, General Partner
Founded 1989. Member: ATA. Translates Russian and German, both from and into English, and Polish, Ukrainian, Latvian, French and Japanese into English. Emphasis on all subject translations. Prospective translators should possess experience, speed and quality at market-level pricing. Resumes are filed against need; translators are then contacted. **Lingua** maintains a pool of 250 translators.

Lingua Language Center, 1730 Main St., Ste. 226, Weston, FL 33326 Phone: (954)349-8088 Fax: (954)349-1799 e-mail: info@linguaschool.com Web site:linguaschool.com Contact: Andreina Ojeda Member: ATA

Lingualink Incorporated, 5777 W. Century Blvd., Ste. 1000, Los Angeles, CA 90045 Phone: (310)642-2920 Fax: (310)642-2945 -mail: lingualinkinfo@ccscom.com Web site: www.ccscom.com/ lingualink Contact: Keir Milan Member: ATA

Linguistic Consulting Enterprises, Inc., 251 W. Marlboro Rd., Oro Valley, AZ 85737 Phone: (520)297-6420 Fax: (520)297-2629 e-mail: LCEAZ1@aol.com Contact: Maria Elisa Rivera

Linguistic Systems, Inc., P.O. Box 390031, 130 Bishop Allen Drive, Cambridge, MA 02139 Phone:(617)864-3900 Fax:(617)864-5186 e-mail: info@linguist.com Web site: www.linguist.com Contact: Martin Roberts, President
Founded 1967. Member: ATA. Uses freelance translators and interpreters. Applicants should have relevant education and experience. Translates mainly Spanish, French, German, Italian, Portuguese, Chinese, Japanese, Korean, Greek and Swedish. Mostly legal, medical and commercial. The company provides translation, interpretation, voiceover, and machine translation editing services. Maintains a pool of about 4000 translators.

Lionbridge, 301 Mission St., Ste. 350, San Francisco, CA 94105 hone: (415)546-6885 Fax: (415)495-4926 Web site: www.lionbridge.com Contact: Allison Smith Member: ATA

Littleton & Associates, Inc., 6006 W. 159th St., Bldg. C, Ste. 2 East, Oak Forest, IL 60452 Phone: (708)429-3336 Fax: (708)429-3414 e-mail: lcs62258@aol.com Contact: James M. Littleton Member: ATA

Lucent Technologies Global Translation, 2400 Reynolda Rd., Winston-Salem, NC 27106 Phone: (336)727-6218 Fax: (336)727-3221 -mail: mrhodes@lucent.com Web site: www.lucent.com/translations Contact: Marta C. Rhodes Member: ATA

LUZ, 202 Potero Ave., San Francisco, CA 941103 hone: (415)241-0520 Fax: (415)241-0504 Web site: www.luz.com Contact: Sanford Wright Member: ATA

-M-

M^2 Limited, 9210 Wightman Rd., Montgomery Village, MD 20886 Phone: (301)977-4281 Fax: (301)926-5046 e-mail: info@m2ltd.com Web site: www.m2ltd.com
Contact: Audrey Moyer
Founded 1979. Member: ATA, STC, World Trade Center. Accepts unsolicted resumes. Applicants should be native speakers of the target language, with 2-5 years minimum experience. Translates mainly Spanish, French, Italian, German, Porutguese, Chinese, Japanese, Korean, Dutch and Russian. Emphasis on Computer Software, technical documentation, web pages and localization. The company does not provide interpreting services. The company has become a specialist in the localization of computer-based equipment and software, and is heavily involved in software development, training, and adaptation of English-language materials for use in other cultures and languages. In addition to translators, the company is interested in proofreaders and editors in all languages. Maintains a pool of 2,000 translators.

M/C International, 7207 Chagrin Rd., Unit #4, Chagrin Falls, OH 44023 Phone:(440)247-2277 Fax:(440)247-0453 e-mail: mcinternational @stratos.net Contact: Mrs. E. Marchbank
Founded 1969. Translates Spanish, French, German, Italian, Portuguese, Russian, Accepts resumes. Translates mainly French, German, Dutch, Italian, Portuguese, Spanish, Arabic, Chinese and Japanese. Emphasis on technical, legal and commercial translation. The company is a full-service translation bureau. It also provides 4-color printing services, desktop publishing and typesetting, both to clients and to other translators. In addition, they operate their own travel agency. Maintains a pool of 50 translators.

MGE Lingual Services, 136 36th St. Drive SE, Ste. A-4, Cedar Rapids, IA 52403 Phone: (319)366-1038 Fax: (319)366-1047 e-mail: mike@mge-lingual.com Web site: www.mge-lingual.com Contact: Michael G. Elliff Member: ATA

MTS Multinational Translating Service, 928 Connetquot Ave., Central Islip, NY 11722 Phone: (631)581-8956 Fax: (631)224-9435 e-mail: mtsvc@optonline.net Web site: www.mtssvc.qpg.com Contact: Lisa Alesci Member: ATA

Madison Linguistic Services, 301 Keezell Hall, MSC 1802, Harrisonburg, VA 22807 Phone: (540)568-3512 Fax: (540)568-6904 e-mail: rethorcx@jmu.edu Web site: www.jmu.edu/forlang/trans Contact: Christophe Rethore Member: ATA

MAGNUS International Trade Services Corp., 1313 North Grand Ave., #280, Walnut, CA 91789
Phone: (909) 595-8488 Fax: (909)598-5852 Web site: www.manuscorp.com Contact: Nora K. Schwartz
Member: ATA, PCLA, HPRMA, LA-FTA, NOTA. Translates Spanish, Chinese, Vietnamese, Tagalog, Korean, Portuguese, French, German and Russian from English, as well as Hindi, Farsi, Armenian, Hmong, Lao and Arabic. Emphasis on Healthcare, Medical, Pharmaceutical, Engineering, Legal, Technical, and General Business translation. Prospective translators should have certification (if possible), appropriate education and field experience. Resumes are responded to with a standard contract, and contractors called as needed.

Mandarin Academy, The Crane Bldg., 40-24th St., Pittsburgh, PA 15222 Phone: (412)434-4771 Fax: (412)434-4772
e-mail: mandarin@stowgate.net
Contact: Helen Liu

Marion J. Rosley Secretarial, Transcription & Translation Services, 41 Topland Rd., Hartsdale, NY 10530 Phone: (914)682-9718 Fax: (914) 761-1384 e-mail: mrosley@rosley.com Web site: rosley.com
Contact: Marion J. Rosley, President
Founded 1977. Member: NYCT, World Trade Council of Westchester, Westchester County Assn., Westconn. Translates all languages. Emphasis on Legal, Medical, Technical, and Business Correspondence translation. The company provides interpreting services in all languages. Prospective translators should have excellent skills and reasonable prices. Resumes are filed for future use. Maintains a pool of "hundreds" of translators. The company provides secretarial, transcription and translation services, including cassette transcription of conferences.

MassLingua, LLC, 5 Stoddard Drive, Worcester, MA 01604 Phone: (508)752-7015 Fax: (508)752-7980
e-mail: ma_lingua@msn.com Web site: www.masslingua.com Contact: Rafael Martinez Member: ATA

MasterWord Services, Inc., 303 Stafford, Ste. 204, Houston, TX 77079 Phone:(713)589-0810 Fax:(713)589-1104
e-mail: masterword@ masterword.com Web site: www.masterword.com Contact: Mila Green
Founded 1993. Member: ATA, Azeri Translators Association. Translates Russian, Spanish, Azeri, Brazilian Portuguese and Chinese, both from and into English. Emphasis on Oil and Gas, Drilling, Legal and Medical translations. Prospective translators should have significant translation experience, especially in the oil/gas or legal areas, and show quality performance on the company's certification exam. All resumes are acknowledged, and after prescreening, ap-proximately 10% are sent an in-house certification exam, primarily in Russian or Spanish. They are then phoned for an in-person interview. The company also has offices in Baku, Azerbaijan, and is involved in ongoing projects in Europe, South America and Asia.They also have affiliates in Washington, DC, New York, London and Moscow. Maintains a pool of 35-50 translators.

Masua Funai Eifert & Mitchell, Ltd., 1701 Golf Rd., Ste. 800, Rolling Meadows, IL 60008
Contact: Yasuyo Wakuta Member: ATA

McDonald's Corporation, 2715 Jorie Blvd., Oak Brook, IL 60521 Phone: (630)623-6085 Fax: (630)623-6143
e-mail: nadia.gould@mcd.com Contact: Nadia F. Gould Member: ATA

McNeil Multilingual, 6564 Loisdale Court, Ste. 800, Springfield, VA 22150 Phone: (703)921-1600 Fax: (703)921-1610
e-mail: rnelson@mcneilmultic.com Web site: www.mcneilmultic.com Contact: George E. Washington, Jr. Member: ATA

ME Sharp, Inc., Publisher, 80 Business Park Drive, Armonk, NY 10504 Phone: (914)273-1800 Fax: (914)273-2106
e-mail: journals@mesharpe.com Web site: www.mesharpe.com Contact: C. P. Chetti Member: ATA

Mena's International Corp., 2548 Nicollet Ave., S., Minneapolis, MN 55404 Phone: (612)872-8392 Fax: (612)872-7861
e-mail: menastrave@aol.com Contact: Maximo Mena Member: ATA

Mendoza-Harmelin, Inc., 525 Righters Ferry Rd., Bala Cynwyd, PA 19004 Phone: (610)668-2700 Fax: (610)668-8412
e-mail: MMendoza@Harmelin.com Contact: Mia Mendoza Member: ATA

Mercury Marine, W6250 West Pioneer Rd., Fond du Lac, WI 54936 Phone: (414)929-5299 Fax: (414)231-8916
email: Gary_Fenrich@mercmarine.com Contact: Gary Fenrich Member: ATA

Metropolitan Interpreters and Translators Worldwide, Inc., 110 E. 42nd St., Ste. 802, New York, NY 10017
Phone: (212)986-5050 Fax: (212)983-5998 e-mail: metlang@aol.com Web site: metlang.com Contact: Joe Citrano

Founded 1990. Member: ATA, NYCT, NAJIT, IAFL. Uses freelance translators and interpreters. Accept unsolicited resumes. Resumes are entered in a database. Translates all languages. Emphasis on legal and law enforcement. About 500 in translator pool.

Monti Interpreting & Translation Services, Inc., 101 S. Wymore Rd., Ste. 315, Altamonte Springs, FL 32714 Phone: (888)686-6007 Fax: (407)830-1860 e-mail: montitrans@yahoo.com Web site: www.montitrans.com Contact: Caroline Montalvo

Founded 1997. Member: ATA. Accepts resumes. Translates mainly Spanish, Creole, Vietnamese, French, Chinese, Arabic, Bosnian, Croatian, Cambodian, Portuguese and Turkish. Mostly medical, legal and corporate literature. Maintains a pool of 50 translators and 500 interpreters.

MooreInterp, Inc., 1251 Century SW, Ste. 102, Grand Rapids, MI 49509 Phone: (616)247-4810 Fax: (616)247-5032 e-mail: mooreinterp@aol.com Web site: www.mooreinterp.com Member: ATA

Morales Dimmick Translation Service, Inc., 1409 W S Slope, Emmett, ID 83617 Phone: (208)365-2622 e-mail: projects@mdtranslation.com Web site: www.mdtranslation.com Contact: Chris

Founded 1989. Member: ATA, IMA. Accepts resumes. Main languages are Spanish, Bosnian, Laotian, Vietnamese and Arabic. Mostly business, medical, legal and insurance. Maintains a pool of 65 translators.

Morgan Guaranty Trust Company, 60 Wall St., 34th Fl., New York, NY 10260 Phone: (212)552-5474 Fax: (212)552-8128 e-mail: lisa.gallo@chase.com Contact: Lisa Gallo Member: ATA

The Multi-Lingual Group, 8 Faneuil Hall Marketplace, 3rd Fl., Boston, MA 02109 Phone: (617)973-5077 Fax: 617)787-3124 e-mail: multilg @aol.com Contact: Felice Bezri

Founded 1994. Member: NAJIT. Translates Spanish, French, Italian and Portuguese, both from and into English, German, Swedish, Arabic and Cantonese into English, and Japanese and Mandarin from English. Emphasis on Medical Studies, Computer, Legal and Military translation. Prospective translators should be ATA members with extensive experience in written translation and specialization in one or more fields. Resumes are reviewed on a regular basis with a particular eye to the experience of the candidate. The company also provides simultaneous interpreting in over 50 languages and offers cross-cultural consulting. Maintains a pool of approximately 320 translators.

MultiLing International, Inc., 32 W. Center St., Ste. 203, Provo, UT 84601 Phone:(801)377-2000 Fax:(801)377-7085 e-mail: translation@ultiling.com Web site: www.multiling.com Contact: Michael V. Sneddon

Founded 1988. Member: ATA, STC, Utah Information Technology Assn., Software Publishers Assn. Translates Spanish, French, Dutch, German, Italian, Japanese, Chinese, Swedish, Danish, Russian and all other languages, both from and into English. Emphasis on High-Tech Product Localization and the translation of related documents. Prospective translators must be native speakers of the target language with an undergraduate and, preferably, a master's degree, with an area of special expertise. They should have a good software and desktop publishing background and several years of experience and accreditation. Resumes, when they meet company requirements, are sent a questionnaire with a request for a sample translation. The company works in all areas of translation, including working with translation software and aiding in its further development. Maintains a pool of1400 translators.

Multilingual Communications Corporation, P.O. Box 7164 Pittsburgh, PA 15213 Phone:(412)621-7450 Fax:(412)621-0522 e-mail: mktg @mccworld.com Web site: www.mccworld.com Contact: Cathy Rosenthal

Founded 1977. Member: ATA. Translates Spanish, French, German, Chinese, Japanese, Russian, Italian, Korean, Portuguese, Arabic and Korean, both from and into English. Emphasis on Technical, Legal and Medical Software translation. Prospective translators should possess native proficiency and background in a specialized field. Resumes are evaluated on receipt, then contacted and tested. Their services include software localization. Maintains a pool of 500 translators.

Multilingual Translations, Inc., 1510 Front St., Ste. 200, San Diego, CA 92101 Phone: (619)295-2682 Fax: (619)295-2984 e-mail: mcardenas@multitrans.com Web site: www.multitrans.com Contact: Michael Ramírez Cardénas, J.D. Member: ATA

Multilingual Word, 2631 Salem Ave. S, Minneapolis, MN 55416 Phone: (952)929-4203 Fax: (952)922-4344 e-mail: mlivon@aol.com Contact: Michelle Livon Member: ATA

-N-

NCS Enterprises, Inc., 1222 Hope Hollow Rd., Carnegie, PA 15106 Phone: (412)278-4590 Fax: (412)278-4595 e-mail: cnagy@ncs-pubs.com Web site: www.ncs-pubs.com Contact: Stephanie Nagy

Founded 1992. Member: ATA. Uses freelance translators and interpreters. Accepts unsolicited resumes. All resume are reviewed and entered into database.

NiS International Services, 1913 Dundin Drive, Old Hickory, TN 37138 Phone:(615)758-6459 Fax:(615)758-6459 e-mail: Nisintl@aol.com Web site: www.nisintl.com Contact: Bill Hollaway

Founded 1987. Member: ATA. Translates Japanese, Korean, Chinese, Spanish, German, French, Italian, and Russian, both from and into English. Emphasis on Automotive, Electrical Engineering, Mechanical Engineering, Patent, Contract and Agreement, and other technical document translation. Prospective translators should send a sample of previous work. A specialized technical background is a plus. Resumes are saved in a database, and the translator Contacted when a job is available. The company provides translation, interpretation, and teaching services. Maintains a pool of 600-700 translators.

N.O.W. Translations, 23054 Covello St., West Hills, CA 91307 Phone: (818)716-9112 Fax: (818)888-6962 e-mail: thomasc@nowtranslations.com Web site: www.nowtranslations.com Contact: Thomas Clement Member: ATA

Narragansett Translations & Interpreting, Inc., 32 East Ave., Pawtucket, RI 02860 Phone: (401)722-1222 e-mail: morra_red@ids.net Contact: Mike D. Chea Member: ATA

Nelles Translations, 104 South Michigan Ave., Room 1004, Chicago, IL 60603 Phone: (312)236-2788 Fax: (312)236-0717 Contact: Lawrence R. Kramer, Product Manager

Founded 1956. Member: ATA, Chicagoland Chamber of Commerce, Chicago Convention & Tourism Bureau. Translates Spanish, French, German, Italian, Portuguese, Polish, Russian, Japanese, Chinese, Korean and numerous other languages, both from and into English. Emphasis on Patent, Print Advertising, Legal, Brochures and Manuals, and Personal Document translation. Prospective translators should be experienced with references. They may be tested at the discretion of the company. Resumes are acknowledged and promising applicants are Contacted. The company provides interpreting and voiceover services in addition to translation.

NetworkOmni Multilingual Communications, 1329 E. Thousand Oaks Blvd., 2nd Fl., Thousand Oaks, CA 91362 Phone: (805)379-1090 Fax: (805)379-2467 e-mail: omni@networkomni.com Web site: www.networkomni.com Contact: Irena Stone

Founded 1978. Member: ATA. Translates French, Italian, German, Spanish, Chinese, Korean and Japanese, both from and into English. Handles a variety of subjects. Excellence is the primary requirement for prospective translators. Re-sumes are followed up with a call and a registration skills packet. The company has five separate divisions: Interpretations, Translations, Teleinterpretations, Transcriptions and Videointerpretations and all are supported by Omni's Quality Control staff. Maintains a pool of 800 translators.

New England Translations, 59 Temple Place, Ste. 204, Boston, MA 02111 Phone: (617)426-4868 Fax: (617)695-9349 e-mail: netranslations@langcenters.com Web site: newenglandtranslations.com Contact: Ken Krall, Director

Founded 1986. Member: ATA. Uses freelance translators and interpreters. Ac-cepts unsolicited resumes. Resumes are entered into databse by language and specialty. Requires experience. Translates Spanish, Portuguese, French, German, Italian, Chinese, Vietnamese, Korean and Japanese from English, and Spanish into English. Emphasis on Finance, Legal, Marketing, Industrial and Medical translation, with specialties in Financial and Medical. Prospective translators should have PC or Mac, fax, modem. A small sample translation should be sent with the resume. Resumes are entered into a database by language pair and technical specialty after qualifications are reviewed. The company is dedicated to the translation of all major languages. It also provides instruction in Spanish only.
Maintains a pool of 800 translators.

Newtype, Inc., 1259 Route 46 E, Bldg. 1, 2nd Fl., Parsippany, NJ 07054 Phone: (973)263-5000 Fax: (973)263-5522 e-mail: tbias@newtypeinc.com Web site: www.newtypeinc.com Contact: Thomas Bias Member: ATA

Nikkei News Bulletin, 1325 Ave. of the Americas, Ste. 2401, New York, NY 10019 Phone: (212)261-6410 Fax: (212)261-6429 e-mail: nnbny@nikkel.com

Northwest Translations, 2636 E. Greentree Ct., Eagle, ID 83616 Phone: (208)938-5005 Fax: (509)351-7529 e-mail: sales@nwtranslations.com Web site: www.nwtranslations.com Contact: Jeff Scott Allen Member: ATA

NovaTrans Enterprises, Inc., P.O. Box 3903, Boca Raton, FL 33427 hone: (561)368-0865 Fax: (954)255-5161 e-mail: mail@novatrans.net Contact: Janet T. Aliaga Member: ATA

-O-

Okada & Sellin Translations, LLC 1950 Addison St., Ste. 101, Berkeley CA 94704 Phone: (510)843-5600 Fax: (510)843-5603 e-mail: okada@ostrans.com Web site: www.ostrans.com Contact: Robert G. Sellin

Founded 1996. Member: ATA, STC. Uses freelance translators and interpreters.
Accepts unsolicited resumes. Resumes are reviewed and graded. Work sample are welcome. Requires e-mail. Translates all major Asian and European languages. Focuses on patents and other technical, scientific, pharma/biotech, and legal subjects.

Omega Translation Service, 331-A North Brand Blvd., Glendale, CA 91203 Phone: (818)545-3626 Fax: (818)545-0364 e-mail: omega2@earthlink.net Contact: Jill Massehian
Founded 1985. Translates Spanish, French, German, Japanese, Italian and Chinese, both from and into English. Emphasis on Scientific, Businese and Computer translation. Prospective translators should have good references. Resumes are filed by specialty and language. The company needs qualified translators and interpreters with various specialty fields. Maintains a pool of 1000 translators.

OmniLingua, Inc., 1010 First St. NW, Cedar Rapids, IA 52405 Phone: (319)365-8565 Fax:(319)365-7893 e-mail: omnilingua @omnilingua .com Web site: www.omnilingua.com Contact: Elizabeth Miller
Founded 1980. Member: ATA, MACHETE, NCATA. Accepts resumes. Translates mainly French, Italian, German, Spanish, Portuguese, Chinese, japanese, Korean, Greek and Russian. Mostly automotive, heavy equipment, medical products, IT, consumer durables and marketing. Prospective translators should complete a written application form and a short translation test. Experience and educational requirements vary; great emphasis is placed on test results. The company also provides desktop publishing services. Maintains a pool of 300 translators, editors, proofreaders, narrators, and word-counters, all freelance.

The One Technology Group, 18101 Von Karman Ave., #650, Irvine, CA 92612
Phone: (949)955-5318 Fax: (949)975-8450 e-mail: candida@theone.com Web site: www.theone.com
Contact: Candida McCollam Member: ATA

OneWorld Language Solutions, 2909 Cole Ave., Ste. 300, Dallas, TX 75204 Phone: (214)871-2909 Fax: (214)871-2907 e-mail: flctans@connect.net Web site: www.oneworldlanguage.com
Contact: Gabriele Hayes, Director
Founded 1990. Member: ATA, META. Uses freelance translators and interpreters. Accepts unsolicited resumes. Requires experience, prefers ATA members. Resumes are entered in database and applicants are Contacted when the need arises. Translates (both ways) mainly Spanish, French, German, Italian, and Russian. Also Japanese, Dutch, and Chinese. Provides interpretation and language training. Maintains a pool of over 400 translators.

Openworld, 2673 NE University Village, Ste. 1, Seattle, WA 98105 Phone: (206)523-1100 Fax: (206)522-3345 e-mail: orders@openworldtranslations.com Web site: www.penworldtranslations.com Contact: Helen Tereshina Member: ATA

Origin - The Language Agency, P.O. Box 1648, Makawao, HI 96768 Phone: (808)573-1453 Fax: (808)573-6446 e-mail: info@origin.to Web site: www.origin.to Contact: Chelsea Hill
Founded 1998. Member: ATA, Aquarius, Proz.com. Accepts resumes via web site. Translates mainly Chinese, Korean, Indian Languages, Spanish, French, Russian, German, Japanese, Ukrainian and Romanian. Mostly medical, computer-related, business, marketing, telecommunications, tourism, pharmaceuticals and automotive. Has a pool of 600 translators.

O'Sullivan Menu Corporation, 110 Triangle Blvd., Carlstadt, NJ 07072
Phone: (201)507-1449 Fax: (201)507-4920 Contact: Adriana Marton Member: ATA

-P-

P.H. Brink International, 6100 Golden Valley Rd., Minneapolis, MN 55422 Phone:(763)591-1977 Fax:(612)542-9138 e-mail: bliaj@phbrink.com Web site: www.phbrink.com Contact: Belia Jimenez-Lorente
Member: ATA. Uses freelance translators and interpreters. Accepts unsolicited resumes. Resumes are screened and best ones are called for test. Requires college degree and native speaking ability. Translates mainly English into major European languages and Japanese. Subjects are mostly technical. Employs 150 full-time translators.

PSC, Inc., 12330 Pinecrest Rd., Reston, VA 20191 Phone:(703)716-5000 Fax:(703)716-5005
e-mail: translat@pscusa.com Contact: Fred Lothrop
Founded 1988. Member: ATA. Translates Spanish (all dialects) to and from English, and Arabic, Chinese (all dialects), Farsi, Haitian Creole, Russian, Serbo/Croatian, Japanese, and Central and West African languages into English. Emphasis on technical (computer, communications, radar), legal, and business translation. Specialty in transcription and translation for law enforcement agencies. Translators must have a specialized area and security clearance before being matched with an appropriate job. Unsolicited resumes for freelance work are processed through internal channels of selection. PSC, Inc. is a privately-owned firm with a major business area, also providing foreign language services for the private and public sectors. Maintains a pool of 1500 linguists.

Pacific Dreams, Inc., 2263 Judson St. SE, Salem, OR 97302 Phone: (503)588-7368 Fax: (503)588-7549
e-mail: pacific.dreams@viser.net Web site: www.pacificdreams.org Contact: Ken Sakai Member: ATA

Pacific Interpreters, Inc., 520 SW Yamhill, #320, Portland, OR 97204 Phone: (800)311-1232 Fax: (800)881-2565

e-mail: recruitment@pacificinterpreters.com Web site: www.pacificinterpreters.com Contact: Joana Laitinen
Founded 1992. Member: ATA, SOMI, NOTIS, NAJIT, ASTM. Accepts resumes. Translates mainly Spanish, Vietnamese, Chinese, Cambodian, Hmong, Laotian, Arabic and Farsi. Mostly health care. Maintains pool of about 100 translators.

Pacific Ring Services, Inc., 1143 Christina Mill Drive, Newark, DE 19711 Phone: (302)269-1518 Fax: (302)269-1618
e-mail: pacific@dca.net Web site: www.pacificring.com Contact: Motoko Yuasa Member: ATA

Pacolet International Translation Co., 11405 Main St., Roscoe IL 61073 Phone: (815)623-1608 Fax: (815)623-1907
e-mail: pacolet@inwave.com Web site: www.pacolet.com Contact: Julie Johnson McKee, President
Founded 1993. Member: ATA, Greater Rockford Chamber of Commerce. Uses freelance translators and interpreters. Accepts unsolicited resumes. Resumes are reviewed for language skills and specialties, and entered in databse. ATA affiliation or translation degree required. Strong professional exeperience preferred. Translates mainly Spanish, French, Dutch, Italian, Portuguese, Swedish, Finnish, Chinese, Japanese, and Korean. Also other European and Asian languages, Arabic and Farsi. Emphasis on technical subjects, heavy equipment, engines, aerospace, food service equipment, business contracts and proposals. Did one millions dollars worth of translation in 1988. Strong background in marketing communications and broadcasting. Company is family-friendly and develops long-term "partnerships" (company-translator-customer are a team). Maintains a pool of 300 translators.

Pangea Lingua, 3620 N. Washington Blvd., Indianapolis, IN 46250 Phone: (317)920-1600 Fax: (317)920-1601
e-mail: staff@pangealingua.com Web site: www.pangealingua.com Contact: Alessandra Matas
Founded 1994. Member: ATA. Accepts resumes. Translates mainly Spanish, Japanese, German, Chinese, French, Dutch, Portuguese and Russian. Mostly medical, pharmaceutical, promotional, legal and automotive. Maintains pool of over 1000 translators.

Para-Plus Translations, Inc., PO Box 92, Barrington, NJ 08007 Phone: (609)547-3695 Fax:(609)547-3345
e-mail: paraplus@erols.com Web site: www.para-plus.com Contact: Sonia Santiago, President
Founded 1981. Member: DVTA, NAJIT, ATA. Translates Spanish, German, French, Creole, Chinese, Japanese, Korean, Italian, Russian, Vietnamese, Arabic and Korean, both from and into English.Emphasis on Legal, Medical, Pharmaceutical and Technical translation. Prospective translators must be native speakers, college graduates, and have areas of special expertise. Candidates should submit a list of equipment available to them, as well as a sample of their work. Resumes are reviewed and a follow-up letter sent in response. The company also provides interpretation services in over 75 language and foreign-language tape translations and transcriptions. Maintains a pool of approximately 95 translators.

Paragon Language Services, 5657 Wilshire Blvd., Ste. 310, Los Angeles, CA 90036 Phone: (323)966-4655 Fax: (323)651-1867 e-mail: info@paragonls.com Web site: www.paragonls.com Contact: Hanne R. Mintz Member: ATA

Peritus Precision Translations, Inc., 727 Industrial Rd., #710, San Carlos, CA 94070 Phone: (650)631-6667 Fax: (650)631-6664 e-mail: info@peritustranslations.com Web site: www.peritustranslations.com Contact: Dagmar Dolatshko Member: ATA

Phoenix Translations, 6306 Highland Hills Drive, Austin, TX 78731 hone: (877)452-1348 Fax: (512)343-6721
e-mail: phoenixtranslations@ev1.net Contact: Deborah K. Cooper Member: ATA

Planet Leap, 220 Fifth Ave., 11th Fl., New York, NY 10001 Phone: (212)726-4061 Fax: (212)726-4020
e-mail: rceruzzi@planetleap,com Web site: www.planetleap.com Contact: Rossana Ceruzzi Member: ATA

Precision Translating Services, 150 W. Flagler St., Penthouse II, Miami, FL 33130 Phone: (305)373-7874 Fax: (305)381-7874 e-mail: vince@pretran.com Web site: www.pretran.com Contact: Vicente J. de la Vega Member: ATA

Premier Translation Services, Ltd., 62 Stonicker Drive, Lawrenceville NJ 08648 Phone:(609)530-0230 Fax:(609)530-0079 e-mail: rzarelli@premiertranslationsusa.com Web site: www.premiertranslationsusa.com
Contact: Renée Zarelli, Esq., President
Founded 1994. Member: ATA. Accepts resumes. Translates mainly French, Italian, Spanish and Portuguese. Emphasis on legal translation and business. Prospective translators should be ATA members, accredited if applicable. Three+ years full-time experience, college education or higher. Equipment should include WP or Word and modem. Resumes are reviewed on a monthly basis. The company specializes in using lawyers and individuals with a strong legal background, in both U.S. and other legal systems, for translation and editing. Ph.D.s in chemistry/physics and engineers are also used for patent translation. Maintains a pool of 150 translators.

Princeton Technical Translation Center, 333 Bolton Rd., East Windsor, NJ 08520 Phone: (609)443-6770 Fax: (609)443-6778 Contact: Charles Teubner, Director

Founded 1982. Member: ATA, STC. Translates French, German, Spanish, Italian, Portuguese, Chinese, Japanese, Russian and Scandinavian languages, both from and into English. Prospective translators should have advanced technical degrees and be proficient in Word/WordPerfect and related software.

Professional Translating Services Inc., 44 West Flagler St., Ste. 540, Miami, FL 33130 Phone: (305)371-7887 Fax: (305)381-9824 e-mail: translate@protranslating.com Web site: www.protranslating.com
Contact: Luis A. de la Vega
Founded 1973. Member: ATA. Accepts resumes. Translates mainly Spanish, Portuguese, French, Italian, German, Japanese, Russian, Chinese, Arabic and Hebrew. Translations are in legal, technical, financial and advertising. Has a pool of over 350 translators.

Professional Translation Services, LLC, 2323 Vista Ave., Ste. 201, Boise, ID 83705 Phone: (208)343-1444 Fax: (208)422-9840 e-mail: daniella@languagesus.com Web site: www.languagesus.com
Contact: Daniella de la Torre Emerson Member: ATA

ProTrans, Inc., P.O.Box 507, 74 Gov. Bradford Dr. Barrington, RI 02806 Phone: (401)245-9535 Fax: (401)245-9534 e-mail: protrans@ids.net Web site: www.protrans1. com Contact: H. Karin Weldy Member: ATA
Founded 1989. Member: ATA, NETA, Greater Providence Chamber of Commerce, WACRI. Uses freelance translators. Accepts unsolicited resumes. Applicants should provide sample translations, references, work history; they need to be *full-time* translators. Resumes usually result in Contact to ask questions, determine fees and check references. Main languages are English into Spanish, Portuguese, French, German, Italian, Japanese, Chinese, and Swedish. Also German, Dutch into English, and English into Cambodian and Laotian. Emphasis on technical manuals, automotive, legal, ad copy, educational, brochures, and catalogs. Maintains a pool of about 350 translators.

ProZ.com, 1448 Madison St., Apt. 410, Oakland, CA 94612 Phone: (510)682-3231
e-mail: henry@proz.com Web site: www.proz.com Contact: Henry J. Dotterer Member: ATA

PTIGLOBAL, 9900 SW Wilshire, Ste. 280, Portland, OR 97225 Phone:(503)297-2165 Fax:(503)297-0655
e-mail: info@ptiglobal.com Web site: www.ptiglobal.com Contact: Mollie Peters
Founded 1977. Member: ATA. Uses freelance translators and interpreters. Accepts unsolicited resumes. Resumes are reviewed, graded, and kept in database. Requires FrameMaker; Trados helpful. Main subjects are technical, software, and web applications.

-Q-

Quality Interpreting, 367 University Ave., Ste. 4, Saint Paul, MN 55103 Phone: (651)244-0066 Fax: (651)312-0270
Contact: Paul Yang Member: ATA

Quantum, Inc., 240 S. 9th St., Philadelphia, PA 19107 hone: (215)627-2251 Fax: (215)627-5570
e-mail: www.quantumtrans@msn.com Contact: Quan Pham Member: ATA

Quintana Multi-Lingual Services, Inc., 3050 W. Cermak Rd., Chicago, IL 60623 Phone: (773)277-0000 Fax: (773)277-1804 e-mail: quintana@compuserve.com Contact: Gloria K. Quintana

-R-

RIC International, Inc., 955 Massachusetts Ave., PMB 342, Cambridge, MA 02139 Phone: (617)666-4555 Fax: (617)666-8896 e-mail: r-i-c.com Web site: www.r-i-c.com Contact: Member: ATA

R.R. Donnelley Financial Translation Services, 75 Park Place, New York, NY 10007 Phone: (212)341-7416 Fax: (212)341-7532 e-mail: FBUTRansServ@rrd.com Contact: Aouck F. Le Fur Member: ATA

Ralph McElroy Translation Company, PO Box 4828, Austin, TX 78765 Phone: (512)472-6753 Fax: (512)472-4591
e-mail: tc@mcelroytranslation.com Web site: www.mcelroytranslation.com Contact: Patricia Bown
Founded 1968. Member: ATA, STC. Accepts resumes. Translates mainly German, Japanese, French, Spanish, Italian, Portuguese, Russian, Chinese, Dutch and Korean. Mostly engineering, technical, medical, legal, pharmaceutical, chemical, patents, localization and high tech. Several hundred active translators.

Rancho Park Publishing, 2203 Balsam Ave., Los Angeles, CA 90064 Phone:(310)470-7488 Fax:(310)470-7930
e-mail: sales@ranchopark.com Web site: www.ranchopark.com Contact: Stan Cheren

Founded 1988. Translates Spanish, French, German, Portuguese and German. Mostly sales and marketing, books and brochures. Prospective translators should have 10+ years experience and full computer /online capabilities. Resumes are filed for future projects. The company also has desktop publishing capabilities. Maintains a pool of over 700 translators.

Rapport International, 3 Stonegate Lane, #3 Middleboro, MA 02346 Phone: (508)946-3443 Fax: (508)946-3533 e-mail: rapport@rapportintl.com Web site: www.rapportintl.com Contact: Lisa Gavigan Member: ATA

Rennert Bilingual Translations, 216 East 45th St., 17th Fl. New York, NY 10025 Phone:(212)867-8700 Fax:(212)867-7666 e-mail: translations@rennert.com Web site: www.rennert.com Contact: Mikael Poulsen, Director
Founded 1973. Member: ATA, New York Circle of Translators. Translates all languages. Emphasis on all aspects of Patent Law, Marketing, Public Relations, Business and Finance, Videos and Educational Material translation, and web site localization. Prospective translators should possess training and experience in the specific fields. Resumes are reviewed for education and experience, and a Rennert application is sent to the translator for completion. Maintains a pool of 3000 translators.

Rescribe, P.O. Box 503981, San Diego, CA 92150 Phone: (858)487-5292 Fax: (858)487-5292
e-mail: erin@rescribe.com Web site: www.rescribe.com Contact: Erin Berzins
Founded 2001. Member: ATA. Accepts resumes. Translates mainly Spanish, French, Chinese, Vietnamese, Japanese, Italian, German, Korean and Russian. Mostly legal, insurance, medical, finance and insurance. Has a pool of several thousand translators.

Richard Schneider Enterprises, Inc., 27875 Berwick Drive, #A, Carmel, CA 93923 Phone: (831)622-0554 Fax: (831)622-0524 e-mail: service@idioms.com Web site: www.idioms.com Contact: Richard A. Schneider Member: ATA

Rosetta, 2261 Market St. #318, San Francisco, CA 94114 Phone: (415) 550-9151 Fax: (415)550-9162 e-mail: oshea@sirius.com Contact: Christina O'Shea, Director
Founded 1995. Member: ATA. Translates Japanese, Chinese, French, German and Korean, both from and into English, and Italian, Spanish, Thai, Swedish, Norwegian, Polish, Danish, Dutch, Portuguese and Russian into English. Emphasis on Computer (hardware and software), Semiconductors, Chemical, Medical, Pharmaceutical, Automotive, Patent, Business, and Marketing translation. Prospective translators should have at least five years experience as translators, plus five years experience in a technical field or in business, and a degree in their area of specialization. Resumes are entered into a data base and sent a test if they fulfill company requirements. The company hires translators with technical specialties as opposed to "generalists" and has every document reviewed for accuracy by a technical editor. Maintains an "active" pool of 50 translators.

Rosetta Stone Associates, Inc., 34 Franklin St., Ste. 200A, Nashua, NH 03063 Phone: (603)883-9388 Fax: (603)595-8673 e-mail: translate@rosettastoneinc.net Web site: www.rosettastoneinc.net Contact: Jana Coughlin
Founded 1972. Member: ATA, STC. Accepts resumes. Translates mainly French, Italian, German, Spanish, Russian, Chinese, Japanese, Arabic, Portuguese and Greek. Mostly industrial, medical, legal, scientific, marketing, computers, software and localization. Uses pool of over 2000 translators.

Russian and Slavic Language Services, 271 Madison Ave., 3rd Fl., New York, NY 10016 Phone: (212)481-4980 Fax: (212)683-4801 e-mail: karina@russiantranslation.com Web site: www.russiantranslation.com Contact: Karina Gukasyan Member: ATA

RussTech, 1338 Vickers Rd., Tallahassee, FL 32303 Phone: (850)562-9811 Fax: (850)562-9815
e-mail: Contact: Cynthia Seaborn Member: ATA

-S-

SBF Translation Services, Inc., P.O. Box 940818, Miami, FL 33194 hone: (305)553-1927 Fax: (305)551-6872 e-mail: SBFTrans@aol.com Contact: Silvia B. Fernandez
Founded 1994. Member: ATA. Accepts resumes. Translates Spanish, Portuguese and Creole. Mostly legal, medical, immigration and Christian books. Has three translators.

SH3, Inc., 5338 East 115th St., Kansas City, MO 64137 Phone: (816)767-1117Fax:(816)767-1727
e-mail: chubbard@sh3.com Web site: www.sh3.com Contact: Cathy Hubbard, General Manager
Founded 1980. Member: ATA, STC. Translates mainly French, German, Spanish, Italian, Dutch, Portuguese, Swedish, Chinese and Japanese. Emphasis on Agricultural and Industrial Equipment, and Consumer Equipment translation. Prospective translators should have Windows-based computer, modem and fax; they should have experience in the agriculture, industrial and mechanical areas. Translator's Workbench is a definite plus. Resumes are reviewed by subject specialty, experience, and language, and flagged for a future Contact.

Does around 20 million words a year. The company deals in high volume, highly technical manuals. Maintains an active pool of 70 translators.

Sally Low and Associates, 600 West Santa Ana Blvd., Ste. #208, Santa Ana, CA 92701 Phone: (714)834-9032 Fax: (714)834-9035 e-mail: slasehabla@aol.com Contact: Lisa Hall
Founded 1979. Member: ATA. Accepts resumes. Translates mainly Spanish, Vietnamese, Korean, Arabic, German, French, Italian, Japanese, Taglog and Chinese. Provides interpreter services. Has a pool of over 300 translators.

SARJAM Communications, Ltd., 4370 NE Hulsey St., Ste. 122, Portland, OR 97213 Phone:(503)287-9277 Fax:(503)287-9277 e-mail: 70314. 1226@compuserve.com Contact: Seth A. Reames
Founded 1987.Member: ATA. Translates Japanese, Korean, Chinese, Spanish, German, French, Italian and Russian, both from and into English. Translates all subjects. Prospective translators should have 5+ years experience, a computer (MAC or PC), fax and modem. Resumes are examined and filed by language. The company also offers desktop publishing and graphic design. Their in-house computers are Macintosh. Maintains a pool of 40-50 translators.

Schreiber Translations, Inc., 51 Monroe St., Ste. 101, Rockville, MD 20850 Phone:(301)424-7737 Fax:(301)424-2336 e-mail: translation@schreibernet.com Web site: www.schreibernet.com Contact: Walter Stankewick, Director, Translation Services
Founded 1984. Member: ATA. Uses freelance translators and interpreters. Accepts unsolicited resumes only on web site. Translates (both ways) mainly Japanese, Russian, German, French, Spanish, Chinese, Italian, Arabic, Korean, Vietnamese, Hebrew, Polish, and Dutch, and close to 90 additional languages and dialects. Emphasis on patents, aerospace, law, medicine, communications, computers, engineering, public relations, military and maritime subjects, chemical subjects, and business and finance. Maintains a pool of over 1300 translators - 350 active, and 200 of those very active. In addition to translation and interpretation, the company produces multilingual brochures and advertisements, prints manuals and business literature in a variety of multinational fonts, and does voiceovers for video and films. Maintains a pool of over 1300 translators - 350 active, and 200 of those very active.

Scitran, 1482 East Valley Rd., Ste. 15, Santa Barbara, CA 93150 Phone: (805)969-2413 Fax:(805)969-3439 e-mail: 71046.1337@compu-serve.com Contact: Revay Seifert
Founded 1972. Accepts resumes. Translates over 45 languages in all scientific disciplines.

Sebastian Lantos, LLC, 5111 East 89th Court, Tulsa, OK 74137 Phone:(918)481-1465 Fax: (918)481-0841 e-mail: language@gorilla.net eb site: lantosconsulting.com Contact: Tanya Shevchuk, Office Manager
Founded 1996. Member: NAJIT. Accepts resumes. Translates mainly Spanish, French, Italian, Chinese, Japanese, Russian, Ukrainian, Korean and German. Mains areas are medical, legal, and federal. The company also specializes in language tutoring, Hispanic personnel bilingual training. Maintains a pool of 20 translators.

Semantics Translations & Publishing, Inc., 3544 NW 99th Ave., Coral Springs, FL 33065 Phone: (954)341-4721 Fax: (954)341-8606 e-mail: getmeaning@sematicstp.com Web site: www.sematicstp.com Contact: Pedro M. Liveira Member: ATA

Semantix, 1660 International Drive, Ste. 400, McLean, Va 22102 Phone: (703)287-0091 Fax: (703)288-4003 e-mail: araswork@sematix.com Web site: www.semantix.com Contact: Andy Ras-Work Member: ATA

Siemens Medical-Ultrsound Group, 22010 SE 51st St., P.O. Box 7002, Issaquah, WA 98029 Phone: (425)392-9180 Fax: (425)557-1780 e-mail: marybeth.sloan@usg.sms.siemens.com Web site: www.siemensultrasound.com Contact: Mary Beth Sloan Member: ATA

SimulTrans, LLC, 1370 Willow Rd., Menlo Park, CA 94025 Phone: (650)969-3500 Fax: (650)969-9959 e-mail: mark@simultrans.co Web site: www.simultrans.com Contact: Mark Homnack, President
Founded 1984. Member: ATA. Translates in all major languages. Covers all major technical areas. Prospective translators should have either a translation degree or professional experience, as well as native fluency. Resumes should be faxed or e-mailed. The company also offers formatting and typesetting services and possesses a digital typesetter for both European and Asian languages. They also provide software localization and desktop publishing. Maintains a pool of in-house translators (in French, German, Italian, Japanese, and Spanish), as well as using freelancers.

SinoMetrics International, Inc., 3503 188th St. SW, Lynnwood, WA 98115 Phone: (425)776-5648 Fax: (425)776-6648 email: info@sinomet.com Web site: www.sinomet.com Member: ATA

Speak Easy Languages, 757 South Main St., Plymouth, MI 48170 Phone:(734)459-5556 Fax:(734)459-1460 e-mail: selanguages@earthlink. net Contact: Cristina Clark

Founded 1980. Member: ATA. Translates all major language pairs. Emphasis on Automotive business, Brochure, Advertising and Legal translation. Prospective translators should be ATA accredited and possess fax and modem capabilities. Resumes are filed and the applicant called upon as the circumstance arises. The company also provides talent for voiceover work. Maintains a pool of 100 translators.

Spectrum Multilanguage Communications, 225 West 39th St., New York, NY 10018 Phone: (212)391-3940 Fax: (212)921-5246 e-mail: 76046.2123@compuserve.com Web site: www.come.to/spectrum Contact: Richard N. Weltz
Founded 1955. Member: ATA, DGA, IDIA. Translates Spanish, French, German, Italian, Japanese, Chinese, Russian, Arabic, Dutch and all major busi-ness languages from English. Emphasis on Marketing, Advertising, Packaging and Public Relations translation. Prospective translators should exhibit a high degree of competence, reliability, and excellent writing style. They should possess a modem, fax, and word processing capabilities. Resumes are reviewed by the language resources manager. Provides complete ad-quality in-house typesetting and color pre-press capabilities in virtually all languages and alphabets.

Square D/Schneider Electric North American Division, 1415 S. Roselle Rd., Palatine IL 60067
Phone: (630)279-2395 Fax: (630)279-3687 email: schreibm@squared.com Web site: www.squared.com
Contact: Marie-France O. Schreiber Member: ATA

Star USA, 477 S. Main St., Plymouth, MI 48170 Phone: (734)416-1865 Fax: (734)416-1867
e-mail: jre@starusa-mi.com Web site: www.starusa-mi.com Contact: Jan R. Eisen Member: ATA

State Farm Insurance, One State Farm Plaza, SC-2, Bloomington, IL 61710 Phone: (309)766-3760
Contact: Joan Epperson Member: ATA

Superior Translations, 1924 Minnesota Ave., Duluth, MN 55802 Phone: (218) 727-2572 Fax: (218)727-2653
e-mail: towardinc@aol.com Web site: www.interpretazioni.com Contact: Elisa A. Troiani
Founded 1993. Member: ATA. Uses freelance translators and interpreters. Accept unsolicited resumes. Resumes for translation and interpretation should be mailed. Applicants are carefully screened and required to submit samples, references, and times tests. Requirements are honesty, accuracy, editing/proofing skills, reason-able rates, punctuality, and an eye for detail. Translates mainly Spanish, French, German, Japanese, Chinese, Russian, Portuguese, Italian, Polish and Hmong. Emphasis on all subject areas. Has 250-300 translators in its pool.

Suzuki, Myers & Associates, Ltd., P.O. Box 852, Novi, MI 48376 Phone:(248)344-0909 Fax:(248)344-0092
e-mail: language@suzukimyers.com Web site: www.suzukimyers.com Contact: Kumiko Oh
Founded 1984. Member: ATA, MITN, Japan-America Society. Translates Japanese and Korean only, both from and into English. Emphasis on Manufacturing-related translation (Autos, Engineering, Quality Design, Robotics, Plastics, Assembly, Electronics, Paint, Contracts, Product Liability).Prospective translators should be competent and diligent. Resumes are responded to with a phone call. The company provides translation, interpretation, and consultation services in North American-Japanese relations. They also provide DTP services. Maintains a pool of about 40 translators.

Sykes Enterprises, Incorporated, 5757 Central Ave., Ste. G, Boulder, CO 80301 Phone:(303)440-0909 Fax:(303)440-6369 e-mail: wpid@corp. sykes.com Web site: sykes.com Contact: Recruiting Coordinator, Worldwide Product Information Development
Founded in 1977. Member: ATA, CTA, LISA, STC. Accepts resumes. Looks for linguists specialized in localization. Requires native language ability. Prefers translation degree. Applicants are tested. Must have full PC processing and communication ability. Main languages are English into all major Asian, Middle Eastern, Latin American, and European languages. Main areas are software, hardware, on-line help, and documentation. Provides information support services. Language services are coordinated from Boulder, Colorado, Edinburgh, Scotland, and Leuven, Belgium.

Synapse Intercultural Communications, 35560 Grand River Ave., Ste. 417, Farmington Hills, MI 48335
Phone: (248)473-4499 Fax: (248)473-1499 e-mail: synintcm@ix.netcom.com Contact: Curt Nielsen, Manager
Founded 1991. Translates German, French, Spanish, Italian, Japanese and Chinese from and into English. Emphasis on technical translations for the automotive industry. Resumes for freelance translation and interpretation are kept on file. Has a few dozen translators in its pool.

Syntes Language Group, Inc., 7465 E.Peakview Ave., Englewood, CO 80111 Phone:(303)779-1288 Fax:(303)779-1232
e-mail: linda.eaton@syntes.com Web site: www.syntes.com Contact: Linda Eaton
Founded 1988. Member: ATA Translates Spanish, French, German, Japanese, Portuguese and Italian both from and into English, and Russian, Chinese and Vietnamese from English. Specialties in Legal, Oil & Gas Patents, Com-puters, Marketing Materials, Video Scripts, Engineering, Medical and Technical translation. The company's work is 60-70% translation and 30-40% interpreting. In addition to translators and interpreters, the company is interested in hearing from detail-oriented editors. Maintains a pool of 1600 translators.

Techno-Graphics and Translations, Inc., 1451 East 168th St., South Holland, IL 60473 Phone: (708)331-3333 Fax: (708)331-0003 e-mail: techno@wetrans4u.com Web site: www.wetrans4u.com Contact: Pinay Gaffney
Founded 1972. Member: ATA. Uses freelance translators and interpreters. Accepts unsolicited resumes. Resumes are entered in database. Requires native ability and technical background. Translates (both ways) mainly European, Asian, and Middle Eastern languages. Main areas are telecommunications, agriculture, industry, automotive, and medical. Worldwide pool of 200 translators.

TechTrans International, Inc., 2200 Space Park Drive, Ste. 410, Houston, TX 77058 Phone: (281)335-8000 Fax: (281)333-3503 e-mail: techtrans@tti-corp.com Web site: www.tti-corp.com Contact: Beth Williams Member: ATA

Techworld language Services, Inc., 1250 W. 14 Mile Rd., Ste. 102, Clawson, MI 48017 Phone: (248)288-5900 Fax: (248)288-7900 e-mail: info@techworldinc.com Web site: www.techworldinc.com Contact: Fred Meinberg Member: ATA

Tele-Interpreters On-Call, Inc., 447 W. Burchett St., 2nd Fl., Glendale, CA 91203 Phone: (818)638-2511 Fax: (818)543-6781 e-mail: dt@teleinterpreters.com Web site: www.tele-interpreters.com Contact: Daniel Trevor Member: ATA

TerraSpan, Inc., 12647 Alcosta Blvd., Ste. 150, San Ramon, CA 94583
Phone: (925)866-3030 Fax: (925)866-3036 e-mail: galiloupour@terraspan.com Web site: www.erraspan.com
Contact: Gloria Aliloupour Member: ATA

TEXTnology CORPoration, 20 Trafalgar Square, Ste. 456, Nashua, NH 03063 Phone:(603)883-8398 Fax:(603)883-8998 e-mail: nadeau@textcorp.com Web site: www.textcorp.com Contact: Ronald Nadeau Member: ATA

Thomas Computer Solutions, 21213-B Hawthorne Blvd., #5367, Torrance, CA 90503 Phone: (310)921-2611 Fax: (310)921-9676 e-mail: info@thomascomputersolutions.com Web site: www.homascomputersolutions.com
Contact: Tracy Zehnder
Founded 1995. Member: ATA. Accepts resumes. Translates mainly Spanish, Russian, Armenian, Chinese, Thai, Arabic, Hebrew, Farsi, Jamaican Patois and Korean. Mostly medical, banking and legal. Has a pool of 300 translators.

3 Way Talk, 2255 Skyfarm Drive, Hillsborough, CA 94010 Web site: www.3waytalk.com
Contact: Dr. B. Goldstein Member: ATA

3DWord, Inc., 4325 Athens High Way, Ste. 4-13, Loganville, GA 30052 Phone: (770)613-0879 Fax: (770)849-9627 e-mail: julieMacgregr@3word.com Web site: www.3word.com Contact: Julie MacGregor Member: ATA

TLS - Translation Service, 69 Broad St., Red Bank, NJ 07701 Phone: (732)530-4542 Fax: (732)530-6755 e-mail: trans90@aol.com Contact: Ingeborg Perndorfer
Founded 1982. Member: ATA. Uses freelancers and accepts unsolicted resumes. Resumes are check and filed until needed. Applicants must show experience. Translates all languages and all subjects. Maintains a pool of 30-50 translators.

Total Benefit Communications, Inc., 5775-B Glenridge Drive, Ste. 120, Atlanta, GA 30328 Phone: (404)256-5042 Fax: (404)256-5101 Contact: Anne McKillips Member: ATA

Total System Services, Inc., 1600 First Ave., TSYS Corporate Campus, 1st Fl., #1318, Columbus, GA 31901
Phone: (706)649-5450 Fax: (706)649-8148 e-mail: Evan Latham Contact: Member: ATA

Toward, 1924 Minnesota Ave., Duluth, MN 55802 Phone: (218)727-2572 Fax: (218)727-2653
e-mail: towardinc@aol.com Web site: www.interpretazioni.com Contact: Dr. Elisa A. Troiani Member: ATA

TRADOS Corporation, 113 S. Columbus St., Ste. 400, Alexandria, VA 22314 Phone: (703)683-6900 Fax: (703)683-9457 e-mail: edith@trados.com Web site: www.trados.com Contact: Edith Westfall Member: ATA

Traducciones LinguaCorp, Poba International, #1-20072, P.O. Box 02-5255, Miami, FL 33102 Phone: 58(2)7625745 Fax: 58(2)7625745 e-mail: linguacorp@compuserve.com Contact: Francisco J. Pance Member: ATA

Trans Global Translation & Immigration Services, 175 Fontainbleau Blvd., Ste. 2G 8, Miami, FL 33172

Phone: (305)552-9793 Fax: (305)223-4080 e-mail: trnsglobal@aol.com Member: ATA

TransACT Inc., 8423 Mukilteo Speedway, Ste. 100, Mukilteo, WA 98275 Phone:(206)348-5000 Fax:(206)348-3095 e-mail: support @transact.com Web site: www.transact.com Contact: Ms. Tomi Renshaw
Founded 1994. Member: ATA, NOTIS, Washington Software Assn., ASCD. Translates Spanish, Russian, Cambodian, Korean, Chinese, Lao, Thai, Arabic, Japanese and Vietnamese from English. Emphasis on Education, Medical and Utilities translation. Prospective translators must have computer skills and PageMaker experience. Resumes are reviewed and applicants contacted if needed. The company specializes in translation and typesetting for school districts in the US. Their software division creates custom CD-ROMs for Mac/Win in all languages. Maintains a pool of 20 translators.

Trans-Caribe Communications, Inc., 9109 Queen Elizabeth Court, Orlando, FL 32818 Phone: (407)260- Fax: (407)260-6349 e-mail: transcc@aol.com Web site: www.iotrak.com/trans-caribe.html Contact: Sherry E. Allen-Diaz Member: ATA

Transcend, 2043 Anderson Rd., Ste. C, Davis, CA 95616 Phone: (530)756-5834 Fax:(756)756-4810 e-mail: end@transcend.com Web site: www.transcend.com Contact: M. Mindlin
Founded 1991. Recruiting translators in Chinese, Korean, Cambodian, Farsi and Lao, from English, and Japanese into English. Prospective translators should have 3+ years experience, accreditation or certification, professional standards, and Internet/FTP capabilities. Resumes are accepted only by fax and only for the languages listed above.

Transemantics, Inc., 4301 Connecticut Ave. NW, Ste. 146, Washing-ton, DC 20008 Phone: (202)686-5600 Fax: (202)686-5603 Contact: M-L Wax Cooperman Member: ATA

Transfirex Translation Services, Inc., 12509 Village Sq. Terr., #201, Rockville, MD 20852 Phone: (301)984-9753 Fax: (630)604-8323 e-mail: info@transfirex.com Web site: www.transfirex.com Contact: Margaret Johnson
Founded 2001. Member: ATA. Accepts resumes. Main languages are Turkish, German, Spanish, Italian, French and Portuguese.Mostly scientific, engineering, social sciences, and safety, emergency and rescue. Has a pool of 12 translators.

TRANSGLOBAL Language Services, 534 Princeton Cove, Memphis, TN 38117 Phone: (901)680-0927 Contact: Robyn Hassell

TransImage Inc., 145 Hudson St., 9th Fl., New York, NY 10013 hone: (212)274-0501 Fax: (212)274-0503 e-mail: Joseph@transimage.com Web site: www.transimage.com Contact: Joseph Ruiz Member: ATA

Transimpex Translations, 8301 East 166th St., Belton, MO 64012 Phone: (816)561-3777 Fax:(816)561-5515 e-mail: transmpx@sound.net Web site: www.transimpex.com Contact: Ingrid Pelger or Doris Ganser
Founded 1974. Member: ATA. Trade Club of Greater Kansas City. Uses freelance translators and interpreters. Accepts unsolicited resumes. Resumes are put in database until needed. Requires degree in linguistics or translation. Main languages translated are German, French, Spanish, Portuguese, Italian, Japanese, Russian, and Arabic. Translates all subjects, with long experience in localization. Has overall pool of some 5000 translators, with about 150 active ones.

Translation Aces, Inc., 29 Broadway, Ste. 2301, New York, NY 10006 Phone: (212)269-4660 Fax: (212)269-4662 Contact: Serge Nedeltscheff
Founded 1952. Member: NY Circle, NY Chamber of Commerce. Translates Spanish, French, German, Japanese Italian, Portuguese, Russian and Greek, both from and into English, as well as *all* other language pairs. Emphasis on Legal, Patent, Medical Financial, Scientific, Advertising, Engineering, and almost all other areas of translation. Prospective translators should have "experience, experience, experience." Resumes are responded to with the company's ap-plication form. The company has 45 years experience in providing the legal, financial, advertising, medical and governmental communities with translation, interpreting, voiceover and consulting services. Maintains a pool of about 400 translators.

Translation Company of America, Inc., 10 West 37th St., New York, NY 10018 Phone:(212)563-7054 Fax:(212)695-2385 e-mail: trude@tcany.com Web site: www.languagematters.com Contact: Trudi Mathys Member: ATA

Translation Company of New York, Inc., 8 South Maple Ave., Marlton, NY 08053 Phone: (856)983-4733 Fax: (856)983-4595 e-mail: tcny2000@cs.com Web site: www.tcny.net Contact: Betsy Lussi
Founded 1983. Member: ATA. Uses freelance translators and accepts unsolicited resumes. Translates mainly French, German,Spanish, Italian, Japanese, Portuguese, Dutch, Russian, Chinese and Swedish. Main areas are pharmaceutical, chemical, medical, engineering, and electronics. Does about 7-8 million words a year. Has active pool of 200 translators.

Translation Services, Inc., 5860 Forward Ave., Office #1, Pittsburgh, PA 15217 Phone: (412)242-8240 Fax: (412)242-1241
e-mail: ATA-info@translations.us.com
Web site: www.translations.us.com
Contact: Lisa M. Heinrich Member: ATA

Translation Services International, Inc., 417 E Blvd., Ste. 204, Charlotte, NC 28203 Phone: (704)375-8530 Fax: (704)375-8540
e-mail: info@tsitranslation.com Web site: www.tsitranslation.com
Contact: Robert E. Krasow Member: ATA

Translations & Language Consulting, 8105 Hearthstone Place, Antelope, CA 95843 Phone: (916)729-4222 Fax: (916)729-4232
e-mail: emorrow@trans-language.com
Web site: www.trans-language.com
Contact: Elena Morrow Member: ATA

Translations Unlimited, 1455 Forest Hill SE, Grand Rapids, MI 49546 Phone: (616)942-5742 Fax: (616)957-8551 e-mail: lmathews@calvin.edu Contact: Leslie Mathews, Director
Founded 1980. Member: ATA. Accepts resumes. Main languages are French, Spanish, German, Japanese, Portuguese, Italian, and Vietnamese. Main areas are patents, sales literature, video scripts, and voice-overs, employee handbooks, sales literature, legal documents, and technical specifications. Translator pool of 25-30.

translations.com, 3 Park Ave., 37th Fl., New York, NY 10016 Phone: (212)689-1616 Fax: (212)685-9797
e-mail: LRC@translations.com Web site: www.translations.com Contact: Pamela Kraljevich
Founded 1999. Member: ATA. Accepts resumes. Translates mainly Spanish, French, German, Chinese, Japanese, Portuguese, Italian, Korean, Norwegian and Swedish. Mostly software, IT-Telecom, finance, travel and medical. Provides full suite of globalization services. Pool of 500 translators.

Translation3, 49 Union Park, #2, Boston, MA 02118 Phone: (617)482-2223 Fax: (617)482-2121
e-mail: jjtranslation3@translation3.com Web site: www.translation3.com Contact: Jacqueline M. Jacquiot Member: ATA

The Translators, PO Box 303, Topsfield, MA 01983 Phone: (508)887-9234 Fax: (508)887-6657
e-mail: trnslate@shore.net Web site: www.thetranslatorsinc.com Contact: Maria Salmon
Founded 1980. Accepts resumes. Translates all languages, mostly medical, patents, human resources, computer, sci-tech, legal, electronic and engineering. Unlimited translator pool.

Translingua, Inc., 5457 Twin Knolls Rd., Columbia, MD 21045 Phone: (410)730-9700 Fax: (410)730-9736
e-mail: moneill@translingua.com Web site: www.translingua.com Contact: Mary J. O'Neill
Founded 1984. Member: ATA, NCATA, STC, CATI. Translates French, Italian, German, Spanish, Japanese, Chinese, Korean, Swedish, Danish, Portuguese, Russian, Hebrew, and Arabic from English. Emphasis on technical, scientific, medical, financial, software, packaging and labeling, marketing and advertising. Specialty in full-service graphics and high resolution double byte output. Prospective translators should have an area of expertise as well as a computer, email, modem, and fax. Resumes are screened, evaluated and databased. The company's translations, often large and multi-lingual, are aimed at publication and the end user. It provides services for the entire process from project management to printing. Maintains a pool of more than 1000 translators.

Transperfect, 2536 Barstow Ave., Clovis, CA 93611 Phone: (554)323-8915 Fax: (554)298-8996
e-mail: mortrans@lightspeed.net Web site: www.thetranslators.com Contact: Morton S. Rothberg
Founded 1992. Member: ATA, Fresno Chamber of Commerce, SJVITA, Hispanic Chamber. Uses freelance translators and interpreters. Accepts unsolicited resumes. Resumes are classified, graded, and filed. Requires college degree with specific language native ability, computer, e-mail. Main languages are Spanish, French, Portuguese, German, Chinese, Japanese, and Arabic. Main areas are food industry and legal. Has affiliate offices in Europe, South America, and the Far East. Pool of 250 translators.

Transperfect Translations International, Inc., 3 Park Ave., 28th Fl., New York, NY 10016 Phone: (212) 689-5555 Fax: (212)251-0981 e-mail: info@transperfect.com Web site: www.transperfect.com Contact: Information Member: ATA

Transtek Associates, Inc., 599 North Avenue, Door 9, Wakefield, MA 01888 Phone: (781) 245-7980 Fax: (781)245-7993 e-mail: michele@transtekusa.com Web site: www.transtekusa.com Contact: Michele Phillips
Founded 1964. Member: ATA. Uses freelance translators and interpreters. Accepts unsolicited resumes.

Tristan Translations, 1130 Taylor St., San Francisco, CA 94108 Phone:(415)474-2611 Fax:(415)928-4755 e-mail: tristant@ix.netcom .com Contact: Marc de Tristan, Jr., Owner.
Founded 1978. Accepts resumes. Translates Spanish, German, Chinese, Japanese, Portuguese, French, Italian, and numerous other languages, both from and into English. Emphasis on Patents, Technical Document, Proposals and RFQ, Discovery Document and Insurance Claim translation. Prospective translators should exhibit fluency in the English resume or phone Contact, education and word processing and file transfer skills. Resumes are read with an eye to flaws, and if approved, entered into a database for future work. Maintains a pool of over 100 translators.

Tru Lingua Language Systems, Inc., 2081 Business Center Drive, Irvine, CA 92626 Phone: (949)955-1151 Fax: (949)955-1153 e-mail: Trulingua@aol.com Contact: Diana Knapstein
Founded 1984. Accepts resumes. Translates mainly Spanish, French, German, Dutch, Portuguese and Japanese. Mostly technical, medical and lega. Prospective translators should be ATA certified, ATA members, and possess wide experience. Maintains a pool of over 350 translators.

Trustforte Language Services, 271 Madison Ave., 3rd Fl., New York, NY 10016 Phone: (212)481-4980 Fax: (212)481-4972 e-mail: aschroeder@trustforte.com Web site: www.trustfortelanguages.com Contact: Jackie Cordero
Founded 1992. Member: ATA. Accepts resumes. Works in most languages. Provides translators and interpreters to a variety of fields, from business to entertainment.

turkishtranslation.com, MSR Consulting Ltd., 33 N. High St., Clinton, CT 06143 Phone: (860)669-2777 Fax: (909)363-9150 e-mail: info@turkishtranslation.com Web site: www.turkishtranslation.com Contact: Asiye Yucel Member: ATA

-U-

Uniscape, Inc., 1292 Hammerwood Ave., Sunnyvale, CA 94089 Phone: (408)743-3500 Fax: (408)743-3600 Web site: www.uniscape.com Contact: Seda P. Mansour Member: ATA

United International Services, Inc., 12701 W. Warren, Dearborn, MI 48126 Phone: (313)846-6903 Fax: (313)846-4278 Contact: Faye Awada Member: ATA

United Nations Translators & Interpreters, Inc., 1515 E. Livingston St., Orlando, FL 32803 Phone: (407)894-6020 Fax: (407)894-6693 e-mail: unti@unti.com Web site: www.unti.com Contact: Fiona Como
Founded 1991. Member: ATA. Accepts resumes. Translates mainly Spanish, Creole, French, German, Arabic, Farsi, Italian, Portuguese and Vietnamese. Mostly legal, medical, technical and INS documents. Uses about 50 translators.

Universal Dialog, 4909 Murphy Canyon Rd., Ste. 301, San Diego, CA 92123 Phone: (858)503-0010 Fax: (858)503-1935 e-mail: email@universaldialog.com Web site: www.universaldialog.com Contact: Alexandra Briskin Member: ATA

University Language Center, Inc., 1313 Fifth St. SE, Ste. 201, Minneapolis, MN 55414 Phone:(612)379-3574 Fax:(612)379-3832 e-mail: translation@ulanguage.com Web site: ulanguage.com Contact: Therese Shafranski, Translation Department Manager
Founded 1986. Member: ATA. Accepts resumes. Translates Spanish, French, German, Italian, Portuguese, Russian, Chinese, Japanese and Hmong, as well as Turkish, Indonesian, Arabic and all Southeast Asian languages. Emphasis in all technical areas. The company handles all phases of production from translation to camera-ready art, including cultural assessment of the source documents. Maintains a pool of 250 translators.

U.S. Translation Company, 3701 Harrison Blvd., Ogden UT 84403 Phone: (801)393-5300 Fax: (801) 393-5500 e-mail: info@ustranslation.com Web site: www.ustranslation.com Contact: David Utrilla Member: ATA

-V-

Vanguard Academy, 6925 Turtlewood Drive, Houston, TX 77072 Phone: (281)530-9895 Fax: (281)575-0301 e-mail: vanguardacademy@hotmail.com Contact: Wendy Wang Member: ATA

Veduccio, Levine, Coleman, Sampson & Partners, 29 Winchester St., Boston, MA
Phone: (617)574-0040 Fax: (617)574-0041 e-mail: Contact@veduccio.com Web site: www.veduccio.com

Contact: Russell Veduccio Member: ATA

Ventwi Technology Partners, 400-1 Totten Pond Rd., Waltham, MA 02451 Phone: (781)890-7007 Fax: (781)890-4433 e-mail: mklinger@ventwipartners.com Web site: www.ventwipartners.com Contact: Michael L. Klinger
Founded: 1993. Member: ATA, NETA, STC. Accepts resumes. Translates mainly Japanese, French, Italian, German, Spanish, Korean, Chinese, Portuguese, Hebrew and Arabic. Mostly software, medical and pharmaceutical. Has a pool of 500 translators.

Vice-Versa Translations, 2707 N. Surrey, Carrollton, TX 75006 Phone: (972)418-6969
e-mail: gqs@earthlink.net Contact: Emilio Santiago Member: ATA

Vital International Programs, Inc., 2300 W. Big Beaver Rd., Ste. 17, Troy, MI 38084 Phone: (248)649-2905 Fax: (248)649- 2962 e-mail: vitalinter@aol.com Web site: www.vitalinternational.com Contact: Member: ATA

Voices for Health, Inc., 894 Fuller NE, #2, Grand Rapids, MI 49503 Phone: (616)458-8388 Fax: (616)458- 8322
e-mail: info@voicesforhealth.com Web site: www.voicesforhealth.com Contact: Scott Van Til, Translations; Iness Quillen, Interpretation.
Founded 1997. Member: ATA. Accepts resumes. Translates mainly Spanish, Vietnamese, Chinese and Arabic. Mostly healthcare and social services. Uses hundreds of linguists.

Vormbrock Translations, Inc., 10415 Jockey Club Drive, Houston, TX 77065 Phone: (281)894-9722 Fax: (281)890-0062 e-mail: VTITrans@pdq.net Web site: www.vormbrock.com Member: ATA

-W-

WKI International Communications, 27 W. 20th St., Ste. 402, New York, NY 10011 Phone: (212)255-6100 Fax: (212)255-8461 e-mail: smwoodruff@wkiintl.com Web site: www.wkiintl.com Contact: Susan Woodruff Member: ATA

Welocalize.com, 241 E. 4th St., Ste. 207, Frederick, MD 21701 Phone: (301)668-0330 Fax: (301)668-0335
e-mail: info@welocalize.com Web site: www.welocalize.com Contact: E. Smith Yewell Member: ATA

Wizards Of The Coast, Inc., P.O. Box 707, Renton, WA 98057 Fax: (425)204-5806 Web site: www.wizards.com
Contact: David Serra Member: ATA

Word for Word, Inc., 325 W. Chickasaw Rd., Virginia Beach, VA 23462 Phone: (757)557-0131 Fax: (757)557-0186
e-mail: wrd4wrd@exis.net Contact: Curtis Hovey Member: ATA

WORDNET, Inc., 282 Central St., Ste. 2, P.O. Box 976, Acton, MA 01720 Phone: (978)264-0600 Fax:(978)263-3839
e-mail: wordnet@wordnet.com Web site: www.wordnet.com Contact: lee Chadeayne
Founded 1985. Member: ATA, German-American Business Council. Uses freelance translators and interpreters. Accepts unsolicited resumes. Resumes are reviews and applicants are sent out forms to fill out, and are periodically tested and evaluated. Main languages translated are French, Spanish, German, Italian, Chinese, Japanese, and Korean. Main areas are technical, medical, machinery, legal, and business/marketing. The company specializes in translation, typesetting and printing, preparing brochures, catalogs, manuals, legal agreements and Web pages.They help companies get started in the international marketplace. Maintains a pool of some 2000 translators.

Worldwide Translations, Inc., 1 Warren Way, Amherst, NH 03031 Phone: (800)293-0412 Fax:(603)672-5574
e-mail: wwtranslate@cs.com Web site: www.wwtranslations.com Contact: Jared Tardie
Founded 1994. Member: ATA, RAPS, FDLI, DIA, NAJIT. Accepts resumes. Translates mainly French, Italian, German, Spanish, Dutch, Portuguese, Greek, Swedish, Japanese and Chinese. Emphasis on Medical, Machinery Manufacture and Computer Products translation. Prospective translators should be native-speaking ATA members with 3+ years technical translation experience and references. Resumes are responded to by telephone when work becomes available. The company is expert in the CE Mark and Medical Device areas and specializes in the translation of instructional manuals. They hold their translators to a high standard of accuracy. Maintains a pool of over 100 translators.

The Write Stuff, 11000 Lake City Way, NE, Seattle, WA 98125 Phone: (206)548-1111 Fax: (206)548-9116
e-mail: translations@writestuff.com Web site: www.writestuff.com Contact: Susan Hedding Member: ATA

Wudang Research Association, 8229 Perry St., Overland Park, KS 66204 Phone: (913)385-1975
e-mail: tmorgan@wudang.com Web site: www.wudang.com Contact: Theresa M. Morgan Member: ATA

APPENDIX F: COMPUTERS, TRANSLATION, AND THE INTERNET

Digital technology as it relates to translation and to almost anything else in today's world is in a constant state of change. In the nearly three years since this handbook was last revised, computers have become more dominant in the translation craft. More work is now being transmitted electronically by e-mail attachment rather than by fax. The Internet has become a routine tool for translators – from work search to word search. And a growing number of translators has become involved in the translation of such computer-based material as websites, a process now generally referred to as localization. All this has resulted in this newly revised and expanded chapter that looks at all the above developments and how they benefit or fail to benefit translators.

Once you have read this chapter you will be glad to find out that one thing has not changed, which should come as no surprise: translation continues to be a human, rather than a machine function. Computers are no closer now to replacing human translation than they were three years ago, or at any other time in the past. Notwithstanding the great benefits translators are deriving from the digital revolution, computers continue to be the tools, rather than the decision-makers of the translation process.

Computers and Related Equipment

As was mentioned before, only a few years ago a translator would use a pen or a typewriter to translate. In 1980, for example, the ultimate text-producing tool in the world was the IBM Selectric electric typewriter, which we thought we would proudly bequeath to our children and grandchildren. All of this changed forever with the birth of the word processor, and more specifically, the PC, or Personal Computer, which is getting better every year, as if it were a magical tool with boundless possibilities. Certainly the PC has changed the lives of translators, increasing their productivity and profitability three- and fourfold, and enabling them to receive and transmit work, look for answers to linguistic questions, communicate around the world, and take advantage of computer-assisted tools (see below) that in certain cases can save a great deal of time and effort.

Bare Minimum Hardware and the Wish List

The electronic age offers a great deal more than the word-processor. There is the fax, modem, optical scanner, e-mail, various types of translation software such as translation memory, and last but not least, the Internet. No doubt, it all seems quite overwhelming. Which is the best tool? How much should I spend? How much do I need?

Perhaps the best way to start is by asking two questions: What is the bare minimum a translator needs to get started, and, if money were no object, what would be my wish list of electronic equipment?

The first thing you need to get is a good, current personal computer. This is a must. The question is whether to get a desktop PC, or a portable notebook? The desktop PC is bigger,
heavier, has a larger, easier-to-read screen, and an easier-to-use keyboard. The notebook, on the other hand, only weighs a few pounds, can fit in your briefcase, can be used anywhere (it has a rechargeable battery that gives you several hours of use), and, like a toothbrush, becomes a truly personal item. This book is being revised on a three-year-old IBM ThinkPad notebook. Though thin (1.8 inches) and flimsy-looking, it is a real powerhouse. The base price was $1,699.00. For $99.98 I upgraded the memory from 32MB RAM (see glossary in the back of the book) to 64MB. For $225.98 I got a second battery for more cordless computing hours while traveling. For $237.98 I got a 3-year warrantee for parts and service. It has a 266MHz Intel Pentium II processor, 3.2GB of hard drive space (upgradable to 6.4GB), a 56K modem, a 3.5 inch disk drive, and a CD-ROM drive which at the moment hosts a disk containing the entire Encyclopedia Britannica. The color monitor, a 12-inch SVGA, has good, sharp resolution. It operates on Microsoft Windows® 98. I use it mainly for word-processing, for e-mail, to surf the net, occasionally for graphics, and sometimes to hear music. At the moment it has some 25 programs, including WordPerfect 6.0 for Windows, MS Word, Lotus Notes, as well as my Internet provider, to mention only a few.

To me as a translator and a writer, this notebook is the best of all possible worlds. On the other hand, many translators prefer a desktop PC for all sorts of reasons, not all of which are known to me. Since I have access to both, it's hard for me to judge. My suggestion to you is to check around and try both, and make your own decision. But again, a translator without a computer in this day and age is like a painter without brushes. One more thing:

The standard computer for translators is the IBM or IBM-compatible. The Macintosh, favored by graphics people, is not nearly as widely used in our circles, so we will concentrate here on the former.

The above configuration of my notebook computer, which one can also get in a desktop PC (except for the batteries), is quite close to what a translator would consider a "wish list" configur-ation. Keep in mind that there is a vast difference between storing text and storing graphics on a hard drive. One hundred pages of text take less disk space that one or two pages of graphics. If your translation work entails extensive graphics, you need a bigger hard drive and a faster computer, and the cost can go up 50%-100%. Most translators, however, do not have such a need. Instead, they can store data on their hard drive, and when it gets too crowded, they transfer files to a disk.

The other item that's a must is a printer. Although you can deliver text on disk or by e-mail, there are many good reasons why you need a printer. First, there is still a widespread requirement for hard copy. Second, you may want to print drafts to check your translation, and third, you need a printer for correspondence, for printing your resume, and certainly for printing an invoice. We recommend the Hewlett Packard family of printers, particularly the LaserJets. Depending on the volume, you can start with a smaller model and go up to the HP 4+ or a newer model, which is a bit faster and better.

The next item that's a must is the facsimile machine, popularly known as the fax. These days information travels very fast, and a sure way to get translation assignments is via the fax. Once you have translated a document, the fastest way to send it back is as an e-mail attachment. In other words, the basic translator tools today are the computer, the printer, the fax and the modem.

Another item you may want to look into is the optical scanner, starting with a recent model of the HP ScanJet family.
Be sure to get it with the OCR, or Optical Character Reader. This optional piece of equipment provides two valuable functions—you can scan text from a page into a disk, which can be a great timesaving shortcut, and you can scan graphics, such as tables and photographs, into your text file.

What about the cost? You can easily spend around $5,000 on the above four items, if you go directly to the top of the line. But you don't have to start at the top of the line. You can start a couple of notches below the top, and still be able to give yourself a decent start.

You could, if you really want to watch your pennies, take advantage of the fact that computers are changing so fast, and look in the paper for a year or two old second-hand computer, but not older. You should be able to find a good one for $400-$800. You can do the same with the printer, by getting a second-hand one for about $100, or a new one for about $300-$400. A good modem (at least a 28.8 or higher) can be found for around $100, although you could spend $300-$400. A plain paper fax machine (thermal paper is out) can be found for around $200-$400, or you could start out by using a local service, like Kinko's. In short, you could get started with the basic equipment for as little as $600-$700 if you had to, and go on from there. As you prosper, you can start upgrading.

Other Useful Kinds of Software

You can use your word-processing software for doing record-keeping and invoicing as well, but if your operation becomes more involved you may want to consider a database program, such as Excel, for record-keeping (and also for other databases, such as glossaries), and some basic invoicing program, which only runs $20-$30.

To protect your computer against computer viruses—the dreaded new computer age affliction—you may want to get a program such as Norton AntiVirus. To be able to retrieve lost text, you need the Norton Utilities program. Both are excellent safety measures. Another safety measure is the constant backing up of all your files. This can be done on the hard drive or on an external medium such as floppy disk or CD disk. Computers are great when they work, but when they fail they can cause you serious losses, which you cannot afford.

For word-processing, translators uses mainly Microsoft Word, but also WordPerfect, the old favorite.

Foreign Language Software

English-language word-processing is the most advanced in the world. Great strides have been made in programs for other languages, but there is still a long way to go. Some languages, such as Russian, Chinese, Japanese, Arabic and Hebrew are simply too complex in either their script or their noun and verb forms or both to lend themselves to, say, spell-check as readily as English. So don't expect to "cruise" as easily in those languages as

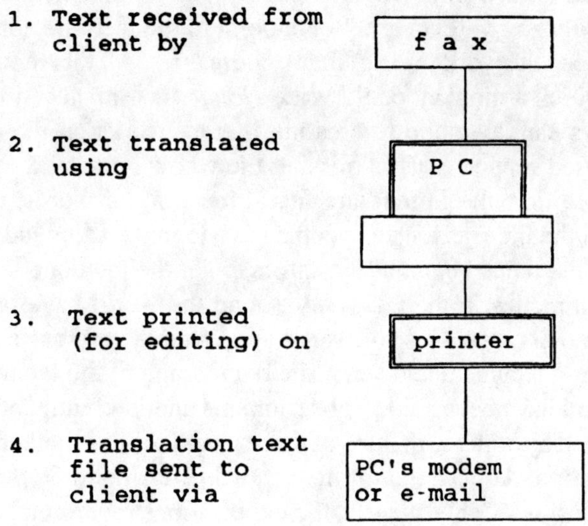

A typical translation process and the required hardware

you do in English. However, if you translate text from English into almost any other language, you are expected these days to deliver the text on electronic media, which means getting in-volved in word-processing in that language (see Appendix 3, Foreign Language Software Sources).

As a translator from English into a foreign language, you need software that accommodates not only your target-language, but also the source-language, namely, English. Sometimes you'll need to include English text in the body of your Chinese or Arabic text. Also, you have to make sure your foreign language software is compatible with English-language software, so that it can interface with your client's equipment. Therefore, we are focusing here on American-made foreign language software, rather than foreign-made.

Foreign Language Software Sources

In recent years the leading source for European languages software was WordPerfect. Its language modules covered a large variety of languages, and there were frequent upgrades. The WordPerfect foreign language modules are still used by many translators, but the trend is shifting to the localized products of Microsoft. These products use the Unicode system which makes Microsoft's English word processing compatible with its foreign versions, enabling the user to use English and foreign word processing in the same document with relative ease. Microsoft's foreign language word processing is now part of its package of English word processing, which eliminates the high cost only a few years ago of buying foreign language modules separately.

Machine Translation Vs. Human Translation

Machine Translation, or MT, is the term used to describe trans-lation performed by a computer software program, as an alter-native to human translation (HT), performed by a human translator. Machine Translation belongs in the area of artificial intel-ligence. Artificial intelligence is the branch of computer science that deals with using computers to simulate human thinking. It looks to create programs that can solve problems *creatively*, rather than merely respond to commands. In other words, to operate just like the human brain.

In the late 1950s people in organizations such as the U.S. Air Force believed that computers would soon be programmed to accept human language input and translate it into English or into any other language. During the following 50 years, millions of dollars were spent by the Air Force and by other U.S. Government bodies and by big business in the hope of having computers take over the human function of translation. So far, the results have been quite limited, for two main reasons: (a) while computers have a seemingly unlimited capacity for processing data, they are a long way from having the capacity to think creatively like human beings; and (b) human language is not merely a collection of signs and symbols that can be easily programmed, manipulated, and computerized. This is true of human language used not only in poetry and philosophy, but also in technical subjects, in which language expresses thought processes far more complicated than merely "one plus one equals two."

Many people today maintain that computers will soon replace translators. Most of those people are not translation experts. In fact, hardly any of them are. Some point to the fact that computers have already replaced typists and secretaries and reduced the work force of many companies. All this reminds me of a remark by George Bernard Shaw, according to which a monkey could write *Hamlet* if it managed to hit all the right keys on the typewriter. Very few translators can lay claim to creating literary works on the order of *Hamlet*, but lumping translators with typists and office support staff is missing the whole point of translation. As long as language continues to communicate more than the immediate literal meaning of words, as long as there are shades of meaning that keep changing all the time, as long as people have to make value judgments about the meaning and intent of a text, one will continue to need human translators to get the job done.

In recent years several companies in the U.S. and around the world have produced software designed to translate from one language into another. This software varies from a very basic word finder for the tourist, to complex programs for translating technical and scientific data. Some of the latter range in price from as low as $250 to as high as $250,000, and have been sold to governments and international organizations. One important lesson, however, has been learned by both the makers of those programs and their consumers. Machine translation does not replace human translation. At best, the former can achieve around 60 percent accuracy, when the goal is as close to 100 percent as possible. Consequently, the expectations regarding MT have been modified, and it is now recognized that to achieve full accuracy such translations must be post-edited by a human translator.

All of the above notwithstanding, Machine Translation does have its uses. Certain limited language environments do allow for machine translation. One example is the Canadian weather bureau, which transmits weather reports in both English and French. The number of words involved in the daily weather report is very limited, and can be easily programmed into a computer for translation from one language into another. Another example is official forms which contain simple basic questions. An organization such as NATO can have forms put out in ten different languages and set up a program to automatically translate each form into those languages. A third example is the Caterpillar company in Illinois that sells its agricultural machinery around the world and maintains operation manuals in various languages. This company has invested millions in its in-house translation software which allows it to update and modify its technical literature in a cost-effective way. In all of the above examples the software was customized for one particular work environment where repetition is the common denominator.

Another use of machine translation is for processing a large body of a foreign language text to find out what the gist of it is, rather than to achieve a fully accurate translation, in order to decide whether on not to select parts of it for accurate (viz., human) translation. This process is only partially reliable.

Translators for the most part are not fond of post-editing machine translation. Often the pay is not adequate, and the work can be harder and more time consuming than translating directly from the original. This certainly applies to freelancers, but also to in-house translators who are on a salary.

At the present time the ones who benefit the most from machine translation are not those who buy such services, but rather the companies who develop and manufacture the software and the translators who work on those machine translation projects either as developers of the programs or editors of the machine-translated text. In other words, machine translation has not made translation cheaper for the average consumer of trans-lation services, and therefore does not pose a real threat to translators.

Translation Memory

One computer tool commonly used today in the area of computer-assisted-translation (CAT) is called translation memory. Here sentences and other parts of translated texts are stored and can be used again when the same or similar translation is required. This tool is best applied to major projects, such as automotive operation manuals that are updated or modified on a regular basis, whereby most of the text remains the same while certain sentences and/or paragraphs are changed.

While this tool has its practical uses, it has been hyped beyond its actual application and has been promoted as a universal aid for translators in nearly all types of translation. Here one should be careful not to invest in this kind of software unless one has a clear ongoing use for it. This applies both to individual translators and to

Example of machine translation from Russian into English:

Raw machine translation: A contemporary airport is the involved complex of engineer constructions and techniques, for arrangement of which the territory, measured sometimes is required by thousands of hectares (for example the Moscow Airport Domodedovo, Kennedy's New York airport).

Text edited by humans: The modern airport is an elaborate complex of engineering structures and technical devices requiring a large territory, which, in some places, measures thousands of hectares (for instance, Domodedovo Airport in Moscow or Kennedy Airport in New York).

translation companies, since in both cases only a small percentage of the work done is of the above-described kind.

Furthermore, as in the case of machine translation and localization (see below), here too the tools are far from able to accomplish their stated goals, and are still being improved upon. Translation memory is certainly not human memory, and while it does work part of the time, human memory remains irreplaceable.

Localization

Localization is defined as "the process of creating or adapting a product to a specific locale, i.e., to the language, cultural context, conventions and market requirements of a specific target market. With a properly localized product a user can interact with this product using his or her own language and cultural conventions. It also means that all user-visible text strings and all user documentation (printed and electronic) use the language and cultural conventions of the user. Finally, the properly localized product meets all regulatory and other requirements of the user's country or region."

Clearly, this definition takes us out of the strict realm of translation into the domain of computer programming and international business. It alludes primarily to the localization of websites (as well as software) in other languages and cultures. Two other terms often used in conjunction with localization are internationalization and globalization. The first refers to the preparation of computer text to be used in localization in such a way that it meets the requirements of the target language and culture. Globalization generally refers to both processes together, namely, internationalization and localization.

With the fast proliferation of websites and the rapid growth of many kinds of computer software, a growing number of translation companies have ventured into the field of localization, and more than a few computer hardware- and software-producing companies (including giants like IBM and Microsoft) have turned to the field of translation as a function of localization.

Thus, localization has been presenting translators with new opportunities and some difficult questions. On the one hand, there is a huge volume of text these days in website and software development that necessitates multilingual translation. On the other hand, for a translator to become involved in localization a specialized knowledge of computers is usually required, since website and software localization requires not only language translation but also adaptation of computer commands to the requirements of the target language. Hence, a translator may want to carefully consider how far he or she may wish to become involved in technical computer work that requires skills and training beyond the scope of actual translation work.

It should be mentioned that localization in the sense of translating a text and adapting it to another culture existed long before the computer age. Thus, for example, an American advertisement company in the pre-computer era that planned an international ad campaign for a company such as Coca Cola, had to study the cultures of other countries and customize the ads not only in terms of the target language, but also the cultural conventions, preferences, taboos etc. of the target country. Furthermore, the act of translating itself is in a sense a form of localization, since language does not exist separately from its culture.

Website and software localization has been around now for several years. It relies heavily not only on human translation but also on machine and machine-assisted translation tools, such as translation software and translation memory. Given the limitations of these tools, the often unrealistic expectations of the marketplace and the eagerness to process a large volume of material in record time, localization has been experiencing many problems, and the goals its pursuers have set for themselves are yet to be realized. One should keep all of this in mind before getting involved in this area of translation.

The Uses of the Internet for Translators

The translation field has become increasingly "wired," witnessing a proliferation of sites relating to professional activities, job-hunting, commercial products, and online reference materials for translators. It is not an exaggeration to say that translators do themselves (and potentially their clients) quite a disservice by ignoring the virtual translation community.

This section will introduce you to a selection of highly-regarded and well-maintained sites of use to translators. It assumes basic Web literacy. Of course, the Internet's ever-changing nature guarantees that certain websites will decline or disappear, while new ones will emerge by the time this book becomes available. So please be aware that you will probably have to do some updating of the following information on your own.

Where We Are on the Web

First, let us invite you to Schreiber Publishing's website. Our address: **schreiberpublishing.com**. It first went online in March 1996. Its objective is to provide reference literature, training materials, and useful information for translators. We fully intend to keep expanding it, and we hope all translators will benefit from it.

Professional Activities

Translators wishing to learn about the state of their profession will benefit from a visit to the American Translators Association's site, **www.atanet.org**. I discuss the ATA in greater detail in the chapter on Translators' Organizations; its Website includes information on the Association's formal activities such as conferences, publications and accreditation procedures. Even if you are not an ATA member, the site is useful because it can guide you to other translation-related sites. Another major website of interest to translators is the site of the international umbrella organization of the world's translator associations, the International Federation of Translators, found on **www.fit-ift.org**.

Aquarius, at **www.aquarius.net.** Claims to be "the world's language network." This commercial website lists translation agencies seeking translators and interpreters who, in turn, can post resumes to make their services known. It also links to other translation sites.

Networking with Other Translators

An extremely popular program on the Internet for translators has been the *Language Forum* of Compuserve, popularly known as FLEFO (Foreign Language Education Forum). You have to subscribe to this forum to be able to participate. You enter FLEFO in the keyword box and you find yourself in a virtual forum full of translators from around the world, who post messages and get answers to almost any question a translator may ask, from the cost of a dictionary, to the meaning of a word, to a social get-together. FLEFO can also link you to translation web- sites.

Another online forum for translators is the newsgroup: subscribers post messages and receive answers (say, to a specialized translation query). A newsgroup for translators is sci.lang. translation.

Reference Materials

The Translator's Home Companion at **www.rahul.net/lai/ companion.html**, provides Links to glossaries, dictionaries, translation publications, and other translators.

The Human Languages Page at **www.june29.com/IDP** provides links to other translation-related sites, including some listed here.

Language Today, an online publication (also available in print; see Bibliography appendix) covering language technology, translation and interpreting: **logos.it/language_today**

Online Dictionary Services

Eurodicautom at **www.europa.eu.int/eurodicautom** is a very useful service, Eurodicauto languages such as Spanish, Portuguese, French, German, Italian, English, Danish and D specialized dictionaries in non-technical, legal and technical areas. Terms are both transla

Online Dictionaries at **www.yourdictionary.com** covers a far greater range of languages It provides links to dictionaries and translations in many specializations.

Glossaries

There are many mediocre glossaries out there in cyberspace, so use caution with this type o are some better ones:

www.refer.fr/termisti/liste.htm

www.yahoo.com/references/dictionaries

U.S. Government agencies provide some very useful glossaries. For example:

www.epa.gov (for environmental terminology).

Finding Cultural Information

A quick way to access cultural and historical information on other countries is via Th **www.embassy.org.** This service provides links to embassy and/or United Nations hom Most countries' pages include links to cultural resources such as online newspapers, libr have to do some digging to find the information you're after, but if it exists online, yo starting here. Also the foreign ministries of various countries are a good source for all so to that particular country.

Shopping for Dictionaries

A prime source for dictionaries is i.b.d. Ltd.'s website is:
www.ibdltd.com.

Another site under construction is: **www.schoenhofs.com**.

Major virtual bookstores also have good selections of dictionaries (see box). Exampl
www.barnesandnoble.com
www.amazon.com
www.borders.com

You may also wish to consult these websites of major dictionary publishers:

Elsevier at **www.elsevier.com**
Routledge at **www.routledge.com**
McGraw-Hill at **www.mcgraw-hill.com**

Machine Translation

If you want to experience some machine translation, try these two sites:
www.babelfish.com/Languages/English/EnglishMachine.shtml
http://babelfish.altavista.com

Example of machine translation from Russian into English:

Raw machine translation: A contemporary airport is the involved complex of engineer constructions and techniques, for arrangement of which the territory, measured sometimes is required by thousands of hectares (for example the Moscow Airport Domodedovo, Kennedy's New York airport).

Text edited by humans: The modern airport is an elaborate complex of engineering structures and technical devices requiring a large territory, which, in some places, measures thousands of hectares (for instance, Domodedovo Airport in Moscow or Kennedy Airport in New York).

translation companies, since in both cases only a small percentage of the work done is of the above-described kind.

Furthermore, as in the case of machine translation and localization (see below), here too the tools are far from able to accomplish their stated goals, and are still being improved upon. Translation memory is certainly not human memory, and while it does work part of the time, human memory remains irreplaceable.

Localization

Localization is defined as "the process of creating or adapting a product to a specific locale, i.e., to the language, cultural context, conventions and market requirements of a specific target market. With a properly localized product a user can interact with this product using his or her own language and cultural conventions. It also means that all user-visible text strings and all user documentation (printed and electronic) use the language and cultural conventions of the user. Finally, the properly localized product meets all regulatory and other requirements of the user's country or region."

Clearly, this definition takes us out of the strict realm of translation into the domain of computer programming and international business. It alludes primarily to the localization of websites (as well as software) in other languages and cultures. Two other terms often used in conjunction with localization are internationalization and globalization. The first refers to the preparation of computer text to be used in localization in such a way that it meets the requirements of the target language and culture. Globalization generally refers to both processes together, namely, internationalization and localization.

With the fast proliferation of websites and the rapid growth of many kinds of computer software, a growing number of translation companies have ventured into the field of localization, and more than a few computer hardware- and software-producing companies (including giants like IBM and Microsoft) have turned to the field of translation as a function of localization.

Thus, localization has been presenting translators with new opportunities and some difficult questions. On the one hand, there is a huge volume of text these days in website and software development that necessitates multilingual translation. On the other hand, for a translator to become involved in localization a specialized knowledge of computers is usually required, since website and software localization requires not only language translation but also adaptation of computer commands to the requirements of the target language. Hence, a translator may want to carefully consider how far he or she may wish to become involved in technical computer work that requires skills and training beyond the scope of actual translation work.

It should be mentioned that localization in the sense of translating a text and adapting it to another culture existed long before the computer age. Thus, for example, an American advertisement company in the pre-computer era that planned an international ad campaign for a company such as Coca Cola, had to study the cultures of other countries and customize the ads not only in terms of the target language, but also the cultural conventions, preferences, taboos etc. of the target country. Furthermore, the act of translating itself is in a sense a form of localization, since language does not exist separately from its culture.

Website and software localization has been around now for several years. It relies heavily not only on human translation but also on machine and machine-assisted translation tools, such as translation software and translation memory. Given the limitations of these tools, the often unrealistic expectations of the marketplace and the eagerness to process a large volume of material in record time, localization has been experiencing many problems, and the goals its pursuers have set for themselves are yet to be realized. One should keep all of this in mind before getting involved in this area of translation.

The Uses of the Internet for Translators

The translation field has become increasingly "wired," witnessing a proliferation of sites relating to professional activities, job-hunting, commercial products, and online reference materials for translators. It is not an exaggeration to say that translators do themselves (and potentially their clients) quite a disservice by ignoring the virtual translation community.

This section will introduce you to a selection of highly-regarded and well-maintained sites of use to translators. It assumes basic Web literacy. Of course, the Internet's ever-changing nature guarantees that certain websites will decline or disappear, while new ones will emerge by the time this book becomes available. So please be aware that you will probably have to do some updating of the following information on your own.

Where We Are on the Web

First, let us invite you to Schreiber Publishing's website. Our address: **schreiberpublishing.com**. It first went online in March 1996. Its objective is to provide reference literature, training materials, and useful information for translators. We fully intend to keep expanding it, and we hope all translators will benefit from it.

Professional Activities

Translators wishing to learn about the state of their profession will benefit from a visit to the American Translators Association's site, **www.atanet.org**. I discuss the ATA in greater detail in the chapter on Translators' Organizations; its Website includes information on the Association's formal activities such as conferences, publications and accreditation procedures. Even if you are not an ATA member, the site is useful because it can guide you to other translation-related sites. Another major website of interest to translators is the site of the international umbrella organization of the world's translator associations, the International Federation of Translators, found on **www.fit-ift.org**.

Aquarius, at **www.aquarius.net.** Claims to be "the world's language network." This commercial website lists translation agencies seeking translators and interpreters who, in turn, can post resumes to make their services known. It also links to other translation sites.

Networking with Other Translators

An extremely popular program on the Internet for translators has been the *Language Forum* of Compuserve, popularly known as FLEFO (Foreign Language Education Forum). You have to subscribe to this forum to be able to participate. You enter FLEFO in the keyword box and you find yourself in a virtual forum full of translators from around the world, who post messages and get answers to almost any question a translator may ask, from the cost of a dictionary, to the meaning of a word, to a social get-together. FLEFO can also link you to translation web- sites.

Another online forum for translators is the newsgroup: subscribers post messages and receive answers (say, to a specialized translation query). A newsgroup for translators is sci.lang. translation.

Reference Materials

The Translator's Home Companion at **www.rahul.net/lai/ companion.html**, provides Links to glossaries, dictionaries, translation publications, and other translators.

The Human Languages Page at **www.june29.com/IDP** provides links to other translation-related sites, including some listed here.

Language Today, an online publication (also available in print; see Bibliography appendix) covering language technology, translation and interpreting: **logos.it/language_today**

Online Dictionary Services

Eurodicautom at **www.europa.eu.int/eurodicautom** is a very useful service, Eurodicautom handles European languages such as Spanish, Portuguese, French, German, Italian, English, Danish and Dutch. Includes many specialized dictionaries in non-technical, legal and technical areas. Terms are both translated and defined.

Online Dictionaries at **www.yourdictionary.com** covers a far greater range of languages than the above entry. It provides links to dictionaries and translations in many specializations.

Glossaries

There are many mediocre glossaries out there in cyberspace, so use caution with this type of online resource. Here are some better ones:

www.refer.fr/termisti/liste.htm

www.yahoo.com/references/dictionaries

U.S. Government agencies provide some very useful glossaries. For example:

www.epa.gov (for environmental terminology).

Finding Cultural Information

A quick way to access cultural and historical information on other countries is via The Electronic Embassy at **www.embassy.org.** This service provides links to embassy and/or United Nations home pages of many nations. Most countries' pages include links to cultural resources such as online newspapers, libraries, and so on. You may have to do some digging to find the information you're after, but if it exists online, you will probably find it by starting here. Also the foreign ministries of various countries are a good source for all sorts of information related to that particular country.

Shopping for Dictionaries

A prime source for dictionaries is i.b.d. Ltd.'s website is:
www.ibdltd.com.

Another site under construction is: **www.schoenhofs.com**.

Major virtual bookstores also have good selections of dictionaries (see box). Examples:
www.barnesandnoble.com
www.amazon.com
www.borders.com

You may also wish to consult these websites of major dictionary publishers:

Elsevier at **www.elsevier.com**
Routledge at **www.routledge.com**
McGraw-Hill at **www.mcgraw-hill.com**

Machine Translation

If you want to experience some machine translation, try these two sites:
www.babelfish.com/Languages/English/EnglishMachine.shtml
http://babelfish.altavista.com

Quick Order Form

Fax orders: (301) 424-2336. Send this form.
Telephone orders: Call 1 (800) 822-3213
(in Maryland: 301-424-7737 ext. 28)
E-mail orders: spbooks@aol.com.

Mail orders to: Schreiber Publishing, 51 Monroe St.,
Suite 101, Rockville MD 20850 USA

Please send the following books, programs, and/or a free catalog. I understand that I may return any of them for a full refund, for any reason, no questions asked:

❑ The Translator's Self-Training Program (circle the language/s of your choice):

Spanish French German Japanese Chinese Italian Portuguese Russian Arabic Hebrew

(U.S. - $69.00 Abroad - $89)

❑ The Translator's Self-Training Program -
Advanced Spanish Legal Translation (U.S. $89 Abroad - $109)
Advanced Spanish Medical Translation (U.S. $89 Abroad - $109)

❑ Multicultural Spanish Dictionary - How Spanish Differs from Country to Country (U.S. $24.95 Abroad -$36)

❑ Spanish Business Dictionary - How Spanish Differs from Country to Country (U.S. $24.95 Abroad -$36)

❑ American English Compendium - The "Odds and End"s" of American English Usage (U.S. $19.95 Abroad $28)

❑ The Translator's Handbook 4rd Revised Edition - The leading guide for translators (U.S. $24.95 Abroad - $36)

❑ Dictionary of Medicine French/English (U.S. $179.50 Abroad - $199.50)

Sales tax: Please add 5% sales tax in Maryland
Shipping (est.): $4 for the first book and $2.00 for each additional product
International: $ $9 for the first book, and $5 for each additional book Order total: ______________

Name: ______________________________

Address: ______________________________

City: ______________ State: ________ Zip: ____________

Telephone: ______________ e-mail: ______________

Payment: ❑ Cheque ❑ Credit card: ❑ Visa ❑ MasterCard

Card number: ______________________________

Name on card: ______________________ Exp. Date: ___/___

Schreiber Publishing – The Translator's Best Friend